LIVING SECURELY
✦IN AN✦
UNSTABLE
W🔒RLD

RICK YOHN
LIVING SECURELY ❦IN AN❦ UNSTABLE W❂RLD

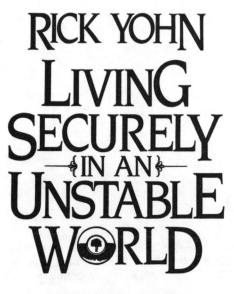

GOD'S SOLUTION
TO MAN'S DILEMMA

MULTNOMAH · PRESS

Portland, Oregon 97266

Unless otherwise indicated, all Scripture references are from the New American Standard Bible, © The Lockman Foundation 1960, 1962, 1963, 1968, 1971, 1972, 1973, 1975, 1977. Used by permission.

Cover design and illustration by Larry Ulmer

LIVING SECURELY IN AN UNSTABLE WORLD
© 1985 by Multnomah Press
Portland, Oregon 97266

Printed in the United States of America

Library of Congress Cataloging in Publication Data
Yohn, Rick.
    Living securely in an unstable world.

    1. Salvation.   I. Title.
BT751.2.Y64   1985   234   85-4895
ISBN 0-88070-082-3 (pbk.)

85 86 87 88 89 90 91 – 10 9 8 7 6 5 4 3 2 1

CONTENTS

PROLOGUE

Anyone thirty five or older can recall a time when security and serenity dominated much of the world's political scene. The war was over. The U.S. and its allies were victorious. It was time for the troops to come home from war and build a house, a family, a business and a future.

The old family radio gave way to a new invention called television. Stereos replaced hi-fi sets. Seventy-eights evolved into forty-fives, which changed to 33-⅓ rpm's. Propeller-driven engines gave way to jet travel.

The new world had a great future. A hope. An optimistic spirit. Eisenhower, our hero on the battle front, was now Commander-in-Chief on the home front. And when he fulfilled his term of duty, the bright future fell into the hands of a young, charismatic personality by the name of Kennedy. Youth had taken charge of America's future. It seemed that the whole Western world had fallen in love with the young, energetic leader, evidenced by the memorable occasion when he stood at the Berlin wall and cried out to the West Germans, "Ich bin ein Berliner!", ("I am a Berliner!"). Spontaneously the people of Berlin echoed, "Ken-ne-dy!", "Ken-ne-dy!"

The response just as easily could have been, "Security!", "Security!"

But on November 22, 1963 an assassin's bullet changed the course of history. Violence replaced serenity. Soon another assassin's bullet brought down civil-rights leader, Martin Luther King, Jr., followed by a third gunshot which ended the life of Bobby Kennedy.

America's confidence in its bright future was shaken. It seemed everything started to go downhill. Unrest over the Vietnam war dogged the entire country. College students burned their draft cards. And when the war was over, returning veterans got no hero's welcome. Instead, they were ignored, ridiculed and insulted.

Enter the new decade.

The seventies gave us Watergate, which so shattered our confidence in government that U.S. citizens began to wonder where one could turn for integrity in high office. The government's clay feet were showing. As confidence in government waned, so did confidence in the family unit.

The epidemic divorce rate of the 70s strained the serenity of the family. As homosexuality as an alternative lifestyle penetrated the social arena, social scientists could no longer agree on a definition of the family.

But if the family unit was being shaken, so was our confidence in nuclear power for peaceful purposes. The accident at the Three Mile Island Plant of Middletown, Pennsylvania, alarmed not only the residents of that state, but resulted in protests all over the country. "Stop building nuclear plants!" was the cry. But man's mistakes were not the only things challenging our security. We also had to cope with Mother Nature.

When Mount St. Helens blew its stack and belched millions of tons of ash over North America, we questioned the security of living in the Northwest. Soon after the disaster in the Northwest, a devastating earthquake levelled the town of Coalinga, California. Not to be outdone, tornados played havoc with the Midwest and floods ravaged towns and farmlands in the Midwest, the East, and the South. Thousands of people were left homeless, crops were irreparably damaged, and millions of dollars of property were lost.

Then the political world became a hotbed of violence once again.

The hostage crisis in Iran showed us how much we were hated by some foreign nations. The Russian invasion of Afghanistan told the world that the Soviets were on the move again. And the rising stockpile of nuclear arms by the U.S. government threw much of the world into panic, convincing man that he no longer lived in security. His world rested on a powder keg, surrounded by governments who play Russian roulette as they light the fuse, watch it burn and then dare anyone to put it out. Our world today is volatile, not secure.

Science has responded by producing weapons that could end man's existence on planet earth. Economists offer little more than mere doomsday forecasts of the distant future. Government is so unpredictable and self-serving that no one can depend on it for security. Even religion has become so fanatical in many parts of the world that it kills rather than heals.

Where, then, can one find security in a hostile and volatile world? The answer lies in a person's relationship with and understanding of God.

Wouldn't you feel more secure knowing that there was a God who planned man's destiny from the beginning to the end, and who then revealed that plan? Wouldn't you sense a greater calm knowing that God made it possible for you to enjoy a significant life now, and guaranteed a life throughout eternity? And wouldn't you certainly enjoy life more if this same God were to offer freedom from the guilt of sin and then guarantee that he would never leave you or forsake you?

Well, here's the good news: That's precisely what the God of the Scriptures has done! He wants to be your security in spite of world conditions. He wants you to enjoy inner peace, even though the world may be filled with turmoil.

You may already know God personally. If you do, this book is for you. As a jeweler slowly turns around a priceless stone with his fingers, gazing upon its exquisite beauty and color, so will you discover many rich components of your salvation.

But that may not be your situation. You may still be searching for an understanding of God, but have not yet established a personal relationship with him. This book is for you, too. It will open the door to greater discoveries of the Person and the works of him who created the heavens and the earth . . . and then made man to enjoy him forever.

It is my sincere hope that after reading the pages of this book, you will not only feel greater security while living in a world of moral challenge, political unrest and spiritual bankruptcy, but also that you come to appreciate the God who created you, and to experience the joy of his salvation.

Read on now and enter into a more in-depth knowledge of the God who drew up a blueprint for life, a plan which explains how he made salvation possible and what he offers to all those who sincerely seek him.

Your first discovery will take you back to eternity past when God initially drew up his masterplan. It's a concept known as predestination.

1

PLANNING AHEAD
PREDESTINATION

A walkway collapses in the Hyatt Regency Hotel in Kansas City, Missouri, in 1981, killing 113 and injuring 186. A section from a bridge on a major turnpike in Connecticut topples the morning of June 28, 1983; three people plunge to their deaths.

In both of these cases there was either a faulty design or a weak link supporting the structures.

In a similar manner, many Christians are able to handle most of their problems and situations in life with what they know about God. But most of us possess inadequate knowledge about God; when certain events test our faith, we may collapse or fall apart at the seams! We don't know how to respond. It's as though God has forsaken us or doesn't have the foggiest idea what is happening to us. Because we are confused, we conclude that God must be confused, or perhaps just doesn't care. But the Bible is very specific about what God knows and what he is doing. The problem is not with God, but with the defective parts of our faith. And since faith is based upon our knowledge of truth, it is imperative that we gain a more accurate understanding of who God is and what he is doing in the lives of men.

Since many of these supporting truths are hidden in a maze of difficult words, such as *predestination, election, reconciliation, redemption,* and *justification,* we tend to shy away from them. But that's a mistake, because these truths are like steel spikes, pins, and clamps that hold our faith together.

Let's begin our venture into knowing God more intimately by looking at predestation. Consider first some underlying truths about God.

What Underlying Truths Will Help Us Better Understand Predestination?

Since predestation is often difficult to understand by itself, let's consider the following underlying truths, which will provide a foundation to help us picture predestation more clearly. We'll begin with the fact of God's sovereign right.

God Is Sovereign and Therefore Has the Right to Do As He Desires

When I refer to "sovereign," I am speaking of that which is supreme, independent in authority or jurisdiction, free. God is the Supreme Being in the universe. His decisions and rule are independent of any created being. He is free to do as he pleases, answerable to no one.

The prophet Isaiah vividly declares God's sovereignty as he queries, "Who has directed the Spirit of the LORD, or as His counselor has informed Him? With whom did He consult and who gave Him understanding? And who taught Him in the path of justice and taught Him knowledge, and informed Him of the way of understanding?" (Isaiah 40:13-14).

Again Isaiah expresses God's sovereign rule over mankind, stating, "Remember the former things long past, for I am God, and there is no other; I am God, and there is no one like Me, declaring the end from the beginning and from ancient times things which have not been done, saying, 'My purpose will be established, and I will accomplish all My good pleasure'; calling a bird of prey from the east, the man of My purpose from a far country. Truly I have spoken; truly I will bring it to pass. I have planned it, surely I will do it" (Isaiah 46:9-11).

PREDESTINATION

Once we truly believe that God has the supreme right to do anything he chooses, the concept of predestination will seem more plausible.

A second truth concerns God's revelation.

God Has Not Revealed Everything About Himself to Man

There are still many truths about God and his way of operating in man's affairs which will never be known this side of eternity. The book of Deuteronomy indicates, "The secret things belong to the LORD our God, but the things revealed belong to us and to our sons forever, that we may observe all the words of this law" (Deuteronomy 29:29).

Jesus himself said before he left the earth, "I have many more things to say to you, but you cannot bear them now" (John 16:12).

Though God has revealed much about himself to mankind, there is a reservoir of information which has never been revealed. But what about the truths that have been revealed? This brings us to the third foundational fact.

Many of the Truths Which God Has Revealed Will Remain a Mystery to Some People

There are two groups of individuals who will have difficulty understanding what God has already revealed in his Word: the natural man and the carnal Christian.

The *natural man* will not understand God's revelation. And who is the natural man? He is the individual who has not established a personal relationship with Jesus Christ. He may possess high moral standards, or be a church member, and perhaps be a very intelligent person. However, because he has never repented of sin and turned to God for salvation, the decisions he makes will originate from a natural mindset, unaided by the Spirit of God.

The Bible describes his response to truth this way: "But a natural man does not accept the things of the Spirit of God; for they are foolishness to him, and he cannot understand them, because they are spiritually appraised" (1 Corinthians 2:14). Consider two problems a natural man faces when he is confronted with spiritual truth.

First, he does not accept or welcome spiritual truth. He has little interest in the true God, though he may admire religion and enjoy helping people. It's just that he is not interested in a personal relationship with God. Nor is he interested in placing himself under the authority of God's Word, because it interferes with the lifestyle he's chosen.

Second, the natural man cannot understand God's revelation. Though he may have the ability to comprehend historical events or even the moral precepts of the Scriptures, he is not able to understand spiritual truth any more than an animal can comprehend computers. God's Word doesn't make any sense to him. It appears to be foolish, so he considers it a waste of his time to bother with such "trivia."

The other individual who has difficulty understanding God's revelation is the *carnal Christian*. This person is motivated by his natural desires, even though he has had a born-again experience. The writer to the Hebrews speaks of this individual when he chides, "Concerning Him [Christ] we have much to say, and it is hard to explain, since you have become dull of hearing. For though by this time you ought to be teachers, you have need again for someone to teach you the elementary principles of the oracles of God, and you have come to need milk and not solid food. For everyone who partakes only of milk is not accustomed to the word of righteousness, for he is a babe. But solid food is for the mature, who because of practice have their senses trained to discern good and evil" (Hebrews 5:11-14).

The writer makes four observations about the carnal Christian: (1) He has become dull of hearing spiritual truth; (2) he can understand only basic truth; (3) he is not accustomed to truth; and (4) he does not practice the truth. The person isolates Christianity from his daily life. Christianity has become a Sunday religion and fails to integrate with his weekly activities.

Another underlying principle to help you understand predestination concerns those who can know God's truth.

Much of God's Revealed Truth Can Be Known
by Many Believers

There are two groups of Christians who have the ability to understand what God is talking about in his Word: those who are spiritual and those who are spiritually mature.

The *spiritual Christian* has tuned into the Holy Spirit. He is walking in the power of the Spirit, obeying what he understands from the Word of God. He maintains an intimate relationship with the Lord, and may be either a young or old Christian. Paul writes of him, "But he who is spiritual appraises all things, yet he himself is appraised by no man" (1 Corinthians 2:15).

The other Christian who is able to understand spiritual truth is the *spiritually mature believer*. He also lives under the control of the Holy Spirit, but has added another dimension to life—he has been a Christian for several years and has grown in his knowledge of God. The writer to the Hebrews informs his readers why this person is mature—"But solid food is for the mature, who because of practice have their sense trained to discern good and evil" (Hebrews 5:14). The spiritually mature Christian is not only capable of understanding the basic truths of Scripture, but he also has the capacity to comprehend the deeper things of God.

One final foundational truth concerns God's all-inclusive plan.

God Has an All-Inclusive Plan and
Sees All Things At a Glance

Man has limited ability to see into the future. Most of the time we have to guess what the future holds; but God is able to see the past, present, and future simultaneously. Suppose you were looking at a painting which depicted some of the great events in history. On one canvas you would observe scenes from the creation, the fall of man, the exodus, the fall of Rome, World Wars I and II, the battle of Armageddon, and the second coming of Christ. In a similar way God has the ability to see all of these things in intricate detail; but he actually sees them taking place simultaneously. And he is not limited to a few scenarios. He sees it all in vivid reality.

The Psalmist speaks of God's infinite ability to see everything, "The LORD nullifies the counsel of the nations; He frustrates the plans of the peoples. The counsel of the LORD stands forever, the plans of His heart from generation to generation.... The LORD looks from heaven; He sees all the sons of men; from His dwelling place He looks out on all the inhabitants of the earth, He who fashions the hearts of them all, He who understands all their works" (Psalm 33:10-11, 13-15).

When God developed his masterplan, he did not consult with his creation, but rather developed his plan with his own wisdom and in line with his holy character. Furthermore, God's plan was not dependent on man's actions. God established his plan according to his own will. That is why he is the sovereign of the universe.

Now, having laid a foundation upon which we can build our understanding of predestination, let's define the term predestination, discover how it works in salvation, learn why God predestines anyone, see what would happen if God were not to predestine men, learn the practical values of predestination, and conclude with finding out how to respond to this rich doctrine.

What Is Predestination?

In answering the question, What is predestination? let's first understand what it is not, and then discover what it is.

Predestination Is Not What Some People Think It Is

There are a number of common misconceptions about predestination. For instance, predestination is not to be equated with *fatalism*. Fatalism is the belief that God or fate has determined all events which occur. Therefore man possesses no free will for decision-making. Many years ago a popular song presented this fatalistic philosophy—"Que será, será, whatever will be, will be. The future's not ours to see. Que será, será."

PREDESTINATION

Though the Bible strongly teaches predestination, it also teaches that man is free to choose and that God holds him accountable for those choices. The apostle Peter preached Christ to the Jewish people on the day of Pentecost, saying, "This Man, delivered up by the predetermined plan and foreknowledge of God [that's God's predestination], you nailed to a cross by the hands of godless men and put Him to death" [that's man's free will in action] (Acts 2:23). On another occasion, Peter reversed the order, first speaking about man's free will and then about God's predestination. He said, "For truly in this city there were gathered together against Thy holy servant Jesus, whom Thou didst anoint, both Herod and Pontius Pilate, along with the Gentiles and the peoples of Israel [man's free will], to do whatever Thy hand and Thy purpose predestined to occur" [God's predestination] (Acts 4:27-28). Predestination is not fatalism. It allows for man to make choices and be held accountable for those choices.

Neither is predestination the *condemnation of some to hell*. Nowhere does Scripture imply that God predestines anyone to hell. Men will experience salvation because God predestined them to experience his blessings. However, they will experience hell because they've rejected the Son of God. Men don't go to hell because they've been predestined to hell. They end up in hell because they have refused to accept God's gift of salvation.

William Jay supports this statement when he writes, "Two grand truths have always seemed to me to pervade the whole Bible, and not confined to a few phrases, namely, that if we are saved, it is entirely of God's grace, and if we are lost, it will be entirely from ourselves."

The apostle John agrees: "For God so loved the world, that He gave His only begotten Son, that whoever believes in Him should not perish, but have eternal life. . . . He who believes in Him is not judged; he who does not believe has been judged already, because he has not believed in the name of the only begotten Son of God. . . . He who believes in the Son has eternal life; but he who does not obey the Son shall not see life, but the wrath of God abides on him"

17

(John 3:16, 18, 36).

Predestination also is not a minute, *detailed plan of your life*. When you look at the life of Jesus Christ, it is obvious that certain specific events in his life were predetermined by God the Father. The place of his birth was predetermined: "But as for you, Bethlehem Ephrathah, too little to be among the clans of Judah, from you One will go forth for Me to be ruler in Israel. His goings forth are from long ago, from the days of eternity" (Micah 5:2). Also, the fact that Jesus would live in Egypt for a period of time was predetermined—"And he arose and took the Child and His mother by night, and departed for Egypt; and was there until the death of Herod, that what was spoken by the Lord through the prophet might be fulfilled, saying, 'Out of Egypt did I call My Son'" (Matthew 2:14-15). The Bible does not say, however, that it was predetermined what Jesus was going to do on a certain day, or when he would get up or go to bed.

Likewise, God gives you a lot of freedom of choice. I don't believe it is predetermined what color of socks you're going to wear in the morning, or what you decide to order at a restaurant. None of us really knows which aspects of our lives have been predetermined and which have been left to our preferences. As far as we are concerned, most of our life is decided by our own free choices. We cannot blame God when things go wrong, or hide behind a fatalistic attitude that says, "I couldn't help myself because God predestined it to happen."

You may be wondering, "Is there any way to know what has been predestined?" The difficulty in answering this question is knowing what is the norm and what is the exception. For instance, several Bible characters were predestined by God to be his messengers. Their occupation was chosen by God before they were ever born. The prophet Jeremiah testifies, "Now the word of the LORD came to me saying, 'Before I formed you in the womb I knew you, and before you were born I consecrated you; I have appointed you a prophet to the nations.' Then I said, 'Alas, Lord GOD! Behold, I do not know how to speak, because I am a youth.' But the LORD said to me, 'Do not say, "I am a youth," because everywhere I send you, you shall go, and all that I command you, you shall speak. Do not be afraid of them, for I am with you to deliver you,' declares the LORD. Then the LORD stretched out His hand and touched my mouth, and the LORD said to me, 'Behold, I have put My words in your mouth. See, I have appointed you this day over the nations and over the kingdoms, to pluck up and to break down, to destroy and to overthrow, to build and to plant'" (Jeremiah 1:4-10).

The apostle Paul gives evidence of a similar appointment. He writes, "But when He who had set me apart, even from my mother's womb, and called me through His grace, was pleased to reveal His Son in me, that I might preach Him among the Gentiles, I did not immediately consult with flesh and blood, nor did I go up to Jerusalem to those who were apostles before me; but I went away to Arabia, and returned once more to Damascus" (Galatians 1:15-17).

I believe that God's plan for me to be a minister of the gospel was decided before the foundation of the world. But I cannot conclude that God predetermines every minister to the ministry or to a specific occupation. Such conclusions may have come more from the inner witness of the Holy Spirit than from hard facts. I am certain, however, that I would never have chosen the ministry as a life-long occupation had not God placed that desire in my heart when I was nineteen years of age.

Is there any evidence that God normally predestines certain aspects of our lives? Possibly. Consider for a moment those areas of your life over which you've had no choice and probably will not have a choice in the future. You did not choose your parents. Nor did you choose the time and place of your birth. And what about your race or skin color? Perhaps you have a birth defect which you did not choose. Then there is your height. Did you have anything to do with that? (Too bad you can't blame your weight on predestination.) You've also had little choice over some difficult trials in your life other than how to respond properly to them. And you will probably have no say about the time of your death.

Some people believe that God has predetermined who they will marry. That's possible in some cases, though it would be difficult to prove as a norm. Most likely the Lord led Abraham's servant to find a wife for Isaac. The servant prayed to God, "'O LORD, the God of my master Abraham, please grant me success today, and show lovingkindness to my master Abraham. Behold, I am standing by the spring, and the daughters of the men of the city are coming out to draw water; now may it be that the girl to whom I say, "Please let down your jar so that I may drink," and who answers, "Drink, and I will water your camels also";—may she be the one whom Thou hast appointed for Thy servant Isaac; and by this I shall know that Thou hast shown lovingkindness to my master.' And it came about before he had finished speaking, that behold, Rebekah who was born to Bethuel the son of Milcah, the wife of Abraham's brother Nahor, came out with her jar on her shoulder. And the girl was very beautiful, a virgin, and no man had had relations with her; and she went down to the spring and filled her jar, and came up" (Genesis 24:12-16).

Is this the norm? I don't know. But I do believe that it is important to bring such matters before the Lord, so that he will give us his guidance and lead us to the same type of success.

By the way, even though Rebekah was God's predetermined choice for Isaac, that in itself did not guarantee a successful marriage. Like any other relationship, their marriage had to be nurtured and developed. Likewise, God may predestine a person to be a minister. But if he is lazy in his study habits, he will not be successful.

What, then, is predestination?

Predestination Is God's Predetermined Plan for His Creation

The word *predestination* derives from two Greek words—*pro* (before) and *orizo* (to appoint, determine). One definition of predestination is "that active exercise of the will of God by which certain results are brought to pass." Another definition states, "God predetermined a purpose and a plan, and then chose just those elements which would promote that purpose and plan."

Whichever definition best clarifies this truth for you, it is important to understand that God is the prime mover, directing all things toward the fulfillment of his predetermined plan. And yet, in that predetermined choice of God, he holds man accountable for his own choices.

I believe that God predetermined Pharaoh's refusal to release Israel when Moses implored him to "let My people go." God told Moses at the outset, "But I know that the king of Egypt will not permit you to go, except under compulsion" (Exodus 3:19). That statement was made before Moses ever reached Egypt. The Bible says both that God hardened Pharaoh's heart (Exodus 4:21; 7:3, 13; 9:12, 35; 10:1, 20, 27; 14:4, 8) and that Pharaoh hardened his own heart (Exodus 8:15, 32; 9:34). Which is correct? Both are accurate statements and combine God's predestination and man's free will. Pharaoh hardened his heart because he wanted to. God just provided the encouragement for him to act out of his evil heart by saying no. Therefore, God is righteous and just to punish Pharaoh for his actions.

I have found that I can cause my dog to do what I want on certain occasions. A few key words cause his ears to prick up and his adrenalin to flow. Words like "bye-bye," "go for a ride," "pussycat," and "dog food" work every time. Then by an act of his own will, he makes a fool out of himself by jumping and barking. I do not force him to do anything. I just provide the incentive and he acts according to his nature.

Likewise, God has merely to provide the incentive and man will respond according to his nature, without any compulsion from God.

Now let's look at another aspect of predestination.

How Does Predestination Work in Salvation?
Though God sees all things simultaneously and knows the beginning from the end because he planned it that way,

we can understand things only in a time sequence. Therefore, from man's perspective here is a possible scenario of
how God's predestination works in salvation.

God's Compassion Saw Man's Helpless Condition

From a Biblical perspective, man is in a *spiritually helpless
condition*. He is spiritually impotent, being spiritually blind
(2 Corinthians 4:4), deaf (Matthew 13:13-15), dead (Ephesians 2:1), and unable to respond to truth unless aided by
God (John 6:44, 65).

Second, man is *enslaved to sin*. This doesn't mean that he
continually commits gross sins, but rather that he doesn't
have the ability to please God. Paul writes, "Do you not
know that when you present yourselves to someone as
slaves for obedience, you are slaves of the one whom you
obey, either of sin resulting in death, or of obedience resulting in righteousness. . . ? For when you were slaves of
sin, you were free in regard to righteousness. Therefore
what benefit were you then deriving from the things of
which you are now ashamed? For the outcome of those
things is death" (Romans 6:16, 20-21). But someone may
say, "Wait a minute! I'm not enslaved to sin. I might sin
once in a while, but I'm certainly not its slave." Jesus re-
sponds to him by saying, "Truly, truly, I say to you, every
one who commits sin is the slave of sin" (John 8:34).

Not only is man spiritually impotent and a slave to sin,
he also is *motivated by satanic forces*. This does not imply that
all men are demon-possessed. However, all mankind is
either energized and motivated by godly forces or by
satanic forces. Concerning the unbeliever, the apostle Paul
writes, "And you were dead in your trespasses and sins, in
which you formerly walked according to the course of this
world, according to the prince of the power of the air, of the
spirit that is now working in the sons of disobedience"
(Ephesians 2:1-2). Therefore, man is in a spiritually helpless condition. What is the result of this condition?

God's Holiness Demanded That Sin Be Punished

Sin is an affront to God's holy character; therefore, God
must judge sin with death: "For the wages of sin is death,

but the free gift of God is eternal life in Christ Jesus our Lord" (Romans 6:23). Because man has sinned against God, someone must die. This brings us to the next principle regarding predestination.

God's Love for Man Motivated Him to Develop a Way to Set Man Free from Spiritual Bondage

God's motivation is love: "For God so loved the world ..." (John 3:16). He saw man's helplessness and knew that sin had to be punished. Therefore, he developed a way to set men free from their bondage. Jesus said, "If therefore the Son shall make you free, you shall be free indeed" (John 8:36). What was involved in this plan?

God's Plan Predestined Christ to Die As a Substitute for Sinful Man

There is no doubt about it, Jesus was predestined to die: "This Man, delivered up by the predetermined plan and foreknowledge of God, you nailed to a cross by the hands of godless men and put Him to death" (Acts 2:23).

In the Old Testament an animal was sacrificed to atone for man's sins. Man's sins were transferred vicariously to the animal and it was killed. The writer to the Hebrews shows how Jesus Christ fulfilled the role of substitute. He writes, "And every priest stands daily ministering and offering time after time the same sacrifices, which can never take away sins; but He, having offered one sacrifice for sins for all time, sat down at the right hand of God" (Hebrews 10:11-12). So Christ was predestined to die as man's substitute for sin. Therefore, in order to assure that Christ's sacrifice would not be ignored by all mankind, God predestined some to enjoy his eternal blessings.

God's Plan Predestined Some to Enjoy His Eternal Blessings

Man was perishing because he rejected God. But in God's love for man, he marked off some to be saved from perishing. The actual choice by God is called "election," a subject we will cover in the next chapter. And yet the Bible does not limit predestination to salvation. God's purposes for predestination are stated in two other ways: to experience a new relationship with God and to develop a new image.

Why Does God Predestine Some People?

To Experience a New Relationship with God

Paul informed the Ephesians, "He predestined us to adoption as sons through Jesus Christ to Himself, according to the kind intention of His will, to the praise of the glory of His grace, which He freely bestowed on us in the Beloved" (Ephesians 1:5-6). These two verses present three aspects of this new relationship.

The relationship is first one of *adopted sons.* Not only are we children of God, but we are also sons of God with all the privileges of sonship. Though the Jewish family was composed of both sons and daughters, it was the son who received his father's inheritance and blessing.

Adoption agencies are springing up all over the world. Many couples who cannot have children of their own, as well as those who may already have children of their own, apply for adoption papers every day. They want to adopt orphans, those who have been left to care for themselves, and those children whose parents could not provide for their needs. When a child is adopted, he is taken from one potential life experience and given another. At the worst many children would die if they were not adopted, and at the best their lives would experience great hardship.

Having become God's adopted sons, we have been removed from one sphere of life and brought into another. The Bible describes this event as being transferred from death to life (John 5:24), from darkness to light (Acts 26:18), and from the dominion of Satan to God (Acts 26:18).

One of the advantages of being an adopted son is that we have received God's Holy Spirit as a guarantee of many other future blessings. "For all who are being led by the Spirit of God, these are sons of God. For you have not received a spirit of slavery leading to fear again, but you have received a spirit of adoption as sons by which we cry out,

Abba! Father!' The Spirit Himself bears witness with our spirit that we are children of God, and if children, heirs also, heirs of God and fellow-heirs with Christ, if indeed we suffer with Him in order that we may also be glorified with Him" (Romans 8:14-17).

This relationship is not only one of adoption, but also one of *intimate fellowship*. We have been predestined unto himself. More important than being an adopted son is being an adopted son of God. Some children are adopted into homes which are not happy, where the husband and wife don't get along with one another. In fact, some people adopt children hoping that this will be the ingredient which reconciles their differences, but often it is the catalyst that encourages a separation.

Furthermore, some children are adopted into homes which really cannot afford one more child, so the life of the adopted child may not be much better than it was previously. Now consider God's adoption agency.

The believer has been adopted as a son of God and is therefore wanted and loved by God. As Father, God abundantly provides for his sons. But there is still more blessing: predestination doesn't stop with adoption and intimate fellowship with God. It also includes a *revolutionary purpose*.

The revolutionary purpose is stated in the following words: "To the praise of the glory of His grace" (Ephesians 1:6). That is a revolutionary purpose because most of what man does is for self-glory or personal praise. But someone who is committed to the praise of another has an entirely new and revolutionary purpose. The apostle Paul presents the same purpose in slightly different terms when he writes, "For the love of Christ controls us, having concluded this, that one died for all, therefore all died; and He died for all, that they who live should no longer live for themselves, but for Him who died and rose again on their behalf" (2 Corinthians 5:14-15).

The basic motivation in a believer's life should be Godward. Even his behavior at work should be Godward— "Whatever you do, do your work heartily, as for the Lord rather than for men" (Colossians 3:23).

In chapter 1 of Ephesians, the phrase "to the praise of His glory" is also used in verses 12 and 14, where we learn that we have not only been predestined to the praise of his glory, but that we should live to the praise of his glory. Furthermore, the Holy Spirit was given to us as a pledge to the praise of his glory. But there is further blessing: Besides a new relationship with God, the believer has been predestined to develop a new image.

To Develop a New Image

The apostle Paul explains this purpose in the book of Romans: "For whom He foreknew, He also predestined to become conformed to the image of His Son, that He might be the first-born among many brethren" (Romans 8:29).

Man was created originally in the image of God. But when he rebelled against God, that image was marred. And so he now conforms himself to the image of the world, which includes "the lust of the flesh and the lust of the eyes and the boastful pride of life" (1 John 2:16). This is why Paul encourages believers, "And do not be conformed to this world, but be transformed by the renewing of your mind . . ." (Romans 12:2). Our lives are not to be patterned after the world's lifestyle and value system, but rather after the inner nature of Jesus Christ. We need to allow the Holy Spirit to develop Christ's character and values in us.

But how can we be certain that God's predestination to a new relationship and new image includes salvation? Paul states, "And whom He predestined, these He also called; and whom He called, these He also justified; and whom He justified, these He also glorified" (Romans 8:30). God has predestined some to a new relationship with him and to develop a new image, which includes a complete salvation. But what if God had not predestined anyone?

What Would Happen If God Had Not Predestined Anyone?

If God had not predestined anyone, I see two results: you would be living life by chance, and God would be subject to man's decisions.

How would you like to live your life by pure chance? It would be terrible to have no sense that what is happening in your life is working toward some divine goal. You'd be a creature of chance and habit rather than one of destiny. Nothing in life would make sense. All things would not be working together for good, but would be occurring haphazardly. There would be neither rhyme nor reason to the circumstances of life. Furthermore, this would place God at man's mercy.

But the Scriptures clearly show that God is not dependent upon man's decisions. When God sent Jonah to Nineveh to inform the people how to avoid his judgment, Jonah went the opposite direction. Was God dependent on Jonah's rebellious decision to get the message to Nineveh? Absolutely not. Jonah was dependent upon God's predetermined choice to get the message to the Ninevites. God merely arranged the circumstances so that Jonah would freely agree with his decision.

Predestination is one of the deeper truths which God has revealed about himself. But this truth is not to be locked up in the archives of the world's seminaries. It is a truth which needs to be understood and regularly practiced by all believers, for it has major practical value.

What Are the Practical Values of Predestination?

As I have studied this doctrine, I've observed five specific values which derive from this truth.

A Sense of Security

Predestination should give you a *sense of security*. Paul told the Roman Christians, "And we know that God causes all things to work together for good to those who love God, to those who are called according to His purpose. For whom He foreknew, He also predestined to become conformed to the image of His Son, that He might be the firstborn among many brethren" (Romans 8:28-29).

First, there is a security of circumstances ("all things"). There are many events in our lives which we do not enjoy or welcome. No one wants to lose a job. No one desires to lose a loved one. None of us enjoys failure. But God can work even these circumstances to our advantage. Even while in prison, Paul knew that the Lord could use his incarceration to great advantage for the gospel, as well as for his personal growth. So whether things go well or whether everything seems to be falling apart, God is able to use those circumstances to great advantage.

There is also security in the process of God's working ("are working together"). We often feel we'll never get through life's troubles. But if we can see that these circumstances are merely pieces of a puzzle being carefully arranged by a skillful developer, we can put greater confidence in the fact that our difficulties are not in vain.

Paul also mentions that there is security in the final product ("for good"). The "good" may not always be your direct good or advantage—it might be for the good of someone else, the good of the gospel, or the good of God's purpose. But goodness can come out of the circumstance, even though it may not be good in itself.

Whenever God operates in our lives, he is either doing it for the good of others or for our good, including discipline: "For they disciplined us for a short time as seemed best to them, but He disciplines us *for our good*, that we may share His holiness. All discipline for the moment seems not to be joyful, but sorrowful; yet to those who have been trained by it, afterwards it yields the peaceful fruit of righteousness" (Hebrews 12:10-11).

There is also a security in your relationship with God ("those who love God" "those called according to His purpose"). God is not working all things together for everyone's good. He is not putting the pieces of life together for every human being. It's only for those who have been predestined, who love God and who are called according to his purpose, that all things are working together for good. So there is security in your relationship with God in that he has called you and you respond to that call by loving him.

PREDESTINATION

Freedom from Jealousy and Competition

Another practical value of predestination is that it can *free you from jealousy and competition with others*. From early childhood we've learned to be competitive. We compete with brothers and sisters, with the other kids on the block, with our schoolmates, and eventually with others out in the job market. When someone gets the position, salary, or attention which we would like to have, we may respond with jealousy. But because God has predestined us by marking off a special life plan, and then controlling circumstances so that we can enjoy that plan, we can free ourselves from jealous competition. Enjoy the freedom to be that person which God has designed you to become.

You and I need to discover the potential God has given to us and then live up to it. He has given us special gifts, a specific personality, different experiences, a certain educational background, so that we don't have to compare ourselves with each other.

The apostle Paul informed the Corinthians, "But now God has placed the members, each one of them, in the body, just as He desired" (1 Corinthians 12:18). We don't all have the same position, gifts, or abilities. But we all have the same Lord. We have all been predestined by God, if Jesus Christ is our Savior. Therefore, our energy should not be used on competing with others, but rather on understanding what it is that God wants us to do in life. When you depart from this life, what special legacy are you going to leave behind? What imprint will you make on the lives of other people? In what way will other people be better off because you lived on earth?

Release from Unnecessary Fears

Predestination can also *release you from unnecessary fears*. Often we worry about so many things over which we have no control. Jesus taught, "For this reason I say to you, do not be anxious for your life, as to what you shall eat, or what you shall drink; nor for your body, as to what you shall put on. Is not life more than food, and the body than clothing? . . . And which of you by being anxious can add a single cubit to his life's span? And why are you anxious about clothing?" (Matthew 6:25, 27-28).

We worry about losing our jobs, about getting sick, about dying, about failure, about not being accepted, and so forth. But our times are in God's hands. And God allows only those things in our lives that will help us to become the people he wants us to be. I am not implying that God predestined everything that happens to us, because many of our circumstances are the result of personal sin. I don't believe God predestines divorce, unwanted pregnancies, immorality, character assassination through gossip, and things of this sort. But even when we reap the devastating results of our own rebellion, the Lord can use those circumstances to shape us into the people he wants us to be.

Greater Patience

Predestination can also help you *experience greater patience*, perhaps the one ingredient most of us are most in need of. And yet when we realize that God's plan always moves according to his time schedule, it can help us develop patience when things don't happen as quickly as we would like. Our responsibility is to relax and fit into his time schedule. When Jesus came to this earth, it was in the "fulness of time" (Galatians 4:4). And the apostle Paul provides an encouraging promise with these words: "And let us not lose heart in doing good, for in due time we shall reap if we do not grow weary" (Galatians 6:9). Too often we miss out on some tremendous blessing of God because we've given up before it was time. We have to give God the time required to work all things together for good.

A Sense of Purpose

The final value of predestination is that it can give you a *sense of purpose in life*. My younger son enjoys working puzzles. In fact, right now on our kitchen table is the frame of a 1500-piece puzzle. Even though it will take him a while before he completes the puzzle, he is able to work on the project contentedly because he knows what the picture is supposed to look like when it's completed.

God, too, is able to see the finished product. He knows what all the pieces of our life are going to look like when they are finally fitted together. But we don't have that advantage. We don't see what the little pieces of life are forming. And that's where faith enters. By faith, we trust that each little piece, no matter what its shape, no matter how large or small, is being fitted neatly by a master craftsman. He knows the end result and we need to trust him to put all those pieces together for good.

Should predestination cause a person to become apathetic? Absolutely not, because God not only predetermines the end, but also predetermines the means to the end. Paul taught the doctrine of predestination and yet was an avid missionary—he knew that salvation will not be completed until men hear and respond to the gospel. The end result is salvation, and the means is preaching or sharing God's living truth with dying men. That's why Paul wrote, "For 'Whoever will call upon the name of the Lord will be saved.' How then shall they call upon Him in whom they have not believed? And how shall they believe in Him whom they have not heard? And how shall they hear without a preacher? And how shall they preach unless they are sent? Just as it is written, 'How beautiful are the feet of those who bring glad tidings of good things!'" (Romans 10:13-15).

How then should we act in light of this doctrine?

How Should We Respond to Predestination?

If you are not certain about your own predestination to a new relationship with God and a new image and life in Christ, you can make sure today. Turn to God by turning your back on the sinful past, and receive Jesus Christ as your personal Savior. Ask him into your life. Ask him to confirm your predestination to you.

Second, recognize that though much of your life has been predetermined by God's personalized masterplan, you cannot know with assurance where his predestination ends and your free will begins. In fact, they actually work hand-in-hand. But it is important that you make your decisions with the mindset that God is at work in you both to will and to work for his good pleasure (Philippians 2:13). Seek his wisdom in your decision making. Don't get paranoid, wondering whether you are in or out of God's will. Just keep bringing your choices to God, continue walking in harmony with his revealed will (the Scriptures), and make decisions with prayer, counsel, and the common sense he gave you.

Rejoice in the fact that you are not a creature of chance, but a person of destiny. God has predestined you. But he didn't stop there. He also chose you to come into a personal relationship with him. You'll learn how and why he chose you in the next chapter.

CHAPTER

2

MAKING THE CHOICE
ELECTION

One of the most surprising elections in American history occurred on November 2, 1948, when Harry Truman defeated Governor Thomas E. Dewey for the presidency of the United States. Everyone expected a landslide victory for Dewey. In fact, the *Chicago Daily Tribune* was so certain of Dewey's victory that it ran headlines for the morning paper declaring Dewey the winner. A historic photograph of the blunder shows a grinning Truman holding aloft that newspaper with its embarrassingly erroneous headline.

But although those election results surprised many, they are insignificant compared to the surprise many have when they read about the election results of the Bible. Man thrives on electing winners who often turn out to be losers. But God exults over losers who eventually become winners.

Another one of those difficult words to understand is "election" as it applies to God's sovereign decision to do whatever fits his predetermined plan. Does God really choose some to salvation and not others? Do the elect alone enter heaven? How can God be loving and just if he doesn't elect everyone?

Let's answer these questions as we investigate another of God's sovereign rights—the right of divine election.

What Should We Know before We Study Election?

Election will make more sense when we study it in light of some other important facts about God and man. *Some of God's truths can only be understood partially in this life.* Though I never did very well in geometry, one principle I did learn is that two parallel lines never meet. The doctrine of election and the free will of man are, from the human perspective, two opposite and somewhat paradoxical concepts. They are like two parallel lines which seem to have no relationship with one another . . . at least in time. But from God's perspective in eternity, these parallel lines do merge.

Election is not the only doctrine that is difficult to understand from a finite vantage point. The doctrine of predestination, the Trinity, and the virgin birth all seem to be equally difficult to fully comprehend. It's like trying to understand electricity. You know that it exists because you see its effects, but it's impossible to fully explain and understand. So don't feel frustrated if, after reading this chapter, you still have unanswered questions about the doctrine of election. I guarantee that you will always wrestle with some of the important doctrines of the Christian faith. God expects you to believe and act upon them, even if you do not fully understand them.

Another important factor to consider before you delve into the study of election is to recognize that *God's reasons for choosing some and not others are not revealed.* Have you ever wondered why God chose Israel to be his special people, and not some other nation? Moses addresses that question, but doesn't give a totally satisfactory answer.

First, Moses says, God's choice has nothing to do with man's merit. "For you are a holy people to the LORD your God; the LORD your God has chosen you to be a people for His own possession out of all the peoples who are on the face of the earth. The LORD did not set His love on you nor choose you because you were more in number than any of the peoples, for you were the fewest of all peoples" (Deuteronomy 7:6-7). Israel certainly was not the largest nation in the world. It got started with just one man, and then one family. Therefore, there was no inherent good in that nation for God to choose Israel.

Moses does point out, however, that God's choice is consistent with his love and faithfulness: "But because the LORD loved you and kept the oath which He swore to your forefathers, the LORD brought you out by a mighty hand, and redeemed you from the house of slavery, from the hand of Pharaoh king of Egypt. Know therefore that the LORD your God, He is God, the faithful God, who keeps His covenant and His lovingkindness to a thousandth generation with those who love Him and keep His commandments" (Deuteronomy 7:8-9).

But why did God love Israel? That is the mystery. And Moses adds no further light on the subject. Therefore, God's choice remains an unrevealed secret.

Consider a third fact which will help you better understand election. *Sinful man will not choose God on his own.* I make this statement on two bases. Adam, who was in a state of innocence, did not choose God. Therefore, how could we expect sinful man to choose God on his own? A second reason sinful man will not choose God on his own is the testimony of Scripture—"There is none righteous, not even one; there is none who understands, there is none who seeks for God; all have turned aside, together they have become useless; there is none who does good, there is not even one" (Romans 3:10-13).

Why does sinful man not choose God? Two reasons given in Scripture are because he does not want to, and because he cannot unless he is aided by God himself (1 Corinthians 2:14; John 6:44). Now with this information as a context, let's investigate the doctrine of election.

How Does Election Differ from Predestination?

Many times *election* and *predestination* are used interchangeably, but there is a distinction between them. *Predestination* defines God's purpose and plan; *election* decides whom God chooses to promote that purpose and plan. Just as a builder first designs a house (predestination) and then chooses those building materials with which he wants to build the house (election), so does God first design his plan (predestination) and then chooses those individuals who will promote that purpose and plan (election).

God's predetermined plan was to provide a sacrifice for sin: ". . . delivered up by the predetermined plan and foreknowledge of God" (Acts 2:23). On the other hand, God's elective choice was to choose Jesus as that sacrifice: "And a voice came out of the cloud, saying, 'This is My Son, My Chosen One; listen to Him!' " (Luke 9:35), and "By this will we have been sanctified through the offering of the body of Jesus Christ once for all" (Hebrews 10:10).

Another way of making the distinction is to say that predestination focuses on the plan, while election highlights the specific individuals involved in that plan. Let's delve a little bit further.

Is Election Limited Only to the Area of Salvation?

The Bible uses the word *elect* in different ways, so it is not limited to salvation. For instance, *God chose one nation over all other nations to be his special people.* "For you are a holy people to the LORD your God; the LORD your God has chosen you to be a people for His own possession out of all the peoples who are on the face of the earth" (Deuteronomy 7:6). Think of the tremendous privilege the nation of Israel has had over the years. Though God loves the world to the point of sending his Son into this world, he has a special affection for the nation of Israel. And he is not through with that nation. That it continues to survive indicates that God still has a purpose and plan for his special people. Many nations of the world believe that Israel is not God's special people. Others think that if they were, he obviously has by now rejected them.

But listen to what Paul has to say about this issue: "God has not rejected His people whom He foreknew. Or do you not know what the Scripture says in the passage about Elijah, how he pleads with God against Israel? . . . For I do not want you, brethren, to be uninformed of this mystery, lest you be wise in your own estimation, that a partial hardening has happened to Israel until the fulness of the Gentiles has come in; and thus all Israel will be saved; just as it is written, 'The Deliverer will come from Zion, He will remove ungodliness from Jacob. And this is My covenant with them, when I take away their sins.' From the standpoint of the gospel they are enemies for your sake, but from the standpoint of God's choice they are beloved for the sake of the fathers; for the gifts and the calling of God are irrevocable" (Romans 11:2, 25-29).

Election is not limited to a nation. *God also chose one man out of all other men from which to build that special nation.* That man was Abraham. "Now the Lord said to Abram, 'Go forth from your country, and from your relatives and from your father's house, to the land which I will show you; and I will make you a great nation, and I will bless you, and make your name great; and so you shall be a blessing; and I will bless those who bless you, and the one who curses you I will curse. And in you all the families of the earth shall be blessed" (Genesis 12:1-3).

God's elective choice even reaches into particular families. For instance, *God chose one brother to serve the other brother.* I'm referring to Jacob and Esau. Paul writes to the Romans, "And not only this, but there was Rebekah also, when she had conceived twins by one man, our father Isaac; for though the twins were not yet born, and had not done anything good or bad, in order that God's purpose according to His choice might stand, not because of works, but because of Him who calls, it was said to her, 'The older will serve the younger.' " (Romans 9:10-12). Did you notice that their goodness or badness had no influence on God's elective decision? In fact, if conduct had been a contributing factor, Esau would have been the favored brother.

God also chose one woman above all other women to give birth to his Son. That women was Mary, the espoused wife of Joseph. The announcement of this miracle is recorded in the Gospel of Luke. "Now in the sixth month the angel Gabriel was sent from God to a city in Galilee, called Nazareth, to a virgin engaged to a man whose name was Joseph, of the descendants of David; and the virgin's name was Mary. And coming in, he said to her, 'Hail, favored one! The Lord is with you.' But she was greatly troubled at this statement, and kept pondering what kind of salutation this might be. And the angel said to her, 'Do not be afraid, Mary; for you have found favor with God. And behold, you will conceive in your womb, and bear a son, and you shall name Him Jesus'" (Luke 1:26-31). Remember that Mary herself was astonished that she was chosen for such a special honor. She was not necessarily the most godly of all the women in the land, but she was God's choice.

Do we see God's elective choice in any other area? Very definitely.

God chose to feed only one widow in the days of Elijah. There were many widows in the day that Elijah preached for God. And yet out of all those widows, God sent him to only one. "But I say to you in truth, there were many widows in Israel in the days of Elijah, when the sky was shut up for three years and six months, when a great famine came over all the land; and yet Elijah was sent to none of them, but only to Zarephath, in the land of Sidon, to a woman who was a widow" (Luke 4:25-26).

And what about the days of Elisha? *God chose to heal only one man of leprosy in Elisha's days.* "And there were many lepers in Israel in the time of Elisha the prophet; and none of them was cleansed, but only Naaman the Syrian" (Luke 4:27). This does not indicate that God disliked the other lepers or that he had no time for the other widows. Because God is sovereign, he does as he pleases, and his will is consistent with his character of holiness, righteousness, and justice. Even today he may choose to heal one person and not another for reasons known only to himself.

What Is Divine Election?

What then is divine election? Divine election is *not what some people think it is.* Many people see election from a negative standpoint, and believe that it is the process of God's choosing some people for hell. But the Bible does not reveal a God of that nature. God neither predestines, nor does he elect anyone to hell. God possesses a compassionate nature. "The Lord is not slow about His promise, as some count slowness, but is patient toward you, not wishing for any to perish but for all to come to repentance" (2 Peter 3:9). Man will not end up in hell because God chose him to go there. He wants man to repent and come to him.

One day many years ago we opened our front door and our beagle scampered out the door, down the street, and out of sight. We called in vain for him to come home. We searched up and down the street, but our efforts were fruitless. We returned to the house and waited a few hours until it was time to go to bed. Before turning in for the evening, we decided to take one more look. I opened the front door and discovered my dog on the doorstep, lying in shock. He had a large gash in his back and his left hind leg was almost completely severed. The dog survived, though his leg had to be amputated. It was not our will or desire that he run out the door. It was our desire that he return to us. But no matter how much we called, he paid no attention. Instead, he returned when he became aware that he had a desperate need.

Likewise, though God is not willing for any to perish, many do perish because they run away from God to do their own thing. They ignore God's constant calling and pleading for them to return to him. They perish because of their choice, not because of his choice.

Another misconception some people have about election is that it bars certain people from heaven. But on the contrary, election excludes no one from heaven. Election is positive. It provides for and guarantees that some will enter heaven. It is man's free choice to neglect God that bars him from heaven. Everyone who ends up in hell will be there by an act of his choice not to accept God's provision for sin.

There are two ways a person can view heaven. One perspective sees multitudes eager to enter heaven, but the gate is locked. Then God comes out to the crowd and chooses certain ones to enter with him, while he pushes the others away from the gate, even though they desperately want in. This is a distorted view of man's desire to find God. It elevates man's goodness and demotes God's justice. The Bible is very clear that God will never turn away anyone who wants to enter heaven: "All that the Father gives Me shall come to Me, and the one who comes to Me I will certainly not cast out" (John 6:37).

The second perspective of heaven is that no one wants to enter on God's terms, and yet the gate is wide open for everyone. But no one shows up or chooses to enter. Therefore, God goes out and persuades some of those who have refused to come to enter with him. The rest of the people stand outside the gate ignoring God's offer. This view is consistent with Jesus' plea, "Come to Me, all who are weary and heavy-laden, and I will give you rest. Take My yoke upon you, and learn from Me, for I am gentle and humble in heart; and you shall find rest for your souls. For My yoke is easy, and My load is light" (Matthew 11:28-30).

If election is not God's choosing some people for hell, or his barring others from heaven, then what is it?

Election is God's choosing specific individuals to accomplish his predetermined plan. Another way of putting it is to say that "election is the process by which God chooses certain individuals for certain purposes while bypassing others."

Election is based upon God's foreknowledge. The apostle Peter tells us this when he writes, "Peter, an apostle of Jesus Christ, to those who reside as aliens, scattered throughout Pontus, Galatia, Cappadocia, Asia, and Bithynia, who are chosen according to the foreknowledge of God the Father, by the sanctifying work of the Spirit, that you may obey Jesus Christ and be sprinkled with His blood: May grace and peace be yours in fullest measure" (1 Peter 1:1-2). Now, this brings up another question—what is foreknowledge? Is it merely preknowledge about the future, or does it imply predetermined knowledge, which is knowledge based on the predetermined plan of God?

The word itself comes from the Greek *prognosis*, from which we derive the same term. Though it means "to know beforehand," it conveys more than the idea of just knowing something about the future. For instance, Israel was fore-known by God: "God has not rejected His people whom He foreknew" (Romans 11:2). Did God just look into the future and see that a nation by the name of Israel was going to appear on the scene, and therefore decide to choose Abraham as the father of that nation? Or did he foreknow the existence of Israel, because he planned the existence of Israel?

The Bible also tells us that God foreknew Jesus Christ. "For He was foreknown before the foundation of the world, but has appeared in these last times for the sake of you who through Him are believers in God, who raised Him from the dead and gave Him glory, so that your faith and hope are in God" (1 Peter 1:20-21). Again, did God look into the future and see someone by the name of Jesus Christ appear on the scene, or did Jesus Christ appear because God the Father planned it that way?

In the same vein, God foreknew believers. "For whom He foreknew, He also predestined to become conformed to the image of His Son, that He might be the first-born among many brethren; and whom He predestined, these He also called; and whom He called, these He also jus-tified; and whom He justified, these He also glorified" (Ro-mans 8:29-30). It is obvious in the first two instances that Israel existed as a nation because God planned for them to exist. Likewise, Jesus Christ came to this earth because God predetermined his arrival. It was through his plan for Israel and for his Son that he foreknew what was going to take place. In the same way, because he predetermined be-lievers to come to him and then chose those who would, he knew beforehand who would come.

When I was a teenager I worked one summer for a builder. Knowing zero about the building trade, I carried out my responsibilities without any idea how my digging ditches or cleaning up debris would play a part in the finished product. But the builder knew exactly what the finished product was going to look like, because he de-signed it. You and I often are unaware of what part our life plays in God's overall plan. But just as the builder chooses various subcontractors to build a house, so does God make his choices according to his predetermined plan. God does not plan because he knows what the future is going to be like; rather, he knows the future because he follows his own plan.

Election is not only based upon God's foreknowledge, it also includes man's responsibility to choose God. Notice how election and responsibility work hand-in-hand. Jesus said, "All that the Father gives Me shall come to Me, and the one who comes to Me I will certainly not cast out. . . . No one can come to Me, unless the Father who sent Me draws him; and I will raise him up on the last day. . . . For this reason I have said to you, that no one can come to Me, unless it has been granted him from the Father" (John 6:37, 44, 65). Only when God's election of man and man's response to God coincide will there be a true new birth.

Let's move on to God's purpose for election.

What Are God's Purposes for Election?

The Scriptures imply five specific purposes why God elects. They include salvation, godly living, witnessing, humility, and productivity.

Salvation

First, God elects so that *some of those who are perishing will be saved.* Paul writes to the church at Thessalonica, "But we should always give thanks to God for you, brethren beloved by the Lord, because God has chosen you from the beginning for salvation through sanctification by the Spirit and faith in the truth" (2 Thessalonians 2:13). The word used in this passage is not the regular word *eklectos*, meaning to elect, but rather *aireo*, meaning to choose. The apostle Paul used this word when he said, "For to me, to live is Christ, and to die is gain. But if I am to live on in the flesh, this will mean fruitful labor for me; and I do not know which to choose" (Philippians 1:21-22). God chooses some for salvation. If he did not so choose, no one would be saved. If you are concerned whether you have been chosen to salvation, all you need to do is to respond to his call. Come to him by faith, and he will not reject you.

But don't stop at this point. Besides appreciating the fact that you have been chosen by God for salvation, also recognize that God has chosen you for another purpose.

Godly Living

God elects individuals so that *they will live godly lives.* Paul writes, "Just as He chose us in Him before the foundation of the world, that we should be holy and blameless before Him" (Ephesians 1:4). He also focuses on the elect's responsibility toward holy living when he tells the Colossians, "And so, as those who have been chosen of God, holy and beloved, put on a heart of compassion, kindness, humility, gentleness and patience; bearing with one another, and forgiving each other, whoever has a complaint against anyone; just as the Lord forgave you, so also should you" (Colossians 3:12-13). No one chooses such a lifestyle on his own. A person may choose a religious life, or even a pious life, but not a Christ-like life with all of its qualities.

Witnessing

Another purpose for election is expressed by Peter. *God has chosen men and women so that they might tell others about him.* Peter says, "But you are a chosen race, a royal priesthood, a holy nation, a people for God's own possession, that you may proclaim the excellencies of Him who has called you out of darkness into His marvelous light" (1 Peter 2:9). This good news of salvation is not to be kept to ourselves. When a young man proposes to his girlfriend and gives her a diamond, she can't wait to share her excitement with her parents and friends. She wants everyone to know about the wise choice her boyfriend has made. She also wants to show everyone her ring and introduce everyone to the one who has chosen her to be his bride. In a similar way, as God has chosen you to live with him throughout eternity and has given you his Holy Spirit as a guarantee of his intentions, it should be just as natural for you to want to introduce others to him.

Humility

A fourth reason God used his prerogative to choose was so that *the elect would live humbly before him.* Humility is not to be confused with low self-esteem. The apostle Paul was a humble man, but he testified, "I can do all things through Him [Christ] who strengthens me" (Philippians 4:13). True humility recognizes that everything one has is a result of God's grace. Though we deserve nothing, God has given us everything. He has given us minds with the ability to think lofty thoughts and create great works. He gives us strength to follow through on projects that we start. He sets us free from the power of sin, so that we can be the kind of people he has chosen us to be.

Though the wise man boasts in his wisdom, the rich in his money, the physically attractive in his looks, and the powerful in his position, the Christian has only to boast in the Lord. Paul put it so well when he wrote, "For consider your calling, brethren, that there were not many wise according to the flesh, not many mighty, not many noble; but God has chosen the foolish things of the world to shame the wise, and God has chosen the weak things of the world to shame the things which are strong, and the base things of the world and the despised, God has chosen, the things that are not, that He might nullify the things that are, that no man should boast before God. But by His doing you are in Christ Jesus, who became to us wisdom from God, and righteousness and sanctification, and redemption, that, just as it is written, 'Let him who boasts, boast in the Lord'" (1 Corinthians 1:26-31). Notice that phrase, "But by His doing you are in Christ Jesus" (v. 30).

Many years ago the great hymn writer Charles Wesley penned these words: "And can it be that I should gain an interest in the Savior's blood? Died He for me who caused His pain? For me, who Him to death pursued? Amazing love! How can it be that Thou, my God, shouldst die for me?" Election should never result in boasting about ourselves. But it should help us to recognize that our salvation is his doing.

Productivity

Another reason for God's election is that *the elect would live productively*. One of the great tragedies of our time is that so many people waste life. They contribute little to the lives of others because they have little interest in them. They live a day at a time, heading in no particular direction. But God has chosen the elect to be productive. Jesus said, "You did not choose Me, but I chose you, and appointed you, that you should go and bear fruit, and that your fruit should remain, that whatever you ask of the Father in My name, He may give to you" (John 15:16). A fruitful life is productive.

This purpose of election is consistent with his purpose for choosing the Hebrews. He made it possible for them to be productive, but they were not. So God sent the prophet Isaiah to awaken their natural conscience that they had failed to live up to God's elective purpose. Isaiah speaks for God, declaring, "Let me sing now for my well-beloved a song of my beloved concerning His vineyard. My well-beloved had a vineyard on a fertile hill. And He dug it all around, removed its stones, and planted it with the choicest vine. And He built a tower in the middle of it, and hewed out a wine vat in it; then He expected it to produce good grapes, but it produced only worthless ones. And now, O inhabitants of Jerusalem and men of Judah, judge between Me and My vineyard. What more was there to do for My vineyard that I have not done in it? Why, when I expected it to produce good grapes did it produce worthless ones? . . . For the vineyard of the LORD of hosts is the house of Israel, and the men of Judah His delightful plant" (Isaiah 5:1-4, 7).

Too many Christians are like the people of Israel in that they were chosen for one purpose but decide instead to live their lives for themselves. Rather than bearing the fruit of the Spirit, they produce sour grapes. Their management of life is little different from that of the unbeliever.

Now, with these purposes in mind, consider the practical values of election.

What Are the Practical Values of Election?

Gratitude

One of the important values of election is that it can *give you a tremendous sense of gratitude.* When you consider that God saw fit to select you out of the billions of people on earth to be his child and to enjoy him forever, there can be only one response—gratitude. Even though he knew you would fail him after you were a believer, he still chose you.

Paul talks about gratitude when he writes, "And let the peace of Christ rule in your hearts, to which indeed you were called in one body; and be thankful" (Colossians 3:15). Too often we Christians behave like the child at Christmas who is deluged by gifts. He reaches out for each gift, opens it, looks at it, puts it aside, and asks, "What else did you get me?"

An unthankful Christian is a paradox. The critical Christian and the believer who wallows in self-pity are equally contradictions. The believer has been given so much. But because his eyes are on his own problems and personal ambitions, he pities himself when things don't go right, criticizes others, and complains that life is treating him badly. Election should send a surge of gratitude through every believer's heart.

A Sense of Responsibility

Another value of election is that it can *give you a great sense of responsibility to live for God.*

His name was Franklin Edward Ray. There was nothing unique about him. He was not a university graduate. He did not hold any political office. Nor was he a wealthy man. Even his occupation was routine. And those who seemed to appreciate him the most were the children who rode his bus each day to school.

But on July 15, 1976, he was catapulted to national attention. For Franklin Ray drove the Chowchilla, California, school bus which was hijacked by three kidnapers.

The kidnapers buried the entire bus, along with its passengers, until a ransom was paid. The children spent fifteen hours entombed in the bus. Some of them gave up hope. But the bus driver refused to give in to despair. With the help of some of the children, Ray freed himself and the passengers and led them to safety. At the news of their release, a group of teary-eyed parents, a town, and an entire nation, rejoiced in the deliverance of these children from near-certain death. And a man who had just hours before lived a relatively secluded life was being proclaimed a national hero. The parents were not only overwhelmingly grateful for what he had done for their children, but they also felt a responsibility to honor the man who had saved their children.

Scripture clearly indicates that we were at one time entrapped and entombed by the power of sin. We lived in despair without hope. There seemed to be no way out of our situation. But then God showed us the way of escape. His Son, the Lord Jesus Christ, led us out of certain death and brought us into a place of life and light. This elective purpose of God should motivate us to honor the One who delivered us. And there is no better way to honor the One who chose you to be his child than to live each day of your life for him.

Paul describes this method of honoring God by writing, "For the love of Christ controls us, having concluded this, that one died for all, therefore all died; and He died for all, that they who live should no longer live for themselves, but for Him who died and rose again on their behalf" (2 Corinthians 5:14-15). Everyone has to live for something or someone. When we were born into this world we lived for ourselves. Now it's time to change masters. There are many examples of people who are ignoring God and living for themselves, and not one of them is experiencing a truly fulfilled life. Instead they are destroying themselves.

Confidence to Share Your Faith

Election can also *give you greater confidence to share your faith*. There is a passage in the book of Acts which unites man's free will with God's election. Paul and Barnabas were on their first missionary journey. They arrived at the city of Antioch and preached Christ in the synagogue. Luke records the scene. "And as Paul and Barnabas were going out, the people kept begging that these things might be spoken to them the next Sabbath. Now when the meeting of the synagogue had broken up, many of the Jews and of the God-fearing proselytes followed Paul and Barnabas, who, speaking to them, were urging them to continue in the grace of God. And the next Sabbath nearly the whole city assembled to hear the word of God. But when the Jews saw the crowds, they were filled with jealousy, and began contradicting the things spoken by Paul, and were blaspheming. And Paul and Barnabas spoke out boldly and said, 'It was necessary that the word of God should be spoken to you first; since you repudiate it, and judge yourselves unworthy of eternal life, behold, we are turning to the Gentiles. For thus the Lord has commanded us, "I have placed You as a light for the Gentiles, that You should bring salvation to the end of the earth." And when the Gentiles heard this, they began rejoicing and glorifying the word of the Lord; and as many as had been appointed to eternal life believed" (Acts 13:42-48).

While the Jews freely refused to listen to the gospel, the Gentiles freely rejoiced that the gospel was available to them and believed. Though the majority of Jews had spurned his message, Paul did not stop preaching. He knew that many had been appointed unto eternal life. He just didn't know who they were. So when the Jews closed the door on the gospel, the apostle did what common sense would dictate. He turned to the Gentiles. It's like the farmer who goes into his orchard to pick fruit. He picks what is ripe and leaves what is not ready.

How did Paul know that God's elect were in the city? Besides seeing some Corinthians trust in Christ, the Lord informed him. "And the Lord said to Paul in the night by a vision, 'Do not be afraid any longer, but go on speaking and do not be silent; for I am with you, and no man will attack you in order to harm you, for I have many people in this city.' And he settled there a year and six months, teaching the word of God among them" (Acts 18:9-11). God promised Paul that many more would come to Christ. Though they were elect, they had to hear the gospel in order to respond in faith. Therefore, Paul was responsible to stay in that city, preach the gospel, and allow God to produce the results.

Assured that God's elect were in every city, Paul was willing to endure persecution and rejection. He testifies to this fact, as he tells Timothy: "For this reason I endure all things for the sake of those who are chosen, that they also may obtain the salvation which is in Christ Jesus and with it eternal glory" (2 Timothy 2:10).

God's elect are in your family, at work, in your neighborhood, and throughout the city. Your responsibility is to pray that God will keep you sensitive to the opportunities for witness. You can be certain that people will respond to the gospel, even though you don't know who they are. So if you feel discouraged because people haven't responded to your witness as you would like, continue to be faithful to God, because he has his elect all around you.

A Knowledge of Your Responsibility

A fourth value of election is that *it distinguishes between your responsibility and God's responsibility.* During my college and seminary days, I always considered it my responsibility to force people to make a decision. I felt that God held me responsible to "get them saved." Whether they were ready to hear the gospel or not, I made certain they got the whole load.

A proper understanding of election distinguishes our responsibility from God's. God holds us responsible to be a faithful witness. Therefore, it is wise to take training in how to become a more effective witness. But God does not hold any of us responsible to save people. That is his responsibility. God changes the unbeliever into a believer. He predestines that unbeliever (Ephesians 1:5), elects him (Ephesians 1:4), gives him the ability to understand the truth (1 Corinthians 2:14; John 6:65), gives him the faith to believe (Ephesians 2:8-9), and then makes salvation so appealing that the unbeliever wants to receive Christ (Ephesians 2:13). Recall that . . . "by His doing you are in Christ Jesus" (1 Corinthians 1:30).

A Better Self-Image

Election can also *give you a better self-image*. Too many people walk around with a negative self-image. They have low self-esteem and feel inferior to everyone else. The apostle Paul encourages believers to maintain a healthy self-image when he says, "For through the grace given to me I say to every man among you not to think more highly of himself than he ought to think; but to think so as to have sound judgment, as God has allotted to each a measure of faith" (Romans 12:3). Your opinion of yourself should neither be exaggerated nor depreciated, but accurate.

What are the qualities of a person who has strong self-esteem? Is he boastful? Obnoxious? Opinionated? No. Such people are usually very productive on the job. They maintain a high moral and ethical sensitivity, have a strong sense of family, experience good inter-personal relationships, and see success more in terms of these relationships than of material possessions. In his book *Self-Esteem, The New Reformation*, Dr. Robert Schuller writes, "Because the human being is created in the image of God, the will to dignity is the irreduceable, psychological, and spiritual nucleus around which the life of the human soul revolves and evolves. The need for dignity, self-worth, self-respect, and self-esteem is the deepest of all human needs."[1] He further states, "Until we are conscious of our belonging to the family of God, we will experience an identity crisis which will create a self-esteem crisis."[2]

We often walk around with low self-esteem because we constantly compare ourselves with those around us. Instead of discovering what God has given to us and wants us to do with our lives, we focus on what other people are able to accomplish. Schuller borrows from an old Norwegian tale that illustrates this point.

A boy in the woods found an egg in a nest, took it home, placed it with the eggs under a goose, and it hatched out—a freakish creature! Its deformed feet—unwebbed, claw-like, made it stumble as it tried to follow the little geese. And his beak was not flat; it was pointed and twisted. Instead of having lovely cream-colored down, it was an ugly brown color. And to top it off, he made a terrible squawking sound! He seemed to be a genetic freak—so ugly and disfigured.

Then one day a giant eagle flew across the barnyard. The eagle swept lower and lower until the strange, awkward little bird on the ground lifted his head and pointed his crooked beak into the sky. The misfit creature then stretched his wings out and began to hobble across the yard. He flapped his wings harder and harder until the wind picked him up and carried him higher and higher. He began to soar through the clouds. He had discovered what he was—he was born an eagle! And he had been trying to live like a goose!"[3]

You are a child of God. You are predestined by God before the beginning of the world and chosen to fit into his masterplan for life. You no longer have to live like the world's crowd, you don't have to live in defeat, or to try to prove yourself worthy. God has selected you just as you are, and with your permission, he will make you into a person of great value. God has not designed you to crawl around on the ground, but rather to soar in the heavens.

How Should We Respond to Election?

What responses might you have to God's election?

You might be surprised, as Harry Truman was when he discovered that he, rather than Dewey, had been elected president. Truman could have responded by saying, "That's not fair. Dewey really should have been elected." Or he might have said with humility, "I don't really feel qualified to be president. What if I blow it? What if I make some wrong decisions? What if I can't live up to what's expected of me?"

History records how Truman responded. He received the news of his election confidently and dedicated the next four years to running the country to the best of his ability. Furthermore, Truman accepted complete responsibility for every decision he made, good or bad—and as a reminder of this, he kept a sign on his desk: "The Buck Stops Here."

Some people respond to their eternal election by arguing over the "fairness" of God's divine choice. From a human standpoint, none of us should have been chosen by God because none of us deserves it. You may want to argue with God about his sovereign choice, but that is futile. I well remember my own reaction toward election when I was first exposed to it as a student in Bible college. I couldn't accept it. I argued with my professor, declaring that God wasn't fair to choose some and not others. But eventually I accepted the truth of election. To the degree you understand election, accept it and move forward in your Christian life to make your calling and election certain (2 Peter 1:10-11).

You should also expect to wrestle with feelings of inadequacy and unworthiness. None of us has anything to boast about in our spiritual life, so a response of humility and gratitude for God's election is quite in order. That's a significant response.

Another reaction to God's elective choice is to commit yourself to the purposes for which God chose you—salvation, godly living, witnessing, humility, and productivity.

The purpose of a traffic light is to control traffic so people can drive in safety. When the light fails, the result can be miles of backed up traffic, frustrated drivers, and potentially serious accidents. In a similar sense, when we fail to carry out the purposes for which we have been chosen, we will experience lives of spiritual stagnation, frustration, and many spiritual and moral accidents.

Election is a precious truth which should alter your lifestyle and give you a lasting appreciation for God. But if election boggles your mind about God's fairness, read on and ask yourself how fair it was for God to send one innocent person to his death for the sake of the multitude who were guilty.

1. Robert Schuller, *Self-Esteem, the New Reformation* (Waco: Word Books, 1982), pp. 33-34.

2. Ibid., p. 59.

3. Ibid., pp. 59-60.

CHAPTER 3

TAKING
YOUR
PLACE
SUBSTITUTION

Substitution is a concept familiar to most people today because it is practiced in so many quarters. The athlete understands substitution because he has either relieved another player in a game or has been relieved himself. A teacher knows about substitution, because he has filled in for an absentee or has had a substitute replace him. Actors have stand-ins prepared to perform if for some reason they, themselves, cannot.

But in each of these cases the substitute is usually considered a lesser light than the person whose place he takes. Furthermore, it is usually to the substitute's advantage to replace the star, because then the substitute has a chance to show what he can do. For instance, Danny White, quarterback of the Dallas Cowboys, was in the shadow of Roger Staubach for many years. But periodically he got the chance to show what he could do. So when Staubach retired from his outstanding football career, White became the number one choice to replace him. Likewise, many great talents in the theater and other professions are discovered when they have to fill in for another person.

But suppose you were asked to substitute for someone who didn't even like you, to take the blame for something you didn't do in the first place. Further, you were told that when you accept the person's blame, you will end your career rather than advance it. Worst of all, you learn that the person whose blame you will take will never appreciate what you do for him. How fast would you volunteer for the job? I doubt any of us would step forward. Yet these were the conditions placed before the One who did volunteer to be a substitute. His name was Jesus of Nazareth. And the task for which he volunteered was to take the punishment for our sins. Let's investigate this astounding concept further by considering what substitution means and how it affects us today.

The Nature of Christ's Substitution

What is the origin of Jesus' substitution? Jesus' substitutionary death on the cross originated in a plan between Father and Son and was foreshadowed in the Old Testament sacrifices. This plan did not develop from the Roman soldiers, nor from the Jewish religious system. It was conceived in eternity past between God the Father and Son. The event is recorded in the book of Hebrews where the Son says to the Father, " 'Sacrifice and offering Thou hast not desired, but a body Thou hast prepared for Me; in whole burnt offerings and sacrifices for sin Thou hast taken no pleasure. Then I said, "Behold, I have come (in the roll of the book it is written of Me) to do Thy will, O God."' . . . By this will we have been sanctified through the offering of the body of Jesus Christ once for all. And every priest stands daily ministering and offering time after time the same sacrifices, which can never take away sins; but He, having offered one sacrifice for sins for all time, sat down at the right hand of God" (Hebrews 10:5-7, 10-12).

Luke records the same plan in the book of Acts when he quotes Peter's sermon: "Men of Israel, listen to these words: Jesus the Nazarene, a man attested to you by God with miracles and wonders and signs which God performed through Him in your midst, just as you yourselves know— this Man, delivered up by the predetermined plan and foreknowledge of God, you nailed to a cross by the hands of godless men and put Him to death" (Acts 2:22-23).

SUBSTITUTION

The Jewish religion is embellished with two types of sacrifices: the non-sweet savor offerings and the sweet savor offerings. The non-sweet savor offerings covered the nation's sins and trespasses and indicated that God cannot abide sin: "... Thou hast not desired ... Thou hast taken no pleasure" (Hebrews 10:5, 6). The sweet savor offerings, which included the burnt offering, the meal offering, and the peace offering, delight the Father. They are sweet to God in view of Christ's perfection.

John the Baptist saw Jesus as a sacrifice for sin when he said, "Behold, the Lamb of God who takes away the sin of the world!" (John 1:29). And as the sacrifices of the Old Testament were made for the benefit of and on behalf of the Jewish people, so Jesus Christ was the Lamb that was to be slain for the benefit of and on behalf of mankind.

What words indicate the concept of substitution? There are two Greek words which imply substitution, though the term itself as applied to Christ's death is not found in Scripture. The idea of substitution is derived from two Greek prepositions. The first one is *huper* meaning "for the benefit of" or "on behalf of." Jesus used this word during the Last Supper: "And when He had taken some bread and given thanks, He broke it, and gave it to them, saying, 'This is My body which is given *for* (*huper*) you; do this in remembrance of Me.' And in the same way He took the cup after they had eaten, saying, 'This cup which is poured out *for* (*huper*) you is the new covenant in My blood'" (Luke 22:19-20). Again, as the Lord spoke about being the Good Shepherd, he told his disciples, "Even as the Father knows Me and I know the Father; and I lay down My life *for* (*huper*) the sheep" (John 10:15).

The other Greek preposition which implies substitution is the word *anti*, meaning "instead of" or "in place of." Again, this term is used by the Lord when he speaks to the disciples about sitting in the kingdom. He said, "Just as the Son of Man did not come to be served, but to serve, and to give His life a ransom *for* (*anti*) many" (Matthew 20:28). Therefore, the death of the Lord Jesus Christ was a death for the benefit of and in place of the sinner.

What does the substitution of Christ mean? It means that

Jesus Christ is the substitute who has taken man's place on the cross, bearing both his sin and his punishment for sin.

Several months ago I saw a tragic incident on *60 Minutes*. The reporter interviewed a man who spent eight years in prison for a crime which he did not commit. But circumstantial evidence and a resemblance to the criminal sent him to prison. In the process, this innocent man paid the penalty of the man who was guilty. He had also been separated from those he loved the most, his wife and child. He was cursed with the label of "convict," alienated from friends, suspected in the eyes of many people, and unable to get a decent job when he was released from prison after the real criminal was apprehended and convicted. During all those years this man was a substitute—though involuntarily—for the guilty man, who remained free.

In a much fuller way the Lord Jesus Christ was our substitute at the cross. As our substitute, the innocent suffered for the guilty. The prophet Isaiah wrote many centuries ago, "He was despised and forsaken of men, a man of sorrows, and acquainted with grief; and like one from whom men hide their face, he was despised, and we did not esteem Him. Surely our griefs He Himself bore, and our sorrows He carried; yet we ourselves esteemed Him stricken, smitten of God, and afflicted. But He was pierced through for our transgressions, He was crushed for our iniquities; the chastening for our well-being fell upon Him, and by His scourging we are healed" (Isaiah 53:3-5). The apostle Peter echoed the same theme, when he wrote, "For Christ also died for sins once for all, the just for the unjust, in order that He might bring us to God, having been put to death in the flesh, but made alive in the spirit" (1 Peter 3:18).

Not only did the innocent suffer for the guilty, but the innocent was also separated from the One he most loved—his heavenly Father. As the Lord hung on the cross, bearing the sins of the world, the Father had to turn his back on that sin. It meant that he also turned his back on his Son (Matthew 27:46).

The innocent became a curse in place of the guilty—"Christ redeemed us from the curse of the Law, having become a curse for us—for it is written, 'Cursed is everyone who hangs on a tree'" (Galatians 3:13).

Jesus' substitution means that he suffered for the guilty, was separated from the One he most loved, and became a curse in place of the guilty. That's the negative side of substitution. But what about the positive side?

The Benefits of Christ's Substitution

Sin's Penalty Is Paid

Out of the many benefits that could be cited, let's consider three advantages Jesus won for us by his death on the cross. First of all, *we do not have to pay sin's penalty*. So many religions in the world teach their followers that somehow they must do something to appease the gods. It may include some form of penance or making some great sacrifice to placate the gods' wrath against mankind. In many religious teachings man has to pay for his own sin. But the good news in Christianity is that the penalty has already been paid.

A college education is not confined to the classroom. This was highlighted for me when my older son related an experience he'll never forget. He was driving with one of his dorm buddies through a small town in Illinois. Apparently his friend had been traveling about forty-five miles per hour in a thirty-five mile-per-hour zone. Like a housefly zooming naively into the web of a spider, my son's buddy drove into the web of a speed trap. The driver saw the flashing lights in his rear-view mirror, pulled over to the side, and was informed that he had violated the speed limit. They were immediately taken to the local jail where they were told that according to Illinois law they either had to pay a fifty-dollar fine or remain in jail overnight. Being typical college students, they had only thirteen dollars between them. Since they were permitted to make one phone call, my son called the dormitory and asked one of his dorm mates to take a collection among the residents and bail them out of their dilemma. They tried to be cheerful during the next one-and-a-half hours of confinement until one of the students arrived with the other thirty-seven dollars.

Once the fine was paid, Rick and his friend had one of two options. They could have stayed in jail that night by refusing to accept the generosity of their fellow students, or they could accept their friends' gracious act and go free. I'm sure I don't have to tell you which option they chose.

And yet so many people refuse Jesus' substitutionary death on the cross as a payment for their sin. They remain imprisoned spiritually, one day going out into eternity having to pay the penalty of their sins. Christ's substitutionary death means that we do not have to pay for sin's penalty. And this isn't the only benefit of the Lord's substitution.

We Can Come to God

A second benefit of Christ's substitution is that *we can come to God*. When a person accepts Jesus' payment for his sin, God no longer is angry with him. Since God's anger is removed, the believer feels free to enter into God's presence.

In the Old Testament tabernacle and temple, a large curtain or veil separated the holy place from the holy of holies (where the presence of God dwelt). The priests could enter the holy place, but they were not permitted to enter the holy of holies. Only the high priest could enter the holy of holies, and that only once a year on the Day of Atonement. But at the crucifixion, something unprecedented took place in the temple—"And Jesus cried out again with a loud voice, and yielded up His spirit. And behold, the veil of the temple was torn in two from top to bottom, and the earth shook; and the rocks were split, and the tombs were opened; and many bodies of the saints who had fallen asleep were raised; and coming out of the tombs after His resurrection they entered the holy city and appeared to many" (Matthew 27:50-53). The tearing of the temple veil showed that access was now available to everyone who wanted to enter the presence of God.

The writer to the Hebrews applied this symbol to the believer's daily life by writing, "Now where there is forgiveness of these things, there is no longer any offering for sin. Since therefore, brethren, we have confidence to enter the holy place by the blood of Jesus, by a new and living way which He inaugurated for us through the veil, that is, His flesh, and since we have a great priest over the house of God, let us draw near with a sincere heart in full assurance of faith, having our hearts sprinkled clean from an evil conscience and our bodies washed with pure water" (Hebrews 10:18-22). No longer do we need to fear God's wrath. Because Jesus died in our place, he made it possible for us to enter the presence of God.

Dying to Sin and Living to Righteousness

A third benefit of Christ's substitution deals with death and resurrection. Because Jesus died in our place, *we can die to sin and live to righteousness*. The apostle Peter wrote, "And He Himself bore our sins in His body on the cross, that we might die to sin and live to righteousness; for by His wounds you were healed" (1 Peter 2:24).

What does it mean to die to sin? Dying to sin begins with one's attitude. The apostle Paul wrote, "Even so consider yourselves to be dead to sin, but alive to God in Christ Jesus" (Romans 6:11). The Scriptures also say, "For as he thinks within himself, so he is" (Proverbs 23:7). Our attitudes toward ourselves often determine our behavior. A person who thinks he's a loser will act like a loser. The one who considers himself a winner will act like a winner. But how does this relate to sin?

Anyone who thinks that he has to yield to sin will yield to it. But the one who believes that both the penalty and the power of sin were nullified at the cross will live as though sin no longer has control over his life. That's why Paul continued, "Therefore do not let sin reign in your mortal body that you should obey its lusts, and do not go on presenting the members of your body to sin as instruments of unrighteousness; but present yourselves to God as those alive from the dead, and your members as instruments of righteousness to God" (Romans 6:12-13). When the Spirit of God has mastery of you, you will not be sinning. Therefore, every time you are tempted to disobey God, recognize that you don't have to yield to that temptation.

The positive side is that you can live to righteousness. You do so by connecting with the Holy Spirit, who is your energy source for living for God.

When I was a child, streetcars were still popular in Lancaster, Pennsylvania. Despite their noise and the hard ride, streetcars were always fun to travel in. And they never had problems with flat tires, since there were no tires. Nor did they ever run out of gas, because they were not fueled by gas. They were powered instead by electricity. That would periodically cause problems.

The power to run the streetcars was in an overhead line, and each streetcar was connected to the line by a long pole. Sometimes at a busy intersection, where a number of the overhead lines were strung, the streetcar's pole would slip off the line. When that would happen, the power was cut off and the streetcar could go nowhere. The driver would have to jump out, walk to the back of the car, and reconnect the pole to the line. Once the car was again in contact with its power source, it was off and running.

We live righteously by remaining connected to the Holy Spirit through prayer, study of the Word, and obedience. Whenever we decide to run life on our own power source, however, we disconnect ourselves from the free flow of the Holy Spirit and make no more progression in our spiritual lives. We indulge in the desires of the flesh and place ourselves under the mastery of sin. The fact that Jesus died in our place allows us to consider ourselves dead unto sin but alive unto righteousness.

Now, having looked at the nature of Christ's substitution and its benefits, let's address the problem of reverse substitution.

SUBSTITUTION

The Problem of Reverse Substitution

In Christ's substitution, the innocent took the place of the guilty; the just died for the unjust. But even after we have accepted Jesus' substitutionary act of love at the cross, it's possible to develop a kind of reverse substitution by choosing the bad in place of the good or replacing the best with the worst. Whenever we select "things" instead of Christ by committing ourselves to them, we are guilty of reverse substitution. What do people normally substitute for Christ?

Personal Interests

Some substitute selfish ambition and personal interests for Christ. The Lord gave a message to the prophet Jeremiah's secretary, whose name was Baruch. He said, "But you, are you seeking great things for yourself? Do not seek them ..." (Jeremiah 45:5). There is nothing wrong with having high goals, as long as they are in line with God's will and character. But some people become consumed with their ambitions and personal interests to the point of willingly violating the known will of God. For instance, Judas was a very ambitious man and was willing to take immoral shortcuts in order to achieve his goals. The apostle John's verdict on Judas is recorded in his gospel. He writes, "But Judas Iscariot, one of His disciples, who was intending to betray Him, said, 'Why was this perfume not sold for three hundred denarii, and given to poor people?' Now he said this, not because he was concerned about the poor, but because he was a thief, and as he had the money box, he used to pilfer what was put into it" (John 12:4-6). Judas was so possessed by his own ambition that he was willing to betray a friend for a few pieces of silver—"Then one of the twelve, named Judas Iscariot, went to the chief priests, and said, 'What are you willing to give me to deliver Him up to you?' And they weighed out to him thirty pieces of silver. And from then on he began looking for a good opportunity to betray Him" (Matthew 26:14-16).

When an individual gets to the place in his life where he is willing to betray his friends or use them for his own selfish purposes, he has substituted ambition and personal interests for Christ.

Tradition

Some substitute traditions and religion for Christ. When I was in seminary, my wife and I befriended a couple with whom we spent a lot of time. He was from a Unitarian background, which denies the deity of Christ and the necessity of the new birth. We had talked frequently about spiritual things, and when on one particular occasion he became very inquisitive I had the opportunity of sharing the claims which Jesus made about himself. After my friend heard that Jesus declared himself God and that he had the authority to forgive sins, I asked, "Do you believe that Jesus was a liar?"

He replied, "No, I believe he was telling the truth."

I then inquired, "If Jesus were telling the truth by claiming not only to be God but also to be the only one who could forgive sins so that man could enter heaven, what does a person need to do to have his sins forgiven and enter heaven?"

He replied, "Apparently he has to ask Jesus to forgive him of his sins."

I continued. "Would you like to receive Jesus Christ as your Savior and have your sins forgiven, so that you may enter heaven?"

He replied, "Yes, I'd like to. However, if I really believe what you told me and act upon it, then I will have to repudiate everything that I've been taught since I was a child. And I just can't bring myself to turn my back on what I've been taught."

Here was a young man who could not give up his religious teaching, even though it opposed the truth in Scripture. He was like the religious leaders of Jesus' day who had a form of godliness, but never experienced the reality of God. Jesus denounced them: "But woe to you, scribes and Pharisees, hypocrites, because you shut off the kingdom of heaven from men; for you do not enter in yourselves, nor do you allow those who are entering to go in. Woe to you, scribes and Pharisees, hypocrites, because you devour widows' houses, even while for a pretense you make long prayers; therefore you shall receive greater condemnation. Woe to you, scribes and Pharisees, hypocrites, because you travel about on sea and land to make one proselyte; and when he becomes one, you make him twice as much a son of hell as yourselves" (Matthew 23:13-15). On another occasion he told the Pharisees, "'Neglecting the commandment of God, you hold to the tradition of men.' He was also saying to them, 'You nicely set aside the commandment of God in order to keep your tradition'" (Mark 7:8-9).

Are you placing your security in a church, a religion, or a tradition? If so, then you are substituting traditions and religion for a personal relationship with Jesus Christ.

Possessions

Some substitute money and possessions for Christ. Remember the account of the rich young ruler who asked Jesus how one gains eternal life? The Lord's response was not what he gave to Nicodemus when he told him, "You must be born again." The Lord realized that what stood between this young man and God was the young man's attitude toward his money and possessions. They were actually his god. Jesus told him he needed to get rid of his man-made god so that he could have a personal relationship with the one and only God. He said, "'You know the commandments, "Do not commit adultery, Do not murder, Do not steal, Do not bear false witness, Honor your father and mother."' And he said, 'All these things I have kept from my youth.' And when Jesus heard this, He said to him, 'One thing you still lack; sell all that you possess, and distribute it to the poor, and you shall have treasure in heaven; and come, follow Me.' But when he had heard these things, he became very sad; for he was extremely rich. And Jesus looked at him and said, 'How hard it is for those who are wealthy to enter the kingdom of God!'" (Luke 18:20-24).

Why is it difficult for the wealthy to enter the kingdom of God? Because wealth too often becomes their god. One does not have to be wealthy for money to become his god, however. Anyone trusting his money or possessions for security makes those things his god.

Even Christians can fall into this dilemma. They begin by making and controlling money, but end up as the slave of their own financial Frankenstein. They find it difficult to be generous toward others, and discover that they are investing a lot of time and energy only to accumulate more things.

Education

Consider another substitute. *Some will substitute education and wisdom for Christ.* The richest man in the world, Croesus, once asked the wisest man in the world, Thales, "What is God?" The philosopher asked for a day in which to deliberate, and then for another, and then for another, and another, and another—and at length confessed that he was not able to answer, that the longer he deliberated, the more difficult it was for him to frame an answer.

The fiery Tertullian, an early church father, eagerly seized upon this incident, saying it was an example of the world's ignorance of God outside of Christ. "There," he exclaimed, "is the wisest man in the world, and he cannot tell you who God is. But the most ignorant individual among the Christians knows God, and is able to make Him known unto others."

The apostle Paul said that by wisdom man failed to know God (1 Corinthians 1:21). "Professing to be wise, they became fools" (Romans 1:22), he wrote about those claiming great wisdom. Some misguided people believe that they are too intelligent for God. They develop their own method of gaining heaven, or they dismiss the existence of heaven and hell entirely and have no concerns about eternity. They hope that by denying the existence of hell, they can somehow escape its penalty.

That's as profound a solution as an individual in a ten-story building who, jumping out the window, tells himself that he's on the first floor and has nothing to worry about. He may deny the existence of the law of gravity. He may even deny the fact that he's jumping from the tenth floor of the building. He can deny all of these facts . . . but only for a few seconds. The coroner could attest to that.

Pleasure

Consider one further substitute. *Some even substitute pleasure for Christ.* The apostle of the first century warned that the pursuit of pleasure would be a characteristic of the last days. "For men will be lovers of self, lovers of money, boastful, arrogant, revilers, disobedient to parents, ungrateful, unholy, unloving, irreconcilable, malicious gossips, without self-control, brutal, haters of good, treacherous, reckless, conceited, lovers of pleasure rather than lovers of God" (2 Timothy 3:2-4). I don't know of a better description of our present generation. Loving pleasure rather than God, however, is not limited to the unbeliever.

During the first century a man named Demas sometimes traveled with the apostle Paul. The Bible doesn't give us too much information about him, but what it does offer is a description of a spiritual drifter.

Demas was with Paul when he wrote his Epistle to the church at Colossae (Colossians 4:14) and when he wrote to Philemon (Philemon 24). Demas had the unique advantage of observing the great apostle first-hand. He witnessed God's power operate through that Spirit-filled believer in many dynamic ways. But though Demas was physically present with Paul and other godly men, his heart was in the world, which lured him to forsake Paul when the apostle needed him most. So in his final letter to Timothy, the apostle Paul wrote, "Make every effort to come to me soon; for Demas, having loved this present world, has deserted me and gone to Thessalonica . . ." (2 Timothy 4:9-10). Demas had every spiritual advantage, but his heart was not committed to God. The world's pleasures became more appealing than pleasing Christ. The writer of Proverbs says, "He who loves pleasure will become a poor man . . ." (Proverbs 21:17). Demas, indeed, became a spiritually poor man because he substituted pleasure for Christ.

This reverse substitution occurs either when we put our confidence in things or when we allow them to consume our interests, time, and energy.

Consider the following questions as you evaluate whether you are involved with reverse substitution.

1. In what are your placing your confidence for security or success?

2. What is consuming the majority of your interests? Your time? Your energy?

3. What do you spend your time talking about most?

We've learned of the nature and benefits of substitution, as well as the problem of reverse substitution. Let's focus now on how one can become Christ's substitute in the world.

How Can We Become Christ's Substitutes in the World?

Get to Know the Holy Spirit

The first step one should take to become the Lord's substitute in the world is to *become acquainted with the Holy Spirit*. It is tragic how little knowledge the average Christian has about the person and ministry of the Holy Spirit. Some perceive the Holy Spirit as a mere force. Others think of him as an angel from heaven. But listen to how the Lord described the Holy Spirit as he gave his farewell address to his disciples. Jesus said, "And I will ask the Father, and He will give you another Helper, that He may be with you forever; that is the Spirit of truth, whom the world cannot receive, because it does not behold Him or know Him, but you know Him because He abides with you, and will be in you. I will not leave you as orphans; I will come to you. After a little while the world will behold Me no more; but you will behold Me; because I live, you shall live also" (John 14:16-19).

In this passage the Lord told his disciples he was sending a Helper who would be with the church forever. He stated further that this Helper is the Spirit of truth and would indwell each believer. The Christian does not live on the earth as a spiritual orphan, since he has experienced the indwelling presence of God's Holy Spirit. And it is through the Holy Spirit that he will be able to take his place in the world for his benefit.

God's Character in You

The second method concerns the believer's character. *Develop the Lord's character in your inner self.*

Perhaps one of the greatest impersonators of the past several decades is Rich Little. He has the ability to capture an individual's voice, gestures, and walk. Jimmy Stewart has said on numerous occasions that Rich Little sounds more like Jimmy Stewart than Jimmy Stewart.

I've always admired people who could imitate the voices and mannerisms of others, wondering how they develop their ability to impersonate. In various interviews Rich Little has divulged a number of his secrets. (1) He studies the individual very carefully; (2) he is an excellent listener not only to what is said but how it is said; (3) he carefully observes the mannerisms of the person he wants to imitate; and (4) he practices the person's voice and mannerisms over and over again. Actually his approach boils down to a strong commitment to carefully observing and practicing the voice and mannerisms of another.

The same qualities are essential if we are going to be Christ's substitutes on earth. Each of us needs to make a strong commitment to carefully observe and practice what the Lord has said and how the Lord behaved. This takes a strong commitment and a lifetime to accomplish. As the Lord was a man of compassion, other-centered, full of grace and truth, always pleasing the Father in what he did, so we need to observe and practice these same qualities.

I know this task is difficult. I've wrestled with many of the Lord's qualities as I've found them lacking in my life. The Lord centered his attention on people, and yet accomplished much. I find it easier to center my attention on many tasks and hope that people's needs are met in the process. The Lord was able to love those who despised him. I find it difficult even to like some people who misunderstand what I'm trying to accomplish or who question my motives. It's not easy to be Christ-like in a world of self-interest. In fact, I would say that without the continual ministry of the Holy Spirit in one's life, the task is impossible.

Finish What He Started

A third aid to becoming Christ's substitute in the world is to *complete what he started*. The Lord began to build his church on the day of Pentecost. He has been building it ever since. Sometimes his Church has become confused with buildings and programs. At other times it is confused with charismatic personalities. Some people equate the church with emotionalism, while others equate it with cold formalism. Many times the light has almost been snuffed out, and the church's voice became practically inaudible.

But the Lord always had a people which he called the church, people who experienced a new birth, individuals who refused to water down the truth for the sake of compromise and convenience.

Building the church of Jesus Christ means building the lives of the individuals who make up the body of Christ. That process includes evangelizing the lost, teaching God's truth to believers, comforting the afflicted, supporting the weak, and giving a cup of cold water in the name of the Savior to those who are thirsty. It also means helping people make the most of the potential which God has entrusted to them. And that demands one's personal commitment to prayer, time, service, and financial support of the ministries of the Church.

Count the Cost

One other method by which we can become Christ's substitutes in the world is to *count the cost and pay the price*. The Lord realized that his entrance into the world would cost him his life. But he counted the cost, and he was willing to pay the price. Too many people count the cost and then refuse to pay the price. Or they volunteer to pay the price before they know the cost, and then walk away from responsibility.

SUBSTITUTION

Jesus highlighted this problem when he told the parable about two sons. Responding to the chief priests and elders of the people who had challenged the authority with which he was speaking and performing miracles, Jesus replied, "'But what do you think? A man had two sons, and he came to the first and said, "Son, go work today in the vineyard." And he answered and said, "I will, sir"; and he did not go. And he came to the second and said the same thing. But he answered and said, "I will not"; yet he afterward regretted it and went. Which of the two did the will of his father?' They said, 'The latter.' Jesus said to them, 'Truly I say to you that the tax-gatherers and harlots will get into the kingdom of God before you. For John came to you in the way of righteousness and you did not believe him; but the tax-gatherers and harlots did believe him; and you, seeing this, did not even feel remorse afterward so as to believe him'" (Matthew 21:28-32).

Some people never volunteer to work for the things of God, thereby neglecting the gifts which God gave them for service. Those who promise a commitment but fail to follow through are no better off. Both groups are poor substitutes for Jesus Christ in the world.

Imagine the Lord refusing to come to this earth and die for man's sins. Or try to imagine him coming to the earth, but refusing to pay the price for man's salvation as the cross drew nearer. Saving his own life, he would have stranded man in a state of hopelessness. But Jesus counted the cost and paid the price willingly, took our place on the cross and experienced the wrath of God for our sin.

Substitution: taking the place of another for the benefit of another. That's what was going on 2,000 years ago on the hill of Golgotha. Now it is your responsibility to become his substitute in the world. You may be the only evidence of a renewed life that some people will ever see. Do your friends know that your life is a replica of Jesus Christ? Do they see his walk and hear his voice as they observe you? That's what it means to be a substitute—taking the place of another for the other's benefit.

To appreciate Christ's substitution even further, consider the transaction which took place when he died on your behalf. In the next chapter you'll discover what you gained as a result of the cross.

CHAPTER

4

CREDITING YOUR ACCOUNT IMPUTATION

I enjoy reading the comic strip *B.C.* Recently it showed a serpent crawling over to a bird and saying, "I'm eternally grateful that the computer has finally taken over." "Why do you say that?" asked the bird. "Up till now, I got all the blame for screwing up the world," the serpent answered.

That comic strip couldn't have appeared at a better time. That same week the television networks broadcast a story about a giant computer foul-up: The computer credited $161 billion dollars and some-odd cents to a woman's account, thus making her a paper billionaire overnight. That was the good news. The bad news? There was no money to back up the computer readout. And until her account was straightened out, she couldn't draw upon it even to buy a newspaper.

Let me tell you about another accounting system, one which never fouls up. It's a system with both debits and credits. Every human being is written in its ledger. You are either on the debit side or the credit side. The side on which your name appears depends on your personal relationship with God. And the process of crediting your account is called "imputation."

This chapter will focus on three aspects of imputation: its meaning, its applications, and its lessons.

What Is the Meaning of Imputation?

The Scriptures provide two Greek words which convey the idea of imputation: *ellegeo* and *logizomai*. Let's consider the first word.

Credit It to My Account

Imputation means to credit to one's account, according to the word *ellegeo*, which is found only twice in the New Testament (Romans 5:13; Philemon 18).

Recall the events that led the apostle Paul to write to Philemon, a personal friend. Philemon was a wealthy slave owner who became a believer in Jesus Christ. One of his slaves, Onesimus, ran away and may have taken some things which belonged to Philemon. Though we're not told how Onesimus met the apostle Paul, the renowned apostle did lead him into a personal relationship with Jesus Christ. As Onesimus grew in the Lord, Paul realized that he would have to send Onesimus back to his master. When Paul considered Onesimus spiritually prepared to return to his master, the apostle sat down, wrote a letter to Philemon, and sent it by Onesimus. The former slave left Paul and returned to his master.

The apostle asked Philemon to receive Onesimus as both a servant and as a brother in Christ. He wrote, "I appeal to you for my child, whom I have begotten in my imprisonment, Onesimus, who formerly was useless to you, but now is useful both to you and to me. And I have sent him back to you in person, that is, sending my very heart, whom I wished to keep with me, that in your behalf he might minister to me in my imprisonment for the gospel; but without your consent I did not want to do anything, that your goodness should not be as it were by compulsion, but of your own free will. For perhaps he was for this reason parted from you for a while, that you should have him back forever, no longer as a slave, but more than a slave, a beloved brother, especially to me, but how much more to you, both in the flesh and in the Lord. If then you regard me a partner, accept him as you would me" (Philemon 10-17).

IMPUTATION

Now notice how Paul uses the word *ellegeo* in his appeal to Philemon. He continues, "But if he has wronged you in any way, or owes you anything, *charge that to my account*" (Philemon 18).

That's imputation. Paul is saying, "Put that on my bill."

This appeal is similar to the account of the Good Samaritan. After the Good Samaritan had aided the man who had been beaten by taking him to an inn and providing food and shelter for him, he told the innkeeper, "Take care of him; and whatever more you spend, when I return, I will repay you" (Luke 10:35). Imputation conveys the idea of crediting something to one's account.

Reckon It to Me

But notice the second meaning of imputation. *The word also means "to reckon" or "to take into account,"* according to the word *logizomai*, which is used forty-one times in the New Testament, eleven of these times in Romans 4. Ten of those occurrences are translated "reckon," and once it is translated "take into account."

An illustration of such reckoning is recorded in the book of 2 Samuel. At this point in Israel's history, David is fleeing for his life. His son Absalom has seized the throne by a coup d'état. As the king and his entourage flee from town to town, the Scriptures say that "when King David came to Bahurim, behold, there came out from there a man of the family of the house of Saul whose name was Shimei, the son of Gera; he came out cursing continually as he came. And he threw stones at David and at all the servants of King David; and all the people and all the mighty men were at his right hand and at his left. And thus Shimei said when he cursed, 'Get out, get out, you man of bloodshed, and worthless fellow!' " (2 Samuel 16:5-7).

Later, Absalom is killed and David returns to Jerusalem as king. As he comes back through the town of Bahurim, Shimei realizes his error. Knowing that the king has power over life and death, Shimei expects to pay the consequences of his uncontrolled tongue. So at the news of David's return, the Scriptures record: "Then Shimei the son of Gera, the Benjamite who was from Bahurim, hurried and came down with the men of Judah to meet King David. And there were a thousand men of Benjamin with him, with Ziba the servant of the house of Saul, and his fifteen sons and his twenty servants with him; and they rushed to the Jordan before the king. Then they kept crossing the ford to bring over the king's household, and to do what was good in his sight. And Shimei the son of Gera fell down before the king as he was about to cross the Jordan. So he said to the king, 'Let not my lord *consider me guilty*, nor remember what your servant did wrong on the day when my lord the king came out from Jerusalem, so that the king should take it to heart. For your servant knows that I have sinned; therefore behold, I have come today, the first of all the house of Joseph to go down to meet my lord the king'" (2 Samuel 19:16-20). That's known as throwing yourself on the mercy of the court. When Shimei pleaded, "Let not my lord consider me guilty," the Hebrew word used conveys the same meaning as *logizomai*, emphasizing taking something into account.

Therefore, to impute means "to attribute something to a person, and then to treat him accordingly." Now that we have an idea of what imputation means, let's discover the various kinds of imputation recorded in Scripture.

What Kinds of Imputation Does the Bible Record?

Adam's Sin

The first imputation occurred when *Adam's sin was credited to the account of the entire human race.* God attributed Adam's sin to mankind and treated it accordingly.

Sin entered into this world through Adam: "Therefore, just as through one man sin entered into the world ..." (Romans 5:12). You might be thinking, "I thought Eve was the one who first sinned against God." That's true. Eve *was* the first human being who sinned against God. But God held Adam accountable for the human race, so it wasn't until he sinned willfully against a direct command of God that humanity was affected. The Scriptures make it very clear that Eve was deceived while Adam knew exactly what he was doing (1 Timothy 2:14).

Therefore, Adam became the federal head of the human race, and the disease of his sin spread throughout his descendants. Adam was like a "Typhoid Mary" who brought the disease into the world and passed that disease from one person to another. Adam's sin was contagious. You suffer today because of one man's sin.

Death, as well as sin, entered the world through Adam: "... and death through sin, and so death spread to all men, because all sinned" (Romans 5:12). Not only does the disease of sin spread throughout the human race, but its penalty is also passed on.

It's a sad commentary on society when drug addiction not only affects adults and teenagers, but infants as well. Each year thousands of babies whose mothers are alcoholics or drug addicts are born with the same addiction. As the disease of the mother is passed on to her child, so are the results of that disease. Likewise, as the disease of Adam's sin was passed on to his descendants, so were the effects: death. When Adam sinned, death penetrated the human body and spirit. People today die in three ways: physically, spiritually, and eternally.

Because Adam sinned against God, he died physically. "So all the days that Adam lived were nine hundred and thirty years, and he died" (Genesis 5:5). Adam's death was the promised result of his rebellion. "And the LORD God commanded the man, saying, 'From any tree of the garden you may eat freely; but from the tree of the knowledge of good and evil you shall not eat, for in the day that you eat from it you shall surely die'" (Genesis 2:16-17). That very day the process of death began in Adam's body, even though it took several hundred years for death to triumph.

Adam died in another way. His spiritual life separated from God: "And the man and his wife hid themselves from the presence of the LORD God among the trees of the garden" (Genesis 3:8). "Therefore the LORD God sent him out from the garden of Eden, to cultivate the ground from which he was taken. So He drove the man out . . ." (Genesis 3:23-24).

One who is alive spiritually is conscious of God and has a personal relationship with him. But anyone who is dead spiritually has either lost his sense of God-consciousness or he has no personal relationship with God.

One of the reasons it's difficult to tell whether some people are spiritually alive or dead is that they are very much alive physically, mentally, and emotionally. They seem to have it all together. They may be wealthy, attractive physically, healthy, and greatly admired by their friends. But if they have not established a personal relationship with Christ, they are spiritually dead.

A third type of death is an eternal separation from God. Eternal death is the continuation of spiritual death. A man who leaves this life apart from God will go into eternity separated from him with no hope of reconciliation. No second chance.

Adam's sin was credited to the entire human race, with the result that sin entered into the world and death entered with it. Some may object, "But that's not fair. Why does God hold me accountable for something that Adam did? Why should I take the blame and pay the penalty for something which I never did?" Let me assure you that though you pay for Adam's sin physically and spiritually, you *can* do something about the problem of spiritual death—and therefore avoid eternal death. This is where the second and third types of imputation become essential.

Credited to Christ

The second aspect of imputation is that *man's sin was credited to Jesus Christ*. As the first imputation demonstrated man's great need, the second imputation secures man's salvation. Jesus Christ became your substitute, dying on the cross for your benefit and in your place. And in the process he was treated both as a criminal and as a sinner.

Notice what Isaiah the prophet said about Jesus' being

treated like a criminal: "All of us like sheep have gone astray, each of us has turned to his own way; but the LORD has caused the iniquity of us all to fall on Him. . . . Therefore, I will allot Him a portion with the great, and He will divide the booty with the strong; because He poured out Himself to death, and was numbered with the transgressors; yet He Himself bore the sin of many, and interceded for the transgressors" (Isaiah 53:6, 12). Luke alludes to this twelfth verse of Isaiah 53 in the New Testament: "He was *classed* among criminals" (Luke 22:37, Moffatt). Here the word *logizomai* is translated "classed." God looked upon Jesus as one would look upon a criminal who had to pay the penalty for his crime.

I don't know if you've ever been treated like a criminal, but when I was a boy of about ten years of age, I was. One Saturday evening, two of my friends and I decided to watch the wrestling matches and swimming meets at a local college. I was familiar with the campus buildings because the college was close to my home and my uncle was the football and basketball coach. "I know a shortcut between the wrestling room and the swimming pool," I told my friends. "Follow me." I led them through the men's locker room, approaching the pool from the back. After watching the swimming meet for about an hour, we made our way back through the locker room to watch the conclusion of the wrestling match, and then went home.

At 7:00 the next morning, our doorbell rang. As my dad greeted the man at the door, I could hear the muffled voice saying, "Mr. Yohn, my name is Detective Mott from the Lancaster Police Department. Some money was stolen last night at the college during the swimming meet and the wrestling match. Your son and two other boys were seen in the men's locker room, and we would like to take him in for questioning."

The next thing I heard was my dad calling, "Rick, get dressed and come on downstairs." I got dressed quickly, ran down the steps, and was introduced to the detective.

He looked down at me and asked, "Son, were you up at Franklin and Marshall College last night?"

I said, "Yes, sir."

He replied, "I want you to come along with me to the police station and answer some questions."

I looked at my dad, who nodded. So I followed the detective out to the police car. One of my friends was already in the back seat. By this time I felt like a criminal. I knew I was innocent, but I began thinking my friend might have been responsible for the missing money. As we sat together in the back seat, the detective drove toward the other boy's house and picked him up.

When we arrived at the police station, the police separated the three of us. One of the other boys was questioned first. While that was going on, I was locked up in a small room as black as pitch, except for a small hole at the top of the door, which allowed a ray of light to shine into the room. I sat there for about half an hour.

I squinted painfully from the glare of light when the police opened the door. They marched me to another room where I sat on a stool, placed my hands on a sign printed with a file number, and was told to look into the camera. The detective said, "I'm going to ask you a question. If the light in the camera flashes, I'll know you are telling a lie." He looked at me and asked, "Did you take the money at the college?"

I said, "Absolutely not." Immediately the flashbulb went off.

The detective growled, "I knew you were lying. Now we'll take you into my office and get to the bottom of this."

He ordered me into his office and began the interrogation. "We know you took the money. We just want to know where you hid it."

"But I didn't take anything," I protested.

He leaned over his desk, gazed into my face, and replied, "You're lying. We know you took it. Your friend has already confessed that the three of you took the money."

I said, "They may have taken some money, but I know that I didn't take anything." The interrogation continued for another twenty minutes. I kept declaring my innocence and the detective kept accusing me of lying.

IMPUTATION

Finally the detective had enough. He said, "OK, if you won't confess, I'll have to take you to the county prison and put you away until you do confess." My friends and I returned to the police car and were driven out to the county prison. As we drove in, the detective said, "I'll give you one more chance. Confess that you took the money, and I'll let you go. But if you refuse to confess, I'm going to put you into this prison, and you won't get out until you're willing to admit what you've done." The three of us continued to claim our innocence.

The detective turned around and smiled. "I didn't think any of you boys really took the money, but I just had to be sure." Then he drove us home. Within two days they found the culprit—one of the college students from a visiting school.

I had never in my life felt more guilty for something I hadn't done. Never before had I been treated like a criminal. And when the Lord Jesus Christ hung on the cross for something he did not do, he too was treated like a criminal. But he was never released. He paid the penalty in full.

The Lord was not only treated like a criminal, he was also treated as a sinner: Our sin was placed upon him, and God's wrath fell upon him. "But the LORD has caused the iniquity of us all to fall on Him" (Isaiah 53:6). The word translated "fall" means "to hit the mark."

I'm amazed at how well skydivers hit the mark from so far up in the air. Sometimes at a football game the announcer will tell the spectators to look up into the air. We raise our heads and see a plane several thousand feet in the sky. Then the announcer shouts, "They've jumped!" As we strain our eyes to see the little dots falling from the plane, suddenly the parachutes open and skydivers descend toward the football stadium. In the middle of the field is a circle. Despite the great distance, the skydivers bypass all of the spectators and hit the center of the mark.

In a similar manner, man's sin fell upon one human being, rather than on the multitudes. And so as Jesus became the target of man's sin, the wrath of God fell squarely on him. Jesus was treated as a sinner. He was never made a sinner, however. This brings us to a third observation.

The Lord was completely sinless. The Bible says, "He [God the Father] made Him [Jesus] who knew no sin to be sin on our behalf . . ." (2 Corinthians 5:21). The Lord never experienced sin, nor did he inherit Adam's nature. He did not die for his own guilt. The prophet Isaiah wrote, "Surely our griefs He Himself bore, and our sorrows He carried; yet we ourselves esteemed Him stricken, smitten of God, and afflicted. But He was pierced through for our transgressions, He was crushed for our iniquities; the chastening for our well-being fell upon Him, and by His scourging we are healed" (Isaiah 53:4-5). The innocent one was declared guilty, treated both as a sinner and a criminal.

Credited to the Believer

But imputation doesn't stop here. The third imputation provides hope for every human being. *God's righteousness was credited to the believer*, guaranteeing man's eternal standing before God. The apostle Paul writes, "For if by the transgression of the one, death reigned through the one, much more those who receive the abundance of grace and of the gift of righteousness will reign in life through the One, Jesus Christ. . . . For as through the one man's disobedience the many were made sinners, even so through the obedience of the One, the many will be made righteous" (Romans 5:17, 19). He says further, "He made Him who knew no sin to be sin on our behalf, that we might become the righteousness of God in Him" (2 Corinthians 5:21).

The word translated "become" means "to become something that one is not." When Jesus came to the earth, the Scriptures declare, "And the Word became flesh, and dwelt among us . . ." (John 1:14). Jesus Christ, the second Person of the Trinity, became something that he was not—flesh.

God's righteousness provides the basis for the believer's acceptance before God. Because God credits his righteousness to our account, he can accept us without reservation. The demands of justice have been satisfied. Jesus has paid our debt.

Anyone who seeks to enter heaven on the basis of his own righteousness has as much chance of achieving that goal as someone who attempts to buy a new car with money from a Monopoly game. Our own righteousness just cannot achieve eternal life. Paul himself confessed, "More than that, I count all things to be loss in view of the surpassing value of knowing Christ Jesus my Lord, for whom I have suffered the loss of all things, and count them but rubbish in order that I may gain Christ, and may be found in Him, not having a righteousness of my own derived from the Law, but that which is through faith in Christ, the righteousness which comes from God on the basis of faith" (Philippians 3:8-9).

In his commentary on the book of Romans, Dr. Donald Grey Barnhouse writes,

> How is it possible to say: "All our sins are blotted out through Jesus Christ"; and to say: "We have been made supernaturally pleasing in the sight of God"; and then to say: "But of course we have to do something in order to be saved." There is the great illogic of the lack of faith. Let us rather say, "God has blotted out all my sins, and God has written down on my side of the ledger the righteousness which is His very own, crediting it to me, imputing it to me, reckoning it to me. Therefore, I have been made supernaturally pleasing in the sight of God, and that is what I am. I am redeemed, justified, and saved. From now on I must recognize the nobility of my position and live in the light of that grace."[1]

We have looked at the meaning of imputation and the three types of imputation. What principles can we draw from this truth?

What Principles Can We Deduce from Imputation?

Spiritual Bankruptcy

I want to draw your attention to two lessons. The first is that *man has a problem with his spiritual accounting system*. He overestimates what he has in heaven's bank account. He begins with a disadvantage, because man puts nothing into the account throughout his life. This is why the Lord on several occasions directed his listeners' attention to the need of laying up treasure in heaven. Jesus taught, "Do not lay up for yourselves treasures upon earth, where moth and rust destroy, and where thieves break in and steal. But lay up for yourselves treasures in heaven, where neither moth nor rust destroys, and where thieves do not break in or steal" (Matthew 6:19-20).

Jesus also spoke of a rich fool who decided to store all his possessions in new and larger barns. Then he planned to sit back and take his ease by eating, drinking, and being merry. Notice God's reply: "But God said to him, 'You fool! This very night your soul is required of you; and now who will own what you have prepared?' So is the man who lays up treasure for himself, and is not rich toward God" (Luke 12:20-21).

It's important to lay up treasures in heaven because all the treasures you and I have on this earth remain on the earth. Scripture clearly teaches this: "For we have brought nothing into the world, so we cannot take anything out of it either" (1 Timothy 6:7).

So man faces a dilemma. He has made no deposits in his heavenly bank account. And yet he makes many attempts to draw on his account, usually when he is in some kind of trouble. He shoots up a prayer to God, hoping for some miracle. That's like the individual who writes checks when he has no money in the bank. He may get away with it for about a month; but eventually it catches up to him.

Man's heavenly account is without funds because he has failed to make deposits. But he is also spiritually bankrupt, and cannot for that reason draw on his heavenly account. The Scriptures declare, "There is none righteous, not even one; there is none who understands, there is none who seeks for God; all have turned aside, together they have become useless; there is none who does good, there is not even one" (Romans 3:10-12). The average person does not understand how distorted a vision he has of his spiritual condition.

He's like those in the church of Laodicea, to which Jesus wrote, "I know your deeds, that you are neither cold nor hot; I would that you were cold or hot. So because you are lukewarm, and neither hot nor cold, I will spit you out of My mouth. Because you say, 'I am rich, and have become wealthy, and have need of nothing,' and you do not know that you are wretched and miserable and poor and blind and naked, I advise you to buy from Me gold refined by fire, that you may become rich, and white garments, that you may clothe yourself, and that the shame of your nakedness may not be revealed; and eyesalve to anoint your eyes, that you may see" (Revelation 3:15-18).

There's another problem with man's spiritual accounting system. He not only overestimates what he has in heaven's account, but he underestimates the debt which he owes God.

You've probably at some time gone grocery shopping to buy a few items, and ended up buying more than you had intended. Then as you checked out at the register, you discovered that your bill was far greater than you had anticipated.

The person without God goes shopping in the world of sin. He decides to buy just a few sinful pleasures here and there. But when he's ready to check out of life, he discovers that his bill comes to a million dollars, and all he has is a twenty-dollar bill. Why does he underestimate the debt which he owes God?

For one thing, he fails to understand how pure God is. The Old Testament prophet Isaiah thought he knew God quite well—until one day when he had a unique vision of God.

"In the year of King Uzziah's death, I saw the Lord sitting on a throne, lofty and exalted, with the train of His robe filling the temple. Seraphim stood above Him, each having six wings; with two he covered his face, and with two he covered his feet, and with two he flew. And one called out to another and said, 'Holy, Holy, Holy, is the LORD of hosts, the whole earth is full of His glory.' And the foundations of the thresholds trembled at the voice of him who called out, while the temple was filling with smoke" (Isaiah 6:1-4).

A match may seem to emit a lot of light in a dark room, but once it is exposed to the brilliance of sunlight it quickly fades into insignificance. Our personal righteousness may seem to shine brilliantly when we compare ourselves with others, but it rapidly fades when compared with the holiness of God Almighty.

Not only does man fail to understand how pure God is, but he also fails to understand how sinful he himself is. When Isaiah saw the holiness of God, he responded, "Woe is me, for I am ruined! Because I am a man of unclean lips, and I live among a people of unclean lips; for my eyes have seen the King, the LORD of hosts" (Isaiah 6:5).

Simon Peter had a similar reaction when he saw the Lord walking along the edge of a lake. Having caught nothing all night long, the disciples were frustrated. When Jesus told them to go further into the water, Simon replied, "'Master, we worked hard all night and caught nothing, but at Your bidding I will let down the nets.' And when they had done this, they enclosed a great quantity of fish; and their nets began to break; and they signaled to their partners in the other boat, for them to come and help them. And they came, and filled both of the boats, so that they began to sink" (Luke 5:5-7). When Simon Peter saw the glory of the Lord in this miracle, he fell down at Jesus' feet, saying, "Depart from me, for I am a sinful man, O Lord!" (Luke 5:8).

I find it difficult to make my way to my bedroom at night right after I have turned out all the lights. My eyes are not able to make a quick adjustment to the darkness. But if I have to get up in the middle of the night to walk to another part of the house, I have little trouble seeing where I'm going. My eyes have had a chance to adjust.

This is part of the spiritual problem which mankind faces. Men have become so accustomed to living in darkness that they don't know that they *are* living in darkness.

The Ultimate Accountant

Another important lesson is that *God is the ultimate accountant*. Because he is the ultimate accountant, you can be certain that he keeps accurate records. The Scriptures refer to various kinds of books, such as those which record the sins of men, the book of life which records all the living, and the Lamb's book of life which records those who are true believers.

Moses talks about God's book when he prays, "'But now, if Thou wilt, forgive their sin—and if not, please blot me out from Thy book which Thou hast written!' And the LORD said to Moses, 'Whoever has sinned against Me, I will blot him out of My book" (Exodus 32:32-33). He is referring to the book of the living. The prophet Isaiah says, "And it will come about that he who is left in Zion and remains in Jerusalem will be called holy—everyone who is recorded for life in Jerusalem" (Isaiah 4:3). Again this refers to the book which records the names of the living. Daniel also refers to such a book when he writes, "Now at that time Michael, the great prince who stands guard over the sons of your people, will arise. and there will be a time of distress such as never occurred since there was a nation until that time; and at that time your people, everyone who is found written in the book, will be rescued" (Daniel 12:1).

The Lord also knows those who belong to him, whose names are written in the Lamb's book of life. Paul, in writing to the church at Philippi, said, "Indeed, true comrade, I ask you also to help these women who have shared my struggle in the cause of the gospel, together with Clement also, and the rest of my fellow-workers, whose names are in the book of life" (Philippians 4:3). In the last book of the Bible, the Lord promises that those whose names are written in the book of life will never be blotted out. He says, "He who overcomes shall thus be clothed in white garments; and I will not erase his name from the book of life, and I will confess his name before My Father, and before His angels" (Revelation 3:5). Later, when the Scriptures refer to those who will inhabit heaven, the apostle John writes, "And nothing unclean and no one who practices abomination and lying, shall ever come into it, but only those whose names are written in the Lamb's book of life" (Revelation 21:27).

The Lord is equally well aware of those who do not have their names in the Lamb's book of life. The Scriptures talk about those living during the tribulation period whose names are not in the book of life: "And all who dwell on the earth will worship him [the beast], every one whose name has not been written from the foundation of the world in the book of life of the Lamb who has been slain" (Revelation 13:8). Again, referring to the antichrist, John says, "The beast that you saw was and is not, and is about to come up out of the abyss and to go to destruction. And those who dwell on the earth will wonder, whose name has not been written in the book of life from the foundation of the world, when they see the beast, that he was and is not and will come" (Revelation 17:8).

Once again, those whose names are not in the book of life are mentioned at the Great White Throne judgment: "And if anyone's name was not found written in the book of life, he was thrown into the lake of fire" (Revelation 20:15). God will never send anyone to hell who doesn't deserve it, nor will he ever allow anyone into heaven on the basis of his own righteousness.

Since God keeps accurate records, he will hold man accountable on the basis of those records. Man will be judged on the basis of his own personal sins. "And I saw the dead, the great and the small, standing before the throne, and books were opened; and another book was opened, which is the book of life; and the dead were judged from the things which were written in the books, according to their deeds. And the sea gave up the dead which were in it, and death and Hades gave up the dead which were in them; and they were judged, every one of them according to their deeds" (Revelation 20:12-13).

IMPUTATION

At this point man will have run out of excuses. He will not be able to say, "I didn't know." Nor will he be able to claim, "I really wasn't that bad." He will be standing before a holy and a just God. He will be reminded of the many opportunities he had to turn away from sin and to turn to God by trusting Jesus Christ as his personal Savior.

As a believer in Christ, you no longer owe a debt. It's been paid in full and you are a spiritual billionaire. All of Christ's righteousness has been transferred to your account.

Imputation—"the transaction by which God turns spiritual paupers into spiritual billionaires." Are you a spiritually wealthy believer living like a pauper? Begin to draw on Christ's righteousness and to live like a child of the King, because that's exactly what you are—God's child, possessing all the spiritual wealth you will ever need to live life to its fullest. Read on to learn how he has removed your problems so you can enjoy what you already possess.

---

1. Donald Grey Barnhouse, *Romans*, vol. 5: *God's Remedy* (Grand Rapids: Eerdmans, 1968), p. 210.

CHAPTER

5

REMOVING
YOUR
PROBLEMS
ATONEMENT

One day when my wife was
making popcorn in a pot, the oil caught fire and flames
shot into the air. My wife instinctively grabbed the pot by
the handle. Not certain what to do with it, she quickly put
it on the floor and grabbed the lid to smother the fire.
Though she solved the fire problem, she created another
one. When she lifted the pot, an ugly scorch mark remained
on the floor. How do you remove a mark which has burned
through part of your linoleum?

Our solution was to cover it with a throw rug. It worked
for a while. Guests would walk through the house and
never notice the mark.

But a few months later we discovered that our home-
owner's insurance would cover the accident. When the ad-
juster came to the house, he concluded that the only way
to get rid of the mark was to replace all of the linoleum.
Covering the mark was only a temporary solution. Removing the mark was the permanent solution.

The event in our kitchen illustrates how God has dealt
with the sin of man from the beginning of creation to today.
When man sinned against God, his soul was marred. God
then provided a temporary solution. The Lord gave Adam
and Eve animal skin clothing. An animal had to die so that
the stain in Adam's soul would be covered.

That solution continued until Jesus was crucified. At the cross God introduced a permanent solution for man's sin. He removed the stain of rebellion and replaced it with the righteousness of Christ.

Both the covering and the removal of sin are known as *atonement*.

The Two Sides of the Atonement

It's easy to become confused when speaking of the atonement, because the word has both a biblical and a theological meaning. Consider first the biblical meaning.

The Biblical Meaning

The biblical word translated *atonement* is the Hebrew *kaphar*, meaning "covering." The word is used seventy-seven times in the Old Testament, fifteen of those in Leviticus 16 alone. It is an Old Testament word exclusively. But if atonement means a mere "covering" of sin, why do we refer to Jesus Christ's death on the cross as an atonement for the sins of mankind?

The Theological Meaning

Atonement also has a theological meaning, and refers to everything that Jesus did at the cross. It means to be "at one" with God by Christ's taking away of sin. Because of Jesus' substitutionary death on the cross, man is now capable of becoming one with God. In fact, if you were to break the word into three syllables—"at-one-ment," the essence of the term will be clear. The Lord Jesus Christ alluded to this when he prayed for his disciples: "I do not ask in behalf of these alone, but for those also who believe in Me through their word; that they may all be one; even as Thou, Father, art in Me, and I in Thee, that they also may be in Us; that the world may believe that Thou didst send Me" (John 17:20-21). The apostle Paul writes, "But now in Christ Jesus you who formerly were far off have been brought near by the blood of Christ. For He Himself is our peace, who made both groups into one, and broke down the barrier of the dividing wall, by abolishing in His flesh the enmity, which is the Law of commandments contained in ordinances, that in Himself He might make the two into one new man, thus establishing peace, and might reconcile them both in one body to God through the cross, by it having put to death the enmity" (Ephesians 2:13-16). Christ's atonement not only brought man to God, but also brought man to man, removing ethnic and racial barriers.

How then does atonement differ from reconciliation? The term *reconciliation* refers to the results of the atonement—man was brought together with God. *Atonement*, on the other hand, focuses on removing sin so reconciliation is possible. You will not find the concept of "removing" sin in the Old Testament, however. And that brings up several built-in weaknesses in the Old Testament concept of atonement.

The Weakness of Old Testament Atonement

The book of Hebrews contrasts the sacrifices of the Old Testament and the sacrifice of the Lord Jesus Christ. Let's look at four weaknesses of Old Testament offerings.

Continual Sacrifice

The sacrifices of the Old Testament were weak in that *many sacrifices had to be made continually*—"For the Law, since it has only a shadow of the good things to come and not the very form of things, can never by the same sacrifices year by year, which they offer continually, make perfect those who draw near. . . . But in those sacrifices there is a reminder of sins year by year. . . . And every priest stands daily ministering and offering time after time the same sacrifices, which can never take away sins . . ." (Hebrews 10:1, 3, 11).

How often did sacrifice have to be made for sin? The high priest made atonement for the nation once a year by entering the holy of holies with the blood of an animal. "You shall not offer any strange incense on this altar, or burnt offering or meal offering; and you shall not pour out a libation on it. And Aaron shall make atonement on its horns once a year; he shall make atonement on it with the blood of the sin offering of atonement once a year through-out your generations. It is most holy to the LORD" (Exodus 30:9-10). As a nation Israel experienced atonement for sin once a year.

But what about the individual who sinned against God? He too needed to make atonement by offering an ani-mal as a sacrifice for his sin. "When a leader sins and unin-tentionally does any one of all the things which the LORD God has commanded not to be done, and he becomes guilty, if his sin which he has committed is made known to him, he shall bring for his offering a goat, a male without defect. And he shall lay his hand on the head of the male goat, and slay it in the place where they slay the burnt offer-ing before the LORD; it is a sin offering. Then the priest is to take some of the blood of the sin offering with his finger, and put it on the horns of the altar of burnt offering; and the rest of its blood he shall pour out at the base of the altar of burnt offering. . . . Thus the priest shall make atone-ment for him in regard to his sin, and he shall be forgiven. Now if anyone of the common people sins unintentionally in doing any of the things which the LORD has commanded not to be done, and becomes guilty, if his sin, which he has committed is made known to him, then he shall bring for his offering a goat, a female without defect, for his sin which he has committed . . ." (Leviticus 4:22-28). Perhaps this is one of the reasons so many people in biblical days had such large herds of animals!

Constant Reminder

The second weakness of Old Testament sacrifices was that *the offender was always reminded of his sin.* The sacrifices vividly portrayed the price of sin. Imagine how you would feel if you were raising sheep, goats, or cattle for food or clothing, but every time you sinned one of those animals had to give its life because of your sin. It was a powerful object lesson that sin is always costly—"Otherwise, would they not have ceased to be offered, because the worship-ers, having once been cleansed, would no longer have had consciousness of sins?" (Hebrews 10:2). Whenever someone observed one of his flock missing, he was reminded of sin.

An Imperfect Priest

Third, in the Old Testament *the priest had to atone for his own sins before he could atone for the sins of others.* The people recognized that he was no better than they. This is what the writer to the Hebrews referred to when he wrote, "Now when these things have been thus prepared, the priests are continually entering the outer tabernacle, performing the divine worship, but into the second only the high priest enters, once a year, not without taking blood, which he offers *for himself* and for the sins of the people committed in ignorance" (Hebrews 9:6-7). God does not permit a sinful man to atone for the sins of others. So the sins of the priest had to be covered before he could atone for others.

An Imperfect Result

One other weakness of the Old Testament was that *the atonement could never remove sin.* "For it is impossible for the blood of bulls and goats to take away sins" (Hebrews 10:4). If these sacrifices did not remove sins, of what value were they? The sacrifices in the Old Testament made it possible for God to pass over the sins of Old Testament believers and withhold immediate judgment. Two Greek words used in the New Testament, contrasting God's dealing with believers in the Old and New Testaments, bear this out.

The word *paresis* is translated "passed over." "For all have sinned and fall short of the glory of God, being justified as a gift by His grace through the redemption which is in Christ Jesus; whom God displayed publicly as a propitiation in His blood through faith. This was to demonstrate His righteousness, because in the forbearance of God He *passed over* the sins previously committed" (Romans 3:23-25). Luke uses a different word in the book of Acts to describe the same process of treating sin in the Old Testament: "Therefore, having *overlooked* the times of ignorance, God is now declaring to men that all everywhere should repent, because He has fixed a day in which He will judge the world in righteousness through a Man whom he has appointed, having furnished proof to all men by raising Him from the dead" (Acts 17:30-31).

God did not treat sin lightly in the Old Testament. But when men brought sacrifices by faith as an atonement for their sin, God was willing to withhold judgment and overlook their sin. The believers of the Old Testament did not have their sins removed; they merely had them covered.

By contrast, today God forgives man by removing sin and its penalty—"Of Him all the prophets bear witness that through His name everyone who believes in Him receives forgiveness of sins" (Acts 10:43). The word translated "forgiveness" is the Greek *aphesis*, meaning "cancellation" or "release." The sins of Old Testament believers were covered over, while in the New Testament they are cancelled, released, or removed.

If you were eating at a restaurant and unintentionally dropped food on your clothes, leaving a grease mark, you would have one of two options: attempt to cover the stain, or use stain remover to remove it. Covering the stain is merely a temporary measure, and it doesn't really solve the problem. To wear those clothes in public again, you need to take the permanent solution and remove the stain.

The sins of Old Testament believers were merely covered by the blood of bulls and goats, so that God would not bring judgment upon the sinner. But Christ's atoning death on the cross removed the stain of sin for believers throughout history.

Let's now consider the cleansing agent for man's sin.

Jesus' Personal Sacrifice Atoned for Man's Sin

The sacrifice of the Lord Jesus Christ contrasts enormously with the sacrifices of Old Testament priests. In fact, it was the insufficiency of Old Testament sacrifices that prompted Jesus to say to his Father before coming to earth, "Sacrifice and offering Thou hast not desired, but a body Thou hast prepared for Me; in whole burnt offerings and sacrifices for sin Thou hast taken no pleasure. Then I said, 'Behold, I have come (in the roll of the book it is written of

Me) to do Thy will, O God'" (Hebrews 10:5-7). The *atoning* agent has always been blood, but the final *cleansing* agent is the blood of Jesus Christ. The songwriter highlights this when he writes, "What can wash away my sins? Nothing but the blood of Jesus. What can make me whole again? Nothing but the blood of Jesus."

The sacrifice of Christ differed from Old Testament sacrifices in at least three ways.

One Sacrifice

The Lord offered only one sacrifice, in contrast to the many sacrifices of the Old Testament. Notice the testimony of Hebrews: "For it was fitting that we should have such a high priest, holy, innocent, undefiled, separated from sinners and exalted above the heavens; who does not need daily, like those high priests, to offer up sacrifices, first for His own sins, and then for the sins of the people, because this He did *once for all* when He offered up Himself. . . . But when Christ appeared as a high priest of the good things to come, He entered through the greater and more perfect tabernacle, not made with hands, that is to say, not of this creation; and not through the blood of goats and calves, but through His own blood, He entered the holy place *once for all*, having obtained eternal redemption. . . . For Christ did not enter a holy place made with hands, a mere copy of the true one, but into heaven itself, now to appear in the presence of God for us; nor was it that He should offer Himself often, as the high priest enters the holy place year by year with blood not his own. Otherwise, He would have needed to suffer often since the foundation of the world; but now *once* at the consummation of the ages He has been manifested to put away sin by the sacrifice of Himself. . . . And every priest stands daily ministering and offering time after time the same sacrifices, which can never take away sins; but He, having offered *one sacrifice* for sins for all time, sat down at the right hand of God" (Hebrews 7:26-27; 9:11-12, 24-26; 10:11-12).

The contrast between Christ's one sacrifice and the Old Testament priests' many sacrifices is seen even today in the contrast between the Protestant and the Roman Catholic churches. The Roman Catholic Church celebrates a mass, where Christ is often offered as a sacrifice. Protestants reject the practice.

In his book entitled *Roman Catholicism*, Dr. Lorraine Boettner quotes from the Creed of Pope Pius IV. The pope wrote, "I profess that in the mass is offered to God a true, proper, and propitiatory sacrifice (that is, sacrifice which satisfies the justice of God and so offsets the penalty for sin) for the living and the dead; and that in the most holy sacrament of the Eucharist there is truly, really, and substantially, the body and blood, together with the soul and divinity, of our Lord Jesus Christ; and that there is a conversion of the whole substance of the bread into the body, and the whole substance of the wine into the blood, which the Catholic Church calls transubstantiation."[1] Then Dr. Boettner quotes from A *Catechism of Christian Doctrine*: "The holy mass is the sacrifice of the body and blood of Jesus Christ, really present on the altar under the appearance of bread and wine, and offered to God for the living and the dead."[2] And finally, from a book entitled *The Dignity and Duties of the Priest*, Boettner quotes, "With regard to the power of the priests over the real body of Christ, it is of faith that when they pronounce the words of consecration, the incarnate God has obliged Himself to obey and come into their hands under the sacramental appearance of bread and wine. We are struck with wonder when we find that in obedience to the words of His priests—*hoc est corpus meum* (this is My body)—God Himself descends on the altar, and He comes whenever they call Him, and as often as they call Him, and places Himself in their hands, even though they should be His enemies. And after having come He remains, entirely at their disposal and they move Him as they please from one place to another."[3]

In contrast, many in the Protestant church view the bread and the wine as symbols of the body and blood of Jesus Christ. Every Memorial Day a wreath is placed on the tomb of the Unknown Soldier, who gave his life for his country once and for all. The soldier does not die every

Memorial Day, but he is remembered. Likewise, when we partake of the bread and the wine, we do not sacrifice the Lord again and again, but rather remember the once-for-all sacrifice which he made on the cross to atone for the sins of mankind.

For All Time

A second contrast between Christ's sacrifice and those of the Old Testament is that *his sacrifice was for all time.* The writer to the Hebrews says, "And He is the radiance of His glory and the exact representation of His nature, and upholds all things by the word of His power. When He had made purification of sins, He sat down at the right hand of the Majesty on high. . . . But He, having offered one sacrifice for sins *for all time,* sat down at the right hand of God" (Hebrews 1:3; 10:12). Today Jesus is seated at the right hand of the Father. His work is finished.

When you put in a hard day of work, you look forward to going home and sitting down. Likewise, when Jesus finished his work on earth, he went home and sat down. The next time you will find the Lord standing is when he is about to bring judgment upon the world during the Great Tribulation—"And I saw between the throne (with the four living creatures) and the elders a Lamb *standing,* as if slain, having seven horns and seven eyes, which are the seven Spirits of God, sent out into all the earth. And He came, and He took it out of the right hand of Him who sat on the throne. And when He had taken the book, the four living creatures and the twenty-four elders fell down before the Lamb, having each one a harp, and golden bowls full of incense, which are the prayers of the saints. And they sang a new song, saying, 'Worthy art Thou to take the book, and to break its seals; for Thou wast slain, and didst purchase for God with Thy blood men from every tribe and tongue and people and nation" (Revelation 5:6-9).

Complete Forgiveness

The third contrast is that *Christ's sacrifice brought complete forgiveness.* When the Lord shed his blood on the cross, sins were not merely covered over, they were removed. "For by one offering He has perfected for all time those who are sanctified.... Now where there is forgiveness of these things, there is no longer any offering for sin." "And you know that He appeared in order *to take away sins*; and in Him there is no sin" (Hebrews 10:14, 18; 1 John 3:5). Another songwriter penned, "There is a fountain filled with blood drawn from Emmanuel's veins, and sinners plunged beneath that flood lose all their guilty stains."

When referring to the atonement of Jesus Christ, therefore, we do not think of the Old Testament concept which emphasizes a covering of sin, but rather the New Testament concept stressing the removing of sin.

The Implications of Christ's Atonement

Jesus' atonement for the sins of men implies at least two things.

The first implication is that *we can't improve on his sacrifice.* There is nothing that man can do to wash away his own sin. There is no offering that he can bring to God that will remove sin. Another songwriter captured this idea when she wrote, "Just as I am without one plea, but that Thy blood was shed for me, and that Thou bidst me come to Thee, O Lamb of God, I come! I come!" The only way to receive cleansing is to come to God just as you are. And yet man has tried to improve on Christ's atoning sacrifice by adding penance, good works, good intentions, and other paraphernalia. But joining a church, getting baptized, giving money, or saying a lot of prayers cannot add anything to the sufficiency of Jesus' atoning death.

The second implication of the atonement is that *we don't have to guess about our relationship with God.* It's a tragedy when a person receives God's forgiveness for his sin and accepts Christ's atoning death, but then lives with the guilt of some past sin. God does not want you to live in guilt. He is not the One who reminds you of past sin. Satan is the accuser of the believer. So if you feel guilty because of something in the past, realize that when God forgave that sin, he also removed the guilt of that sin. King David testified, "I acknowledged my sin to Thee, and my iniquity I did not hide; I said, 'I will confess my transgressions to the LORD'; and Thou didst forgive the guilt of my sin" (Psalm 32:5). Hebrews puts it this way: "For if the blood of goats and bulls and the ashes of a heifer sprinkling those who have been defiled, sanctify for the cleansing of the flesh, how much more will the blood of Christ, who through the eternal Spirit offered Himself without blemish to God, cleanse your conscience from dead works to serve the living God?" (Hebrews 9:13-14).

Appreciating Christ's Atonement

Jesus was willing to offer himself as a sacrifice on our behalf in order that we might have complete forgiveness and removal of sin's penalty. We can add nothing to what he has already provided. But we can show our appreciation for Christ's atonement.

Because the central focus of Christ's atonement is his sacrifice on the cross, we can be thankful by offering spiritual sacrifices to him—"You also, as living stones, are being built up as a spiritual house for a holy priesthood, to offer up spiritual sacrifices acceptable to God through Jesus Christ" (1 Peter 2:5). The sacrifices that the Lord would appreciate are not animal sacrifices. He takes no delight in them. But the Scriptures do suggest a variety of spiritual sacrifices we can offer to God.

Thanksgiving

The Psalmist speaks about a sacrifice of *thanksgiving*—"Offer to God a sacrifice of thanksgiving. . . . He who offers a sacrifice of thanksgiving honors Me; and to him who orders his way aright I shall show the salvation of God" (Psalm 50:14, 23). The Psalmist again declares, "Let them give thanks to the LORD for His lovingkindness, and for His wonders to the sons of men! Let them also offer sacrifices of thanksgiving, and tell of His works with joyful singing" (Psalm 107:21-22).

I'm sure you've felt disappointed when you've gone out

of your way to help a person but haven't received a thank you. Even though you're not looking for the praise of men, it's nice to know that you've been appreciated for your help. God rendered us such a priceless service when he sent Christ to atone for our sins that Jesus' sacrificial act should challenge all of us to continually offer up sacrifices of thanksgiving.

There are so many negative and critical people in the world today. The Church has its quiver full of those who feel chosen to tell you what is wrong while neglecting to say anything that is right. I have discovered that it's difficult to be critical and negative when I'm full of thanksgiving. So offer up a sacrifice of thanksgiving, not only for his atonement, but also for the many specific ways in which he blesses you.

Our Bodies

Another sacrificial offering which we can make in appreciation for Christ's atonement is to *offer him our bodies*—"I urge you therefore, brethren, by the mercies of God, to present your bodies a living and holy sacrifice, acceptable to God, which is your spiritual service of worship" (Romans 12:1). Paul says that such a sacrifice is our spiritual service of worship. The bodies we have are the only ones we will receive this side of eternity. We know that they have their limitations and are susceptible to sickness, disease, and accidents. But many of our physical problems are self-induced. When we abuse our bodies, we are abusing the temple of the Holy Spirit (which doesn't belong to us in the first place, 1 Corinthians 6:19). How can we offer our bodies as a living sacrifice to God?

One way is to take care of yourself. Eat the right kinds of food, the proper amounts of food, and get the proper amount of rest and exercise. I don't know of any Old or New Testament saint who "burned out" for God. When a person abuses his body "for the sake of Christ," he does not stand on biblical grounds.

Another way to offer your body as a living sacrifice is to use it for the honor of God. This includes how you dress.

ATONEMENT

Do you realize that your outward appearance makes a statement to other people? That statement may be intentional or unintentional, but your appearance does say something to others.

Picture how you think the following individuals would dress. "I'm a tough guy." "I'm successful." "I'm sexy and available." "I'm a rebel." "I'm a non-conformist." "I don't care how I look."

Now which of those individuals do you believe honors the Lord with the way he or she dresses? Which one of these individuals places a high value on developing his or her character?

How you dress tells people more about yourself than you may want them to know.

Another way to use your body for his honor is in the way you relate to the opposite sex. Do you treat the opposite sex as something to use for self-gratification, or someone to respect for whom he or she is? Presenting your body as a living sacrifice is an excellent way of showing the Lord you appreciate Christ's atoning death.

Money

Financial commitment is another type of sacrifice to offer God. When the apostle Paul received financial help from the church at Philippi, he told them, ". . . no church shared with me in the matter of giving and receiving but you alone; for even in Thessalonica you sent a gift more than once for my needs. Not that I seek the gift itself, but I seek for the profit which increases to your account. But I have received everything in full, and have an abundance; I am amply supplied, having received from Epaphroditus what you have sent, a fragrant aroma, *an acceptable sacrifice*, well-pleasing to God" (Philippians 4:15-18). The writer to the Hebrews also mentions this sacrifice when he writes, "And do not neglect doing good and sharing; for with such sacrifices God is pleased" (Hebrews 13:16).

I was very touched recently when I received a letter from a friend in our church who has been unemployed for five months. This person wrote, "How I know the Lord has something exciting for me to do in the near future. I will not wait to commit myself or my anticipated income or postpone it until 'times are better.' I will give a tithe of what I have. I never thought I would tithe what I anticipated rather than what I earned, but here I am 'proving the Lord' and trusting Him to provide that which I need and that which He wants me to have and be a steward of in the future." That, my friend, is a sacrifice pleasing unto the Lord.

Humility

The Scriptures also refer to a sacrifice of *humility*. In his prayer of confession, David prayed to God, "For Thou dost not delight in sacrifice, otherwise I would give it; Thou art not pleased with burnt offering. The sacrifices of God are a broken spirit; a broken and a contrite heart, O God, Thou wilt not despise" (Psalm 51:16-17). The humble always receive more of God's grace while he resists the proud: "But He gives a greater grace. Therefore it says, 'God is opposed to the proud, but gives grace to the humble'" (James 4:6).

Humility is not to be confused with low self-image. God is not honored when we flay ourselves, crying, "I am nothing!" or "I am a loser!" A humble attitude recognizes that in spite of our unworthiness, God has gifted us and empowered us with his Spirit. He considers us important individuals whom he wants to work into his overall masterplan. The apostle Paul maintained a healthy self-attitude, admitting his personal insufficiency while recognizing God's sufficiency. He writes, "For I am the least of the apostles, who am not fit to be called an apostle, because I persecuted the church of God. But by the grace of God I am what I am, and His grace toward me did not prove vain; but I labored even more than all of them, yet not I, but the grace of God with me" (1 Corinthians 15:9-10). Humility recognizes God's ability working within our lives, so that we can successfully fulfill his purposes in the world.

Faith

Another sacrifice to consider as an offering to God is the sacrifice of *faith*. Paul refers to this sacrifice in his letter to the believers at Philippi. "But even if I am being poured out as a drink offering upon the sacrifice and service of your faith, I rejoice and share my joy with you all" (Philippians 2:17). In what way did the Philippians offer their faith as a sacrifice to God? The emphasis of sacrifice is not what one loses, but rather what one freely offers. When the believers at Philippi confronted difficulties and persecutions, they offered a sacrifice of faith by trusting God through those difficulties. James writes, "Consider it all joy, my brethren, when you encounter various trials, knowing that the testing of your faith produces endurance. And let endurance have its perfect result, that you may be perfect and complete, lacking in nothing" (James 1:2-4).

You may also offer a sacrifice of faith when you trust God in the midst of problems, even though you don't understand the why or the what of God's purpose. You pray, "Lord, even though I don't understand and don't know how it's all going to turn out, I know you're in control and I trust you to work it out."

Success

One final way in which we can show our appreciation for Christ's atonement is to offer the sacrifice of our *successes*. In writing to the believers at Rome, the apostle Paul refers to the salvation of the Gentiles as his offering to God. He says, "But I have written very boldly to you on some points, so as to remind you again, because of the grace that was given me from God, to be a minister of Christ Jesus to the Gentiles, ministering as a priest the gospel of God, that my offering of the Gentiles might become acceptable, sanctified by the Holy Spirit" (Romans 15:15-16).

Paul was not boasting in evangelistic statistics. He credits the grace of God for producing his success in winning Gentiles to the Lord. But he does offer these Gentiles to God as trophies of God's grace, thereby giving honor to whom honor was due.

We can show our appreciation for Christ's atonement by offering to him spiritual sacrifices. But there is another way to express gratitude.

Qualities Greater Than Sacrifices

We can thank God for Christ's atonement by offering him *that which is greater than sacrifices*. What could possibly be greater than sacrifices? Loyalty and faithfulness.

God spoke to his people through the prophet Hosea, asking, "What shall I do with you, O Ephraim? What shall I do with you, O Judah? For your loyalty is like a morning cloud, and like the dew which goes away early. . . . For I delight in loyalty rather than sacrifice, and in the knowledge of God rather than burnt offerings" (Hosea 6:4, 6).

All of us expect loyalty from our friends and from our spouses. Should we think that God demands any less from us after he has given us so much? You may think, "I've been pretty loyal to God." That's good to know, if the statement is accurate. I'm afraid I cannot say that my own loyalty and faithfulness to him have always held fast. His values have not always been my values, nor his priorities my priorities. His plans have not always been my plans, nor his will my will. His interests have not always been my interests, nor his concerns my concerns. His timing is not always my timing, nor his methods my methods. How would you rate your loyalty?

Showing compassion toward others is another quality greater than sacrifices. As Jesus dined with Levi and his tax-gatherer friends, the Pharisees accused him of wrongdoing. The host, Levi (Matthew), describes the scene: "And it happened that as He was reclining at table in the house, behold many tax-gatherers and sinners came and were dining with Jesus and His disciples. And when the Pharisees saw this, they said to His disciples, 'Why is your Teacher eating with the tax-gatherers and sinners?' But when He heard this, He said, 'It is not those who are healthy who need a physician, but those who are sick. But go and learn what this means, "I desire compassion, and not sacrifice," for I did not come to call the righteous, but sinners'" (Matthew 9:10-13). The Pharisees were willing to give their time and their tithes to God, but refused to show compassion.

ATONEMENT

On another occasion the Lord rebuked them for failing to be compassionate, though they were keeping the external requirements of the law. Jesus scolded, "Woe to you, scribes and Pharisees, hypocrites! For you tithe mint and dill and cummin, and have neglected the weightier provisions of the law: justice and mercy and faithfulness; but these are the things you should have done without neglecting the others" (Matthew 23:23).

Do you know someone who is hurting physically, emotionally, or spiritually? Is it possible that God wants you to show compassion to that person? Perhaps just a word of encouragement or financial aid. Or perhaps you need to sit down and listen to those inner hurts.

A third quality more important than sacrifice is obedience to God's truth. In the days of King Saul's reign over Israel, God sent the prophet Samuel to deal with Saul's disobedience. When the prophet asked the king why he did not obey the voice of the Lord, the king replied, " 'I did obey the voice of the LORD, and went on the mission on which the LORD sent me, and have brought back Agag the king of Amalek, and have utterly destroyed the Amalekites. But the people took some of the spoil, sheep and oxen, the choicest of the things devoted to destruction, to sacrifice to the LORD your God at Gilgal.' And Samuel said, 'Has the LORD as much delight in burnt offerings and sacrifices as in obeying the voice of the LORD? Behold, to obey is better than sacrifice, and to heed than the fat of rams.' " (1 Samuel 15:20-22).

King Saul assumed that as long as he was willing to make a sacrifice to the Lord, he could do his own thing. It's the same philosophy that many live by today. They willfully sin against God and then try to make up for their sin by sacrificing their time or money to help someone. But the Lord is more concerned about total obedience than he is about the things we offer him.

Even in the New Testament the mark of the disciple is not a willingness to make sacrifices, but rather a desire to obey. "Jesus therefore was saying to those Jews who had believed Him, 'If you abide in My word, then you are truly disciples of Mine; and you shall know the truth, and the truth shall make you free'" (John 8:31-32).

What would you rather receive from your own children? A gift or some sort of obedience? The mark of a true disciple of Christ is total obedience to the revealed will of God—like the Lord's own obedience when he left the glories of heaven, took upon himself a human body, and came to earth. Paul records Jesus' obedient spirit in his letter to the Philippians: "Who, although He existed in the form of God, did not regard equality with God a thing to be grasped, but emptied Himself, taking the form of a bond-servant, and being made in the likeness of men. And being found in appearance as a man, He humbled Himself by becoming obedient to the point of death, even death on a cross" (Philippians 2:6-8).

The atonement is God's love gift to mankind. It is God's personal sacrifice of his Son, Jesus' unequivocal obedience to his Father.

The atonement of Jesus Christ was made once for all time. But the gift of the Lord and his salvation is offered to all generations. The gift just keeps going on, so that whoever believes in him shall not perish, but have eternal life. Aren't you glad you already possess that gift? Why not share it with someone this week, so he too can have his sins removed?

Have you ever wondered how God could accept Jesus' death to atone for your sins? You'll discover the answer to that in the next chapter.

---

1. *The Creed of Pope Pius IV,* quoted in Lorraine Boettner, *Roman Catholicism,* p. 169.

2. *A Catechism of Christian Doctrine,* quoted in Boettner, *Roman Catholicism,* p. 175.

3. *The Dignity and Duties of the Priest,* quoted in Boettner, *Roman Catholicism,* p. 175.

CHAPTER
6

SATISFYING YOUR JUDGE
PROPITIATION

We live in a generation that places a high priority on options and choices. When the Model-T first arrived on the scene, you had only one color choice—black. Today you can drive a yellow, blue, white, or even pink automobile. It may be striped or plain, with or without letters or numbers painted on its sides, customized or off the lot, stripped or fully optioned.

When I was growing up, the options for eating out also were greatly limited. Ninety-nine percent of my breakfasts, lunches, and dinners were eaten at home. Eating at home for many families today is the exception rather than the rule. Not only do you find McDonalds, Wendys, Taco Bell, and Wienerschnitzels, but now you can eat breakfast, lunch, or dinner at many of these fast food restaurants.

Years ago most people walked to the corner mom-and-pop grocery store, which offered a limited choice in food selection. Now there are not only supermarkets, but chains of supermarkets offering an unlimited variety of foods. Even pharmacies used to offer only pharmaceutical products. But today you can purchase magazines, cameras, small appliances, and a host of other items there.

God also offers variety. He has created a wide variety of people. He uses many different methods to accomplish his purposes. He allows his people to worship him in a variety of creative ways and at different times of the day. The Scriptures tell of a variety of spiritual gifts, a variety of ministries, and a variety of effects (1 Corinthians 12:4-6).

But there are some aspects of life where no options exist. There is only one true God who created the heaven and the earth and who controls the affairs of men. There is only one way to reach this God, as Jesus claimed for himself when he said, "I am the way, and the truth, and the life; no one comes to the Father, but through Me" (John 14:6). There is only one reason why God is able to receive sinful man. (And it has nothing to do with something we have done to please or satisfy him.) It is because of what Jesus has done for us, the only option which was open to God to bring man to himself—*propitiation*.

The Meaning of Propitiation

Out of all the different aspects of salvation, perhaps the most difficult to understand—and to pronounce—is propitiation. Webster defines propitiation as, "to appease and render favorable" or "to conciliate." From a theological perspective he says that propitiation is "the self-sacrifice and death of Jesus viewed as appeasing divine justice and effecting reconciliation between God and man."

The Greeks used the term *hilasmos*, meaning "appeasing" or "satisfying." When a person commits a crime and is not brought to trial, justice is not satisfied. But when that individual pays for his crime, justice is accomplished. Propitiation therefore focuses on *turning away wrath by satisfying justice which has been violated*. It answers the question, "How can a holy and just God clear the guilty?"

In order to better understand this concept, let's see how it relates to other truths about salvation.

What Did Jesus accomplish at the Cross?

- He took your place (substitution).
- He removed your sin (atonement).
- He credited his righteousness to your account (imputation).
- He satisfied your judge (propitiation).

PROPITIATION

What Benefits Do You Derive from Jesus' Death at the Cross

- You can start life over again (regeneration).
- You have been released from the slavery of sin (redemption).
- Your spiritual slate has been wiped clean (forgiveness).
- You have been declared righteous (justification).
- You have been brought to God (reconciliation).
- You have been committed to a higher purpose in life (sanctification).
- You have gained status in the family of God (adoption).

Let's diagram this to show the cause and effect relationship between what Jesus did for you and what you receive from his great sacrifice.

Because Jesus Did This:　　　　**You Experience This:**
　　　　(The Cause)　　　　　　　　　　(The Effects)

Substitution　　　　　　　　　　　Regeneration Reconciliation
Atonement　　　Redemption　 Forgiveness
Imputation　　　　　　　　　　　　Sanctification Adoption
Propitiation　　　　　　　　　　　 Justification

Now let's consider three reasons propitiation was necessary.

The Need for Propitiation

All Have Sinned

The first cause for propitiation is that *man has offended God's holy character.* The Scriptures declare, "For all have sinned and fall short of the glory of God" (Romans 3:23). The word translated "have sinned" means "to miss the mark."

Each summer in Pennsylvania, archers from the

Atlantic seaboard converge on the campus of Franklin and Marshall College in Lancaster for a week of stiff competition. It's fascinating to watch the precision with which each archer handles his or her equipment. Their accuracy is just as amazing. But in spite of their greatly developed skill, not all the arrows hit the bull's-eye. Many of them hit the outer rings, and some miss the target altogether. The archers' aim is good; but even the best will miss. It is to their credit that at least they aim at the mark.

I have never seen any archers direct their aim toward passing cars, houses across the street, or at the gallery of observers. They all try to hit the target in front of them. That's better than man's aim in life.

The word translated *sin* in this passage indicates both a "missing of the mark" and an "aiming at the wrong target." Man not only falls short of God's standard and his holy character, but he also turns away from that standard and aims his life in many other directions. So he both misses the mark and aims at the wrong target.

Sin Must Be Punished

Propitiation is also necessary because *justice demands sin be punished*. Paul informed the believers at Rome, "The wages of sin is death . . ." (Romans 6:23). God never takes sin lightly. He doesn't look at man and say, "I know man is weak, so I'll overlook his sin." Some defense lawyer in our judicial system today may take that approach and plead that society or his defendant's home life or some other outside force caused the accused to rob or kill someone. But God holds each individual accountable for his or her choices in life. And sin must be punished. In the Old Testament alone, God's wrath against sin is mentioned 585 times. Even in the New Testament it is clear that God's wrath is in force: "For the wrath of God is revealed from heaven against all ungodliness and unrighteousness of men, who suppress the truth in unrighteousness, because that which is known about God is evident within them; for God made it evident to them" (Romans 1:18-19).

PROPITIATION

God's Wrath Rests on the Unbeliever

Propitiation is also necessary because *God's wrath abides upon the unbeliever.* Jesus said, "He who believes in the Son has eternal life; but he who does not obey the Son shall not see life, but the wrath of God abides on him" (John 3:36). The word translated *abide* means "to remain." God's wrath is like a ticking time bomb which explodes at death and thrusts man out into eternity, separating him from God forever. Though God is loving and full of compassion, he is also just. And because man has violated his holy character and his revealed will, the unbeliever must pay sin's penalty: separation from God.

Someone may object that this makes God a vengeful deity. Not at all. God is just, righteous, and holy in all of his dealings. Though he demands complete satisfaction of his righteousness, his love caused him to provide the one sacrifice which would satisfy both his justice and righteousness. He offered his only begotten Son as the propitiation or satisfaction for man's sin. The time bomb of God's wrath can be defused immediately when the unbeliever is willing to acknowledge his sin and turn to Jesus Christ for salvation.

Propitiation is essential because man has offended God's holy character. That offense must be punished, and God's wrath abides on the sinner.

But what is the source of this idea, that God's wrath may be turned away so that he may show mercy? What is the background of propitiation? Let's look into the Old Testament judicial system to discover the answer.

The Old Testament Roots of Propitiation

The idea of satisfying God's holy character and justice is found in Israel's worship of Jehovah God. During Israel's earlier years, the place of worship was the tabernacle. The tabernacle was divided into two rooms. The larger room was called the holy place and contained the table of shewbread, the golden candlestick, and the altar of incense. The smaller room was the holy of holies and contained only

113

one piece of furniture—the ark of the covenant, covered by a lid known as the mercy seat. This piece of furniture symbolized God's provisions for man and man's rejection of those provisions.

The ark of the covenant was a small acacia wood box covered with gold. God gave Moses specific details for the construction of this ark. "And they shall construct an ark of acacia wood two and a half cubits long, and one and a half cubits wide, and one and a half cubits high. And you shall overlay it with pure gold, inside and out you shall overlay it, and you shall make a gold molding around it" (Exodus 25:10-11). And what would be placed in the ark? According to the book of Hebrews, three special items were put into this ark. "And behind the second veil, there was a tabernacle which is called the Holy of Holies, having a golden altar of incense and the ark of the covenant covered on all sides with gold, in which was a golden jar holding the manna, and Aaron's rod which budded, and the tables of the covenant. And above it were the cherubim of glory overshadowing the mercy seat; but of these things we cannot now speak in detail" (Hebrews 9:3-5). Let's look into that box and learn the significance of those items which symbolized God's provision and man's rejection of that provision.

The Jar of Manna

First of all, notice the golden jar of manna. Manna was God's provision for the people's physical needs. As the people trekked through the wilderness, they were hard pressed to find food. So they grumbled and complained against the Lord and his servant Moses. "Would that we had died by the LORD's hand in the land of Egypt, when we sat by the pots of meat, when we ate bread to the full; for you have brought us out into this wilderness to kill this whole assembly with hunger" (Exodus 16:3). The Lord responded to their cry by promising them manna. "And the house of Israel named it manna, and it was like coriander seed, white; and its taste was like wafers with honey. Then Moses said, 'This is what the LORD has commanded, "Let an omerful of it be kept throughout your generations, that they may see the bread that I fed you in the wilderness, when I brought you out of the land of Egypt.'" And Moses said to Aaron, 'Take a jar and put an omerful of manna in it, and place it before the LORD, to be kept throughout your generations" (Exodus 16:31-33).

Picture yourself in the wilderness. The temperature may be in the 70s or 80s. When you awake one morning, you walk out of your tent and see a strange-looking white substance lying on the ground. It's as though a light snow had just fallen. How did the people respond to that sight?

"When the sons of Israel saw it, they said to one another, 'What is it?' For they did not know what it was. And Moses said to them, 'It is the bread which the LORD has given you to eat. . . .' And they gathered it morning by morning, every man as much as he should eat; but when the sun grew hot, it would melt" (Exodus 16:15, 21).

Why didn't God provide for Israel in another way? Couldn't he have given them livestock for food? Couldn't he have told them to remain in the wilderness and attempt to grow some crops? Surely. But he chose to give them manna, and the reason for that choice is revealed in the book of Deuteronomy. "And you shall remember all the way which the LORD your God has led you in the wilderness these forty years, that He might humble you, testing you, to know what was in your heart, whether you would keep His commandments or not. And He humbled you and let you be hungry, and fed you with manna which you did not know, nor did your fathers know, that He might make you understand that man does not live by bread alone, but man lives by everything that proceeds out of the mouth of the LORD. . . . In the wilderness He fed you manna which your fathers did not know, that He might humble you and that He might test you, to do good for you in the end" (Deuteronomy 8:2-3, 16).

God wanted to do what was good for the nation. He wanted his people to depend upon him for their daily needs. It was not his purpose to hurt them or to cause them great pain. Rather he wanted to help them see their need daily to depend upon him.

Daily dependence on God is a difficult lesson to learn. Our natural desire is to handle our own affairs, to be dependent on no one. But even in the model prayer which the Lord taught his disciples, he emphasized the need of daily dependence upon God: "Give us this day our daily bread."

God also outlined the procedure which the people were to follow as they gathered the manna: "'This is what the LORD has commanded, "Gather of it every man as much as he should eat; you shall take an omer apiece according to the number of persons each of you has in his tent."' And the sons of Israel did so, and some gathered much and some little. When they measured it with an omer, he who had gathered much had no excess, and he who gathered little had no lack; every man gathered as much as he should eat" (Exodus 16:16-18). No one was to hoard God's provision. He was to take only what was needed.

This dependence upon God lasted for forty years. God constantly proved himself faithful. But no matter how faithful God was to Israel, the nation continually complained and wanted more than what God had provided.

Aaron's Rod

The second item placed within the ark of the covenant was a rod that budded. It was God's way of reminding Israel that he was the One who chose the leadership of the nation. He chose Moses as the main leader and Aaron as high priest. To understand the significance of this rod that budded, you should recall that the authority of both Moses and Aaron was being undermined and challenged by those within the ranks.

In the events which led to the budding rod, Aaron was challenged by Korah. Both men came from the tribe of Levi, but God chose Aaron as high priest, which brought jealousy to Korah's heart. So Korah gathered some sympathizers and challenged Aaron's authority. As 250 leaders of the congregation arrived, ". . . they assembled together against Moses and Aaron, and said to them, 'You have gone far enough, for all the congregation are holy, every one of them, and the LORD is in their midst; so why do you exalt yourselves above the assembly of the LORD?'" Jealousy drove Korah to a false assumption. Neither Moses nor Aaron exalted themselves to positions of leadership. They never asked for those positions. So Moses reacted with a crushed spirit: "When Moses heard this, he fell on his face; and he spoke to Korah and all his company, saying, 'Tomorrow morning the LORD will show who is His, and who is holy, and will bring him near to Himself; even the one whom He will choose, He will bring near to Himself'" (Numbers 16:4-5).

The next day God made his choice clear to the people by giving Moses a plan of action as well as by bringing judgment upon Korah and the rebels. He told Moses to take a rod from each of the fathers' households, and to put the twelve rods in the tabernacle in front of the tablets on which God's law was written. Then he said, "And it will come about that the rod of the man whom I choose will sprout. Thus I shall lessen from upon Myself the grumblings of the sons of Israel, who are grumbling against you" (Numbers 17:5). So Moses did what God required.

"Now it came about on the next day that Moses went into the tent of the testimony; and behold, the rod of Aaron for the house of Levi had sprouted and put forth buds and produced blossoms, and it bore ripe almonds. Moses then brought out all the rods from the presence of the LORD to all the sons of Israel; and they looked, and each man took his rod. But the LORD said to Moses, 'Put back the rod of Aaron before the testimony to be kept as a sign against the rebels, that you may put an end to their grumblings against Me, so that they should not die'" (Numbers 17:8-10). It is the Lord who chooses his leaders.

Aaron's rod that budded was both a symbol of God's provision of leadership for the people and a sign of man's rebellion against God's choice.

The Law of God
The third item placed into the ark of the covenant was the law of God written by God's finger on two tablets of

stone. Moses told his people that having followed God's command, "I turned and came down from the mountain, and put the tablets in the ark which I had made; and there they are, as the LORD commanded me" (Deuteronomy 10:5).

The law of God was a description of his holy character. Many of the pagan gods possessed the character of mere men, with human vices and frailties. But the God of Israel was unique in every respect. He was holy, full of compassion and mercy, a God of love.

The tablets of stone on which God's law was written also informed men of what God expected from them. As God's chosen people, the Israelites were to reflect his character in their dealings with one another, as well as in their dealings with other nations.

The Mercy Seat

But besides the ark of the covenant, another very important piece of furniture covered the ark. It was called *the mercy seat*. God also instructed Moses in the building of the mercy seat, telling him, "And you shall make a mercy seat of pure gold, two and a half cubits long and one and a half cubits wide. And you shall make two cherubim of gold, make them of hammered work at the two ends of the mercy seat" (Exodus 25:17-18).

Some commentators believe that the two cherubim represented both the righteousness and the justice of God. Because they faced downward upon the three items within the ark, they looked upon God's provision and man's rebellion. Man rebelled against God's provision of physical needs, his choice of a high priest, and his holy character and expectations of man. Rebellious man deserved God's judgment. So the mercy seat was actually a symbol of judgment.

But the mercy seat was also a place where God wanted to meet man, and where he made it possible for man to meet him. He told Moses, "And there I will meet with you; and from above the mercy seat, from between the two cherubim which are upon the ark of the testimony, I will

speak to you about all that I will give you in commandment
for the sons of Israel" (Exodus 25:22). God could not meet
with man until his holy character, which man had violated,
was appeased or satisfied. So how was this problem going
to be solved? Through atonement.

God told Moses, "Then Aaron shall offer the bull of the
sin offering which is for himself, and make atonement for
himself and for his household, and he shall slaughter the
bull of the sin offering which is for himself. . . . Moreover,
he shall take some of the blood of the bull and sprinkle it
with his finger on the mercy seat on the east side; also in
front of the mercy seat he shall sprinkle some of the blood
with his finger seven times" (Leviticus 16:11, 14).

Though the mercy seat at first was a symbol that man
deserved judgment, the sins of the people were covered
once blood was sprinkled on it. As the cherubim looked
upon the blood, God's justice could say, "I'm satisfied because the death penalty has been paid. I will withhold
judgment." Furthermore, God's righteousness could say, "I
am no longer offended because the evidence of man's sin
has been covered by the blood of the innocent animal." So
God showed his mercy and withheld his judgment.

But what does this have to do with the Lord Jesus
Christ? How is he involved with propitiation and the mercy
seat?

The New Testament Fulfillment of Propitiation

God's Total Provision

Jesus fulfills God's total provision for man. You've already observed the three objects in the ark of the covenant: the
manna, the rod that budded, and the law. Each of these
items was a symbol of God's provision for his people, as
well as a symbol of man's rejection of those provisions.
Each of these symbols is fulfilled by Christ in the New Testament.

Jesus, for example, is God's bread of life. Like the
manna from heaven, Jesus was God's bread which came
down from heaven. When the Lord was speaking to the

Jews, he told them to believe in him because he was sent by God. But they wanted to see a sign ... some miracle which he would perform. They reminded him how God had performed a sign in the Old Testament in the form of manna, saying, "Our fathers ate the manna in the wilderness; as it is written, 'He gave them bread out of heaven to eat.'" The Lord responded, "Truly, truly, I say to you, it is not Moses who has given you the bread out of heaven, but it is My Father who gives you the true bread out of heaven. For the bread of God is that which comes down out of heaven, and gives life to the world" (John 6:31-33).

Jesus then declared, "I am the bread of life. Your fathers ate the manna in the wilderness, and they died. This is the bread which comes down out of heaven, so that one may eat of it and not die. I am the living bread that came down out of heaven ..." (John 6:48-51a).

Jesus tells them that, like the manna, he gives life to those who are willing to take it: "If any one eats of this bread, he shall live forever; and the bread also which I shall give for the life of the world is My flesh" (John 6:51b). As Israel depended upon God's daily provision of physical bread, so must man depend upon this living bread so that he may have eternal life.

Jesus is not only God's bread of life, but he is the Lord's chosen High Priest. As Israel rejected God's provision of manna and God's choice of Aaron as high priest, so did the Jews reject Jesus as the bread of life and as God's chosen One.

Jesus fulfills his role as high priest by offering a permanent sacrifice for sin: "But when Christ appeared as a high priest of the good things to come, He entered through the greater and more perfect tabernacle, not made with hands, that is to say, not of this creation; and not through the blood of goats and calves, but through His own blood, He entered the holy place once for all, having obtained eternal redemption. For if the blood of goats and bulls and the ashes of a heifer sprinkling those who have been defiled, sanctify for the cleansing of the flesh, how much more will the blood of Christ, who through the eternal Spirit offered

Himself without blemish to God, cleanse your conscience from dead works to serve the living God?" (Hebrews 9:11-14).

As high priest Jesus Christ both offered a permanent sacrifice for sin and satisfied God's justice: "Therefore, He had to be made like His brethren in all things, that He might become a merciful and faithful high priest in things pertaining to God, to make propitiation (satisfaction) for the sins of the people" (Hebrews 2:17).

Jesus also fulfilled the symbol of God's law which was written on the two tables of stone. He not only kept the Old Testament law perfectly, but he himself was the living Word, demonstrating the character of God and declaring the expectations of God. The writer to the Hebrews states, "And He [Jesus] is the radiance of His glory and the exact representation of His nature . . ." (Hebrews 1:3). The Scriptures also declare that Jesus is the Word of God: "In the beginning was the Word, and the Word was with God, and the Word was God. . . . And the Word became flesh, and dwelt among us, and we beheld His glory, glory as of the only begotten from the Father, full of grace and truth" (John 1:1, 14). Jesus further declared himself to be equal with God when he said, "I and the Father are one" (John 10:30). He later said, "He who has seen Me has seen the Father . . ." (John 14:9).

Jesus Christ fulfilled the provisions symbolized by the Old Testament items in the ark of the covenant. The Lord not only proved himself to be the bread of life, God's chosen one, and the exact essence of God, he also provided for man by satisfying God's justice and righteousness.

God's Justice Satisfied

Notice the two ways in which *Jesus satisfied God's justice and righteousness*. First of all, Jesus is declared to be the mercy seat, "whom God displayed publicly as a propitiation in His blood through faith. This was to demonstrate His righteousness, because in the forebearance of God He passed over the sins previously committed" (Romans

3:25). The word translated *propitiation* is the word for *mercy seat*. God was able to pass over the sins of Old Testament believers who brought sacrifices because he looked forward to the cross and saw his Son's personal and perfect sacrifice for sin. That's why Jesus said, "I am the way, and the truth, and the life; no one comes to the Father, but through Me" (John 14:6). As the mercy seat, Jesus is the meeting place for man and God.

The Lord was not only the mercy seat, but he was also the satisfaction of God at the mercy seat—"My little children, I am writing these things to you that you may not sin. And if anyone sins, we have an Advocate with the Father, Jesus Christ the righteous; and He Himself is the propitiation [satisfaction] for our sins; and not for ours only, but also for those of the whole world" (1 John 2:1-2). John also wrote, "In this is love, not that we loved God, but that He loved us and sent His Son to be the propitiation [satisfaction] for our sins" (1 John 4:10).

Jesus made the believer right with God. Because he took our place on the cross and satisfied God by shedding his own blood, God's anger was withdrawn from the believer. As a Christian you don't have to live under the anxiety that God's wrath is upon you, because that wrath has been removed. Jesus perfectly satisfied his Father. That's why the apostle Paul could rejoice in the love of God, writing, "What then shall we say to these things? If God is for us, who is against us? He who did not spare his own Son, but delivered Him up for us all, how will He not also with Him freely give us all things? Who will bring a charge against God's elect? God is the one who justifies; who is the one who condemns? Christ Jesus is He who died, yes, rather who was raised, who is at the right hand of God, who also intercedes for us. Who shall separate us from the love of Christ? Shall tribulation, or distress, or persecution, or famine, or nakedness, or peril, or sword? Just as it is written, 'For Thy sake we are being put to death all day long; we were considered as sheep to be slaughtered.' But in all these things we overwhelmingly conquer through Him who loved us. For I am convinced that neither death, nor life, nor angels, nor principalities, nor things present, nor things to come, nor powers, nor height, nor depth, nor any other created thing, shall be able to separate us from the love of God, which is in Christ Jesus our Lord" (Romans 8:31-39).

Thank God that he does not condemn you, if you belong to him. He does not stop loving you. He is not angry with you. Even when you fail him, as a loving father encourages his child who slips, our loving Father picks us up, encourages us with a warm hug, and sets our feet on firm ground to walk once again with him.

Let no man condemn you. Let no man judge you, for God accepts you as you are. But when the Spirit of God brings to your mind through the Word certain areas which need to be evaluated and perhaps changed, cooperate with him. Confess whatever sin is brought to mind and move on without fear of condemnation. Move on with courage, knowing that you are doing what he wants you to do. Like the apostle Paul, press on in order to lay hold of that for which Christ laid hold of you. Forget what lies behind and reach forward to what lies ahead, pressing on toward the goal for the prize of the upward call of God in Christ Jesus.

How can God be just and at the same time release the guilty? The answer lies in the truth of propitiation. Jesus satisfied God's justice by taking our penalty of death, and he satisfied God's holiness by being the perfect sacrifice for sin.

And how should the believer take advantage of God's mercy seat? The writer to the Hebrews said it best: "For we do not have a high priest who cannot sympathize with our weaknesses, but one who has been tempted in all things as we are, yet without sin. Let us therefore draw near with confidence to the throne of grace, that we may receive mercy and may find grace to help in time of need" (Hebrews 4:15-16). And it is God's grace that helps you start over again.

CHAPTER

7

STARTING
OVER
AGAIN
REGENERATION

To possess something new: this is one of the American consumer's greatest desires, and the marketing industry has exploited this to the hilt. The promise of the new entices even the most sales-resistent customer. Its appeal blocks the consumer's reasoning powers and entices his emotions.

The potential buyer dreams of a new car, a new house, or a new wardrobe. Every September sports fans anticipate the beginning of a new football season, while TV addicts crave the new program schedule. Every December we prepare for the new year by making a series of promises. But when the new year arrives, little more has changed than the date.

Most people would like to start some aspect of their lives over again if they could. But even with the best of intentions, the path of least resistance replaces the promise of a new commitment.

There is, however, a way to start over again. The Bible promises that all things in life can become new. And the foundation for the new life can be established immediately, although the building of that life will take years to complete.

The Bible has a name for beginning this new life. It's called regeneration.

The Meaning of Regeneration

What It's Not

Before we define regeneration, it's important to eliminate some misconceptions about it. So consider first *what regeneration is not.* There are those who confuse regeneration with reformation. It is common for people to evaluate their lives as they approach the end of a year. They look back on the past year's successes and failures. As they observe how they've treated people, their attitudes toward others, their jobs or themselves, they may desire to make some major changes. But a change of a habit, attitude, or behavior is only a reformation of one's life; it should not be confused with the biblical concept of *regeneration.*

Some people have another misconception about regeneration. They equate it with baptism. Some churches teach that baptism guarantees a place in heaven, believing that a child becomes part of the family of God on the basis of his parents' faith. But if this were the case, you would expect the apostle Paul to be a great promoter of baptism, since he dedicated his life to win people to Christ. Is that the case? Listen to him: "I thank God that I baptized none of you except Crispus and Gaius, that no man should say you were baptized in my name. Now I did baptize also the household of Stephanas; beyond that, I do not know whether I baptized any other. For Christ did not send me to baptize, but to preach the gospel, not in cleverness of speech, that the cross of Christ should not be made void" (1 Corinthians 1:14-17). If baptism regenerated a person, why would Paul place such a low priority on it?

Another concept of regeneration to avoid is equating it with adopting a new belief or religion. Some people change denominations or religions, expecting that by accepting a new philosophy or religious practice, they will gain eternal life. People who join churches, have religious experiences, and adopt various philosophies of life may feel better and even have a better outlook on life, and yet still not be regenerated.

REGENERATION

What It Is

What then is regeneration? The term comes from two Greek words: *palin,* meaning "again" and *genesis* meaning "birth." Regeneration therefore means to "be born again." Let's look at three of its characteristics in order to get a better grasp on this subject.

A *new birth.* Regeneration is a new birth. Jesus spoke of the necessity of the new birth when he conversed with a religious leader by the name of Nicodemus. Though Nicodemus was part of the Jewish Sanhedrin, Jesus told him that he had to be born again in order to enter the kingdom of God (John 3:3, 5). Then he went on to explain the nature of the new birth, telling Nicodemus that it came from above, originating in heaven rather than on earth: "Jesus answered and said to him, 'Truly, truly, I say to you, unless one is born again, he cannot see the kingdom of God'" (John 3:3). The phrase "born again" could be translated "born from above" or "born anew." This is a new birth which has no relationship to physical birth. God is the source of the new birth: "But as many as received Him, to them He gave the right to become children of God, even to those who believe in His name, who were born not of blood, nor of the will of the flesh, nor of the will of man, but of God" (John 1:12-13).

This new birth also originates from the Holy Spirit. "Jesus answered, 'Truly, truly, I say to you, unless one is born of water and the Spirit, he cannot enter into the kingdom of God. That which is born of flesh is flesh, and that which is born of the Spirit is spirit. Do not marvel that I said to you, "You must be born again." The wind blows where it wishes and you hear the sound of it, but do not know where it comes from and where it is going; so is every one who is born of the Spirit'" (John 3:5-8).

The new birth is a Spirit birth, originating with the Holy Spirit.

You might wonder, "If the Bible says you must be born of the water and the Spirit, doesn't this indicate that you must also be baptized?" First, recognize that baptism is not a part of the context of this passage. Furthermore, in the same Gospel the Lord Jesus Christ referred to the Holy Spirit as "living water." He said, "'. . . If any man is thirsty, let him come to Me and drink. He who believes in Me, as the Scripture said, "From his innermost being shall flow rivers of living water."' But this He spoke of the Spirit, whom those who believed in Him were to receive; for the Spirit was not yet given, because Jesus was not yet glorified" (John 7:37-39).

Therefore, rather than reading this verse as "the water *and* the Spirit," it can also be read "the water *even* the Spirit." There is a physical birth and a spiritual birth. The physical birth originates from the natural order, while the spiritual birth derives from the spiritual order. The physical birth originates from the will of the flesh and the will of man, while the spiritual birth derives from the will of God. The physical birth is earthly in origin, while the spiritual birth is heavenly.

Though there are differences between these two births, there are also similarities. Both the physical and spiritual birth begin with an act of love and an implanted seed. The new birth comes from the love of God—"For God so loved the world, that He gave His only begotten Son . . ." (John 3:16)—and an implanted seed—"For you have been born again not of seed which is perishable but imperishable, that is, through the living and abiding word of God" (1 Peter 1:23).

Also, although gestation may take a while in both physical and spiritual birth, the actual birth is instantaneous. Both physical and spiritual birth usually need help in delivery. When a person is brought into a relationship with God, someone is usually present to help him through the process of receiving Jesus Christ as his personal Savior, and encouraging him to take his first spiritual breath. After both births, as well, there needs to be a lot of tender, loving care, so that the newborn is able to develop a healthy life in an atmosphere of love and acceptance.

A *spiritual resurrection.* Regeneration is a new birth. But it is also a spiritual resurrection. Man is unable to respond to God on his own, because he is "dead in trespasses and sins" (Ephesians 2:1). He needs to be brought to life by the Holy Spirit.

In the Old Testament Ezekiel was given a vision of dry bones lying in a valley. As he looked upon the bones, God asked whether he believed these bones could live. Then he asked Ezekiel to prophesy to the bones. As the prophet spoke to the bones, they came together, grew flesh, and were covered with skin. But there was no breath in them. Then Ezekiel was told to prophesy to the breath, that it might enter the bones. When the prophet obeyed the command, breath came into the bones, they came to life and stood on their feet like an exceedingly great army.

Then God interpreted the vision, saying, "'Son of man, these bones are the whole house of Israel; behold, they say, "Our bones are dried up, and our hope has perished. We are completely cut off." Therefore prophesy, and say to them, "Thus says the Lord GOD, 'Behold, I will open your graves and cause you to come up out of your graves, My people; and I will bring you into the land of Israel. Then you will know that I am the LORD, when I have opened your graves and caused you to come up out of your graves, My people. And I will put My Spirit within you, and you will come to life, and I will place you on your own land. Then you will know that I, the LORD, have spoken and done it,' declares the LORD."'" (Ezekiel 37:11-14).

Like the dry bones, man is alive physically, emotionally, and mentally, but is dead spiritually. He needs to experience the breath of God, which is the Holy Spirit. When the Holy Spirit enters a person's life, a spiritual resurrection occurs and the individual receives new life.

A *new creation*. Regeneration is a new creation. The Scriptures teach that the believer has been created for good works (Ephesians 2:10), in righteousness and holiness (Ephesians 4:24). This new creation completely changes the individual: "Therefore if any man is in Christ, he is a new creature; the old things passed away; behold, new things have come" (2 Corinthians 5:17). The one who has been born again has been given a new ability to please

God. Peter writes, "For by these He has granted to us His precious and magnificent promises, in order that by them you might become partakers of the divine nature, having escaped the corruption that is in the world by lust" (2 Peter 1:4).

As a child receives the nature of his parents, so does the regenerated individual receive God's divine nature. The Scriptures refer to this nature as the "new man." Paul writes, "Therefore consider the members of your earthly body as dead to immorality, impurity, passion, evil desire, and greed, which amounts to idolatry. For it is on account of these things that the wrath of God will come, and in them you also once walked, when you were living in them" (Colossians 3:5-7). Paul continues, "But now you also, put them all aside; anger, wrath, malice, slander, and abusive speech from your mouth. Do not lie to one another, since you laid aside the old self with its evil practices, and have put on the new self who is being renewed to a true knowledge according to the image of the One who created him" (Colossians 3:8-10). Then the apostle lists several qualities of the new self: "And so, as those who have been chosen of God, holy and beloved, put on a heart of compassion, kindness, humility, gentleness and patience; bearing with one another, and forgiving each other, whoever has a complaint against anyone; just as the Lord forgave you, so also should you. And beyond all these things put on love, which is the perfect bond of unity" (Colossians 3:12-14).

Regeneration is not a mere reformation, a baptism, or an adoption of a new belief or religion. No, regeneration is a new birth, a spiritual resurrection, and a new creation, at which time the believer receives the divine nature.

The Means of Regeneration

Since regeneration originates with God, what means does he use to bring new birth into someone's life? He uses many ways, but three of his tools are highlighted in Scripture.

REGENERATION

People

God uses the human instrument to accomplish his purpose of regeneration. Paul referred to himself and others as messengers of reconciliation (2 Corinthians 5:18-19). These messengers focus their messages on a variety of issues. Some of God's messengers emphasize the dangers of hell, from which one needs to escape. Other messengers will highlight God's ability to heal the human soul and spirit. Still others emphasize God's ability to give man both a fulfilled earthly life and eternal life. People respond to the message which focuses on their own felt needs. But they can respond only when they've heard the message (Romans 10:13-17).

So what happens when God's people are not faithful in sharing their faith? Does it prevent God's truth from reaching its intended target? Will the lost never hear the truth and lose out on regeneration? I do not believe that would be the result, because God is sovereign and his purposes will be accomplished, whether we are faithful or not. On the other hand, Scripture shows how God deals with those who claim to be born again, but who refuse to tell the good news to anyone else.

When Jonah refused to convey God's message to the city of Nineveh, the Lord disciplined the prophet by taking him through a period of great difficulty in his life. Eventually Jonah fulfilled God's command, and a city which was under the judgment of God experienced God's mercy instead.

God may place other believers on the shelf and commission someone else to convey his message. The nation Israel was to be God's spokesman and lighthouse to the world. But when it was unfaithful in pointing people to the one true God, God set it aside and created another people whom he calls "the church."

Another way in which God deals with those who refuse to communicate their faith is to allow spiritual stagnation to form, like barnacles encrusted on an old ship. The spiritual life begins to slow down. The Word of God becomes boring. Prayer becomes ineffective and God seems to become more and more distant. Some of the most exciting Christians I know are those who are out on the front lines, consistently witnessing to those in the clutches of the enemy.

Scripture

God not only uses human instruments, but *he also uses the Scriptures* to accomplish his purpose of regeneration. Many have given testimonies describing how they came into a personal relationship with God by reading the Scriptures in a motel room, in a car, or some other isolated place where the Spirit of God was able to speak to them.

One of the greatest theologians of all time was Augustine, a man who formerly lived a loose and morally degrading existence. But he was born again when he picked up the book of Romans and read this passage: "And this do, knowing the time, that it is already the hour for you to awaken from sleep; for now salvation is nearer to us than when we believed. The night is almost gone, and the day is at hand. Let us therefore lay aside the deeds of darkness and put on the armor of light. Let us behave properly as in the day, not in carousing and drunkenness, not in sexual promiscuity and sensuality, not in strife and jealousy. But put on the Lord Jesus Christ, and make no provision for the flesh in regard to its lusts" (Romans 13:11-14).

The Scriptures can penetrate the inner recesses of the heart: "For the word of God is living and active and sharper than any two-edged sword, and piercing as far as the division of soul and spirit, of both joints and marrow, and able to judge the thoughts and intentions of the heart" (Hebrews 4:12).

God revealed the power of his Word to the prophet Isaiah when he said, "For as the rain and the snow come down from heaven, and do not return there without watering the earth, and making it bear and sprout, and furnishing seed to the sower and bread to the eater; so shall My word be which goes forth from My mouth; it shall not return to Me empty, without accomplishing what I desire, and without succeeding in the matter for which I sent it" (Isaiah 55:10-11).

The Holy Spirit

God also uses the Holy Spirit to accomplish regeneration. One who is born again is born "out of" the Spirit (John 3:6). It is the Holy Spirit who convicts men of their sins (John 16:8-11) and gives them the ability to understand truth (John 16:13). He also actually produces the new birth: "He saved us, not on the basis of deeds which we have done in righteousness, but according to His mercy, by the washing of regeneration and renewing by the Holy Spirit, whom He poured out upon us richly through Jesus Christ our Savior" (Titus 3:5-6). Regeneration is a washing or a cleansing of spiritual filth, as the Holy Spirit renews the individual's inner self.

The Responsibility of Man for Regeneration

If God is responsible to regenerate an individual, what is man's responsibility in the process?

To Recognize His Condition

It is obvious that man must first *recognize his spiritually dead condition.* Until someone discovers that he has a problem, he will not look for a solution. Consider the person who is unaware he has cancer. He will continue living his life believing that he is perfectly healthy, until he is finally made aware of the problem.

That awareness may come through signs of illness, such as a rapid weight loss, a change in complexion, or a continued state of nausea. When these symptoms linger, he recognizes that a problem exists. Sometimes the Lord allows a person to pass through great difficulties—such as divorce, the loss of a job, the loss of a loved one, a business failure, or some other tragic event—in order to bring to the person's attention a more deeply-seated problem.

Or perhaps someone discovers his condition accidentally (from a human perspective). One of the men on our church staff in Fresno was in a serious automobile accident. He escaped serious injury, but went to see a doctor just to be certain that everything was all right. During the check-up, he showed the doctor a mole on his chest. Subsequent examination showed the mole to be malignant, though fortunately none of the tissue around the mole was cancerous. The doctor told Scott that had he waited another month, the malignancy would have spread throughout his body.

As you read this chapter, you may be unaware of your spiritual condition. You may be unaware that a spiritual cancer is spreading throughout your soul. If you have not been regenerated, it is just a matter of time before this cancer will take its toll. Though many forms of this disease in the body are incurable, the cancer of the soul, which is sin, does have a cure. But there is only one Physician who can heal the soul. His name is Jesus Christ.

Believe God Can Regenerate

Once the individual recognizes his spiritual condition, *he must believe that God can regenerate him.* Some people do not believe in doctors. Others are afraid of doctors and will never go to one. They hope that by avoiding doctors they will remain healthy. That is as logical as saying, "If I never talk about death, I'll never die." Unless one believes that God can solve his spiritual dilemma, he will never remedy the problem. Unless he believes that God can put his life back together again, his life will remain fragmented. He must believe that God has the ability to impart new life.

Make Contact

The next step to take is to *make contact with the power source of new life.* People who live in snowbelt areas usually carry jumper cables, because their car batteries often die. When the cables are connected between the good battery and the dead battery, there is a good chance that the car will start. But if contact is never made with the good battery, your prospects for getting the car started diminish enormously. In the same way, someone can believe that God has the capacity and the willingness to impart his divine nature to man. But if he never makes contact with God through the Lord Jesus Christ, his spiritual life will remain dead.

Receive Christ

The fourth responsibility of man in regeneration is *to allow Jesus Christ to enter his life*: "But as many as received Him, to them He gave the right to become children of God, even to those who believe in His name" (John 1:12).

One of the most frustrating experiences that children have at Christmas time is to receive an exciting toy which is able to make noises, move, and respond to the wishes of the child, but sits idle because someone forgot to buy the batteries. The most expensive or enjoyable battery-operated toy is useless without a power source.

When a person is born into this world, he usually comes with all of his parts intact. Most of the time everything functions well and he is on his way to maturity. Like most battery-operated toys, however, he does not come with a spiritual power pack. His only power for living is what he can generate on his own. And that is insufficient to live a spiritually motivated life or to get him to heaven. He needs to receive Christ into his life and live by his power.

Therefore, though regeneration originates with God, man is responsible to recognize his need, believe that God can regenerate him, make contact with God, and then allow Jesus to enter his life.

The Evidences of Regeneration

When you come into a personal relationship with God, a whole new world opens up. You get a new perspective on life, a new hope, a new purpose, new friends, a new direction, a new sense of security, and much more. But as I've observed various changes in the lives of those who are born again, four outstanding qualities emerge most consistently.

A Greater Awareness

The first noticeable quality is that *the person develops a greater awareness*. You've experienced coming out of a dark room into a bright light. Your eyes have difficulty focusing, don't they? Everything doesn't come into sharp focus immediately. So it is with a babe in Christ. There is a growing awareness of God. God becomes a real Person, rather than an impersonal force or power somewhere in outer space. And the more time spent with him, the more real he becomes.

At the same time, the awareness grows that God is at work in his life and in the lives of others. So often it's difficult to see how God is working in our lives, especially when we go through times of stress and testing. Someone who observes an artist splashing an array of color on his canvas may be puzzled over what the artist is painting. He sees only the strokes of the brush as the artist paints; but the artist sees the completed picture.

In a similar way, when anyone trusts Christ as his Savior, it becomes increasingly clear that God is operating in his life and is working out a plan for his life. But often it's only in retrospect that he sees the life portrait coming to life under the various strokes of God's brush.

A new relationship with the Lord also creates a greater awareness of God's people. A stranger is always suspect until you find something that you have in common with him. And so it is with the people of God. What once was merely a group of strangers soon becomes part of the family.

A new believer begins to see a contrast between his new friends and many of his old friends, as Peter so ably wrote. "For the time already past is sufficient for you to have carried out the desire of the Gentiles, having pursued a course of sensuality, lusts, drunkenness, carousals, drinking parties and abominable idolatries. And in all this, they are surprised that you do not run with them into the same excess of dissipation, and they malign you; but they shall give account to Him who is ready to judge the living and the dead" (1 Peter 4:3-5).

An awareness of sin also develops. I've talked to new Christians who have experienced greater struggles in life after they became Christians than before. They are shocked over the various sins they see in their lives. They feel more sinful after conversion than before. What's the problem? Actually, there is no problem. It's the natural result of the new birth. Someone who is dead in his trespass and sins feels little guilt for the things he does. He justifies his sinful behavior and attitudes, and compares himself with all of his friends who do the same things. But once he comes into a personal relationship with God, he begins to understand what God expects of him and soon recognizes how far away from God he really was. And the Spirit of God uses the Word of God to convict him so that he will confess his sins and live cleanly.

Suppose a young boy who lived in the ghettos all his life was adopted by a millionaire living in a large mansion. The very first meal could prove a great embarrassment for the boy. Because the millionaire and his family developed acceptable social graces over the years, they know which fork to use for the salad and which to use for the main course. They hold their utensils properly and transfer the napkins from the table to their laps. But the untrained boy from the ghetto would eat as he was taught by his peers. He would be confused by the extra silverware on the table. He probably would not understand the purpose of the napkin. His table manners might appall those who were reared in the millionaire's home. As he was exposed daily to the proper way of eating, he would begin to see just how many bad social habits he had developed over the years.

So it is with the individual who becomes a child of God. He turns away from his old life and enters into a new one, which demands new habits, new attitudes, and a new lifestyle. And as he compares his former life with his new life, he begins to realize just how far from God he was. He becomes aware of wrong attitudes and wrong behavior in his personal life which at one time were quite acceptable.

A Greater Enjoyment

A second evidence that an individual has been regenerated is that *he has a greater enjoyment of life*. Life begins to make sense. He realizes there is One who is in control of man's destiny. The Scriptures become more enjoyable. It's like meeting the author of a book: If you are impressed with him as a person, you will want to read his book. And so it is when people meet the Author of the Scriptures. They become greatly impressed by him and want to read his book. It's exciting to observe the growth of those who have recently come to know the Lord. Their eyes have a sparkle and they develop an insatiable appetite for the truth of the Scriptures. They follow Peter's injunction: "Therefore, putting aside all malice and all guile and hypocrisy and envy and all slander, like newborn babes, long for the pure milk of the word, that by it you may grow in respect to salvation" (1 Peter 2:1-2).

The regenerated also enjoy praying. Praying is a treat because they can talk to God about anything, no matter how intimate it is. Furthermore, seeing direct results of their prayers encourages them to pray even more. It's refreshing to hear a new Christian pray, because he hasn't learned all the jargon which many Christians have developed. He doesn't put on holy tones or use flowery phrases. He just talks to God from the depths of his heart with sincerity and expectation that God is going to do something about what he has asked.

Life in general becomes more enjoyable because he realizes that God has a plan for him, and he doesn't have to prove himself to anybody. He learns to put up with the imperfections of others, because he is aware of his own deficiencies. He realizes that he doesn't have to take himself so seriously. He can enjoy life to the fullest.

I know of no one who has regretted committing himself to Jesus Christ. On the other hand, I know of many people who have lived in regret for not committing themselves to the Lord earlier in life.

A Greater Desire to Conform to God
Another evidence of the person who has been regenerated is that *he develops a greater desire to conform his life to God's standards.* He begins to ask himself how he can please God. Most of his life he's tried to please people. He's attempted

to please his parents, his teachers, his friends, and his boss. Sometimes he succeeds, but often he fails. But when he comes to know the Lord in a personal way, he realizes that it is God alone he needs to please. The apostle Paul wrote, "But just as we have been approved by God to be entrusted with the gospel, so we speak, not as pleasing men but God, who examines our hearts" (1 Thessalonians 2:4).

Whether it be in a large corporation, in the political arena, or even in the church, there are always special interest groups who feel their cause alone is just. And when leadership doesn't give attention to the cause, complaints run rampant. The apostle's words need to be taken seriously. God has not called us to please special interest groups. He *has* called us to please him by meeting the needs of others. Rather than ask the question, "What will people think?" the newborn begins to ask, "What does God think about what I'm doing (or not doing)?"

Along with the desire to please God, the regenerate desires to learn how to please him. I learned how to please my father by being around him. I knew as a child that I could please him by running down the street to meet him as he walked home from work. I also knew that I did not please him when I would bring a pack of stray dogs to the house.

Born-again people also desire to conform their lives to God's standards by loving God's people. The apostle John emphasized this when he wrote, "We know that we have passed out of death into life, because we love the brethren" (1 John 3:14). He also said, "Beloved, let us love one another, for love is from God; and everyone who loves is born of God and knows God" (1 John 4:7). He continues, "Whoever believes that Jesus is the Christ is born of God; and whoever loves the Father loves the child born of Him" (1 John 5:1).

A Greater Victory

There is one other evidence of the new birth. He who comes to know God personally and is born of the Spirit *develops a greater victory over sin.* He begins to practice what is good and wholesome. The apostle John writes, "If you know that He is righteous, you know that everyone also who practices righteousness is born of Him. . . . No one who is born of God practices sin, because His seed abides in him; and he cannot sin, because he is born of God" (1 John 2:29; 3:9). Of course, John is not saying that believers never sin. But he does emphasize that if a person is truly born again, he will spend more time practicing righteousness and less time committing sin. Anyone who claims to have experienced a new birth, but has had no change in his lifestyle, is contradicting the clear teaching of Scripture.

Every child inherits certain traits and abilities from his parents. If he happens to be born into a musical family, most likely he will possess some inherent musical ability. Music may become important to him because of the natural ability he inherits from his parents, his constant exposure to music, the encouragement from his parents to develop that ability, and the opportunity to develop it. Likewise, the child of God inherits special abilities and desires from his heavenly Father. His Father continually encourages him to a godly lifestyle and provides many opportunities for him to develop that lifestyle.

As the spiritual newborn begins to practice what is right, he also overcomes the world system, described by John in his warning, "Do not love the world, nor the things in the world. If anyone loves the world, the love of the Father is not in him. For all that is in the world, the lust of the flesh and the lust of the eyes and the boastful pride of life, is not from the Father, but is from the world (1 John 2:15-16).

If you are overcoming the world you are not participating in its lust. You don't spend your time looking at porno magazines, going to suggestive films, reading trashy novels, or feeding on soap operas. Instead you feed your mind and soul with knowledge that is helpful and profitable for your spiritual growth. You develop a greater sensitivity toward the Spirit of God.

How can one overcome the world? Every believer has

two instruments at his disposal: his faith (1 John 5:4-5), and the Holy Spirit (1 John 4:4). His faith includes his trust in the authority of Scripture. He believes the Word when it says, "Flee from youthful lusts" (2 Timothy 2:22), and "abstain from every form of evil" (1 Thessalonians 5:22). He takes the Word of God seriously when it tells him that his body is a temple of the Holy Spirit (1 Corinthians 6:19). He ceases to compromise with the world system. He does not feel that the Scriptures are a great burden upon his shoulders, but instead believes biblical truth gives principles of freedom which enable a person to live a truly abundant life. John writes, "For this is the love of God, that we keep His commandments; and His commandments are not burdensome. For whatever is born of God overcomes the world; and this is the victory that has overcome the world—our faith; and who is the one who overcomes the world, but he who believes that Jesus is the Son of God?" (1 John 5:3-5).

Regeneration helps you start life all over again. It gives you a new capacity to be yourself and to please God at the same time. It helps you to fit into God's plan for your life. You lose nothing and gain everything.

"Therefore if any man is in Christ, he is a new creature; the old things passed away; behold, new things have come" (2 Corinthians 5:17).

So the first great benefit derived from Jesus' death on the cross is a new beginning. But there are other benefits. Read on and discover what it means, after you have been purchased and set free from spiritual bondage, to belong to someone else.

8

PAYING
THE
PRICE
REDEMPTION

During the Great Depression of the 30s and the devastating recessions of the 70s and early 80s, many businesses, small and large, filed for bankruptcy. The financial strain was too great. Cash flows dried up. Creditors demanded payment. But the reservoir was depleted, and no one came to the rescue by paying the debts and delivering the businessmen from their financial bondage.

The Bible speaks about another type of indebtedness, one beyond the ability of anyone to pay. The indebtedness is spiritual; so is man's bondage. He is spiritually bankrupt.

But there is One who has come to the rescue by paying all of man's spiritual debts. He is called the Redeemer and his act of freeing man is *redemption*, another of those tough words. As you delve into this chapter, however, you will discover that the word is not as difficult as you might think. Let's take a closer look.

What Is Redemption?

The word *redemption* is not totally unfamiliar to contemporary man. Many cities have "redemption centers," where people trade in green savings stamps, yellow stamps, and red stamps for appliances and other merchandise. In the Christian arena, the word *redemption* is more familiar. The average Christian probably knows that Jesus Christ is the Redeemer, and that the believer himself has been redeemed. But what does it all mean?

Webster defines redemption as "deliverance from the bondage and consequences of sin, as through Christ's atonement." Redemption includes an act of deliverance. Redemption further implies that mankind is in bondage to sin. And the agency through which this deliverance is achieved is Christ's atonement. Now we have a little more light on the subject. But let's look at redemption from the perspective of the New Testament, highlighting four of its significant emphases about redemption.

The Act of Buying

The act of buying is the first emphasis we'll consider. In the days of the New Testament, much of a town's social life was spent in the *agora*, the common marketplace. The marketplace of that day was quite different from those of today.

One of the famous tourist attractions in Lancaster, Pennsylvania, is the local farmers' market, where many of the Amish and other farmers sell their homegrown fruits and vegetables. It's a place of teeming activity between narrow aisles. Inside a building dating from the 1700s, you can buy a variety of pastries, from freshly baked "sticky" buns to shoo fly pie. Or you can purchase cabbage slaw, apple butter, and homemade potato salad. You also have a choice of baked ham, smoked ham, or boiled ham at the meat counter. Whatever your palate desires and your pocketbook can afford is available for purchase.

The markets of the New Testament days offered similar opportunities to purchase essentials, but they provided many other activities. Children played and sang in the marketplace (Matthew 11:16-17). Often the unemployed would stand around the marketplace, hoping to be hired for the day (Matthew 20:3). The Pharisees enjoyed walking around the marketplace because the townspeople would give them respectful greetings, thus satisfying their religious egos (Matthew 23:6-7). Often when Jesus entered a village, the people would bring the sick and lay them in the marketplace, hoping he would pass by and restore them to health (Mark 6:56). When Paul and Silas hurt the profits of some unscrupulous businessmen who were using a demon-possessed girl to make money, they were dragged into the marketplace and brought before the chief magistrate (Acts 16:19-21). Also, when Paul entered a new city, he not only preached Christ to the Jews in the synagogue, but also to the Gentiles who bought and sold in the marketplace (Acts 17:17).

One other event carried out in the marketplace was slave trading. Slaves were dragged into the marketplace and sold to the highest bidder. When a slave owner purchased a slave from the agora, his action was known as redemption.

Paying the Price

Redemption also emphasizes *paying the price*. The focus is on setting a person free, but this word (*lutrosis*) includes the idea of making a payment. Redemption cannot be finalized until the price has been paid. One of the questions most commonly asked by a young family man as he decides to make a major purchase is, "How much are the monthly payments?" He may want to purchase a house, a car, or a TV, but until he pays the asking price, that item does not belong to him. So redemption is not merely buying something, it also includes paying a price. But there is something more.

Releasing

The third emphasis of redemption is *releasing*. The word used to emphasize this is the same Greek word *lutrosis* along with the added prefix *apo*, which means "to set free *from*." An illustration would be the granting of pardon to a prisoner, setting him free from prison.

I'm sure you've seen a number of those "B" movies where the condemned-but-innocent man is sitting on death row. Moments before he is to be electrocuted, his cell door rattles open. "It's time to take that long walk," the warden says. He slowly gets up from his bunk, walks out the cell door, and flanked by the warden, a couple of guards, and a priest, begins his long trek down the corridor. As he passes the many cells, some of his buddies call out a few words of encouragement. From down the hall come the mournful strains of "Swing low, Sweet chariot." The condemned prisoner arrives at the chamber housing the electric chair. As the door slowly opens, the prisoner's eyes fix on the ghastly sight before him. The priest puts his hand on the prisoner's shoulder and says, "God be with you, my boy." The prisoner, choked with fright, attempts a smile. The guards grab him by each arm and shove him into the chair, shackling his legs and hands. One of the guards straps a leather and metal band around his head. Everything is now in place for the terrifying moment when a tremendous jolt of electricity will shoot through the innocent victim's body and end his life. But just as the executioner is about to pull the switch, the shrill ring of the phone pierces the silence. "Wait!" says the warden. "It might be the governor." And sure enough, it is the governor, pardoning the innocent man and delivering him from certain death.

The root word *luo*, from which *apolutrosis* is taken, is used by Jesus after he calls Lazarus to come out of the tomb. The Bible says, "He who had died came forth, bound hand and foot with wrappings; and his face was wrapped around with a cloth. Jesus said to them, 'Unbind him, and let him go.' " (John 11:44). The command, "Unbind him," is the word *luo*, emphasizing unbinding, releasing, or setting free.

Owning

The fourth emphasis of redemption is on *owning*. When the Greeks used the word *peripoier*, they focused on buying something for oneself. Sometimes slave owners sent others to buy their slaves for them. When that buyer redeemed a slave, the slave did not belong to him, but to the one who paid the money. A similar procedure is followed today at auctions.

Though it is normal for the buyer himself to go to an auction, those buyers who spend hundreds of thousands of dollars for luxury items often send a representative to do their purchasing for them. And when the price has been paid, the item belongs, not to the representative, but to the absentee purchaser.

Suppose you decide to buy a car for yourself. You pay the agreed price. Once that price is paid, the ownership of that vehicle is transferred from the dealer's name to your name and is verified by a pink slip. The dealer no longer has any rights to that car. He may not even get in it without your permission. The ownership has been transferred. You now own the car.

Redemption is no different. When an object has been redeemed, the ownership is transferred from one person to another. This means that the former owner has no rights or privileges over the purchased object.

Now, having looked at these four emphases of redemption, let's ask another question.

What Are the Implications of Redemption?

Man Lives under Enslavement

One significant implication of redemption is that *man lives under the enslavement of Satan and sin.*

The apostle John wrote, "We know that we are of God, and the whole world lies in the power of the evil one" (1 John 5:19). The world system is under the influence of Satan. He is "the prince of the power of the air" (Ephesians 2:2), or as Jesus put it, "the ruler of this world" (John 12:31). All those who live outside of Christ are under his control. This is why the apostle could write, "And you were dead in your trespasses and sins, in which you formerly walked according to the course of this world, according to the prince of the power of the air, of the spirit that is now working in the sons of disobedience. Among them we too all formerly lived in the lusts of our flesh, indulging the desires of the flesh and of the mind, and were by nature children of wrath, even as the rest" (Ephesians 2:1-3). Though the natural man feels that he has total freedom to do as he pleases, in reality he is walking according to the course which the prince of the power of the air has laid out for him. He is like the man in prison who is free at certain times of the day to go out in the prison yard and play baseball. He is free to walk to the cafeteria, or to the prison library. But all his freedom is restricted to the confines of the prison.

So it is with the unbeliever. He has a certain amount of freedom to do as he pleases, but he pleases to do according to the dictates of Satan. As we become aware of this, we should evaluate our attitude toward those outside of Christ. Too often Christians mistake the unbeliever as the enemy rather than as a victim of the enemy. The unbeliever needs to be set free, to be released from Satan's stronghold.

Man is not only enslaved to Satan, but he is also enslaved to sin. Obviously this idea is not too popular with the unbelieving world. The typical person on the street would never consider himself enslaved to sin. But both Scripture and experience prove that this is true. It was Jesus who said, "Truly, truly, I say to you, everyone who commits sin is the slave of sin" (John 8:34). Have you ever committed a sin? Have you ever gone a week without sinning? As the apostle Paul looks back on the former life of the Christian, he writes, "But thanks be to God that though you were slaves of sin, you became obedient from the heart to that form of teaching to which you were committed. . . . For when you were slaves of sin, you were free in regard to righteousness. Therefore what benefit were you then deriving from the things of which you are now ashamed? For the outcome of those things is death" (Romans 6:17, 20-21).

What's the implication? Precisely this: the unbeliever cannot stop himself from breaking God's laws and violating God's holiness. He may be selective about which moral or spiritual laws he will break, but I guarantee that he will break them. He cannot help himself. Paul testified of this as he groaned, "For we know that the Law is spiritual; but I am of flesh, sold into bondage to sin. For that which I am doing, I do not understand; for I am not practicing what I would like to do, but I am doing the very thing I hate. But if I do the very thing I do not wish to do, I agree with the Law, confessing that it is good. So now, no longer am I the one doing it, but sin which indwells me. For I know that nothing good dwells in me, that is, in my flesh; for the wishing is present in me, but the doing of the good is not. For the good that I wish, I do not do; but I practice the very evil that I do not wish. But if I am doing the very thing I do not wish, I am no longer the one doing it, but sin which dwells in me. I find then the principle that evil is present in me, the one who wishes to do good. For I joyfully concur with the law of God in the inner man, but I see a different law in the members of my body, waging war against the law of my mind, and making me a prisoner of the law of sin which is in my members. Wretched man that I am! Who will set me free from the body of this death? Thanks be to God through Jesus Christ our Lord! So then, on the one hand I myself with my mind am serving the law of God, but on the other, with my flesh the law of sin" (Romans 7:14-25).

Look around you at the various lifestyles of the people who surround you. You'll see ample evidence that many are enslaved to harmful habits such as smoking, drinking, lust, gluttony, anger, jealousy, and feelings of inferiority. Many times these habits are debilitating and can even kill.

Man Is Indebted

Man's indebtedness is another implication of redemption. *Man is highly indebted to God*, and he needs to be released from that debt. When a man breaks society's law, he is indebted to society. If convicted, he must pay his debt. Because man has broken God's moral and spiritual laws, he is indebted to God and must pay with his life, since the wages of sin is death (Romans 6:23).

Have you ever been up to your ears in debt? Heavy debts often produce terrible emotional strain. But imagine a debt so enormous that you could not possibly pay it. This is the condition of the unbeliever. The Bible clearly states that there is a certificate of debt which is against him (Colossians 2:14). And until that debt is paid, he will constantly live under God's judgment.

Man Cannot Pay His Debt

This brings us to the third implication of redemption. Because man lives under the enslavement of Satan and sin, and because he is indebted to God, it is obvious that *he cannot pay the price to free himself.* Men try to pay for their sin, but their efforts are futile.

Some attempt to pay back God by giving money to the church or to charitable organizations. But it is impossible for anyone to buy his way into heaven. If this were the way to salvation, only the wealthy could achieve it. The apostle Peter makes it clear that money is insufficient to pay for one's redemption: "Knowing that you were not redeemed with perishable things like silver or gold from your futile way of life inherited from your forefathers" (1 Peter 1:18).

Another insufficient payment for redemption is religion. If religion could pay the debt of man's sin, Jesus never would have told Nicodemus (a very religious man), "Truly, truly, I say to you, unless one is born again, he cannot see the kingdom of God" (John 3:3).

A third insufficient payment for redemption is sincerity. There are many sincere people in the world, but that doesn't count toward getting them to heaven.

Jim Marshall played for the Minnesota Vikings in the team's early years. During a nationally televised game, Marshall intercepted a pass and began to run toward the goal line. He was so determined to reach the end zone that he didn't hear his own players running down the sidelines with him and shouting at him. He thought they were cheering him on. He was so proud of himself when he finally crossed the goal line, and very impressed with himself because he outran every player from the opposing team. Caught up in his moment of glory, he hadn't realized that he had made a major mistake. Marshall had run the wrong way, and scored for the opposing team. He was very sincere. He did everything in his power to accomplish what he thought was the right thing to do—get a touchdown. And he achieved his goal. It's just that the points went to the opposing team. The book of Proverbs says, "There is a way which seems right to a man, but its end is the way of death"

(Proverbs 14:12). Sincerity is good, but not good enough to achieve redemption.

Men also attempt to purchase redemption through good works. They see God as holding a big balance in the sky. One side weighs the sins which a person has committed, while the other side weighs his good deeds. Since most people grade themselves on the curve, they are convinced that God uses the same measurement. Therefore, in their own evaluation they usually come out on top. Convinced that their good works outweigh their bad deeds, these people seldom worry about not making it.

Do the Scriptures agree with this concept? In no way. The apostle Paul is very clear that redemption is not achieved like that. He writes, "For by grace you have been saved through faith; and that not of yourselves, it is the gift of God; not as a result of works, that no one should boast" (Ephesians 2:8-9). He also writes to Titus, "He saved us, not on the basis of deeds which we have done in righteousness" (Titus 3:5).

Your own righteousness will never merit heaven. The book of Romans points out that this was Israel's great mistake in trying to establish a relationship with God. "Brethren," Paul writes, "my heart's desire and my prayer to God for them is for their salvation. For I bear them witness that they have a zeal for God, but not in accordance with knowledge. For not knowing about God's righteousness, and seeking to establish their own, they did not subject themselves to the righteousness of God" (Romans 10:1-3). Anyone who declares, "I'm good enough," is only kidding himself.

The Only Sufficient Price

What then is sufficient for man's redemption, to set him free from the bondage of sin and Satan? Who can pay the insurmountable debt man owes God? The sufficient price and the only person who qualifies as a Redeemer is stated clearly in Scripture.

Man cannot free himself from that debt. The only sufficient price accepted by God for man's redemption is the blood of Jesus Christ. Peter says, "Knowing that you were not redeemed with perishable things like silver or gold from your futile way of life inherited from your forefathers, but with precious blood, as of a lamb unblemished and spotless, the blood of Christ. For He was foreknown before the foundation of the world, but has appeared in these last times for the sake of you who through Him are believers in God, who raised Him from the dead and gave Him glory, so that your faith and hope are in God" (1 Peter 1:18-21). Again Peter writes, "Peter, an apostle of Jesus Christ, to those who reside as aliens, scattered throughout Pontus, Galatia, Cappadocia, Asia, and Bithynia, who are chosen according to the foreknowledge of God the Father, by the sanctifying work of the Spirit, that you may obey Jesus Christ and be sprinkled with His blood: May grace and peace be yours in fullest measure" (1 Peter 1:1-2). Paul wrote to the Ephesians, "In Him we have redemption through His blood . . ." (Ephesians 1:7).

Though liberal theologians are often offended by the emphasis which evangelicals place on the blood of Christ, hymn writers down through the centuries have written unequivocally about this unique price which alone can set a man free from bondage. One lyricist has penned, "What can wash away my sin? Nothing but the blood of Jesus. What can make me whole again? Nothing but the blood of Jesus." Another wrote, "Would you be free from your burden of sin? There is power in the blood, power in the blood. Would you o'er evil a victory win? There is wonderful power in the blood." Another familiar hymn says, "There is a fountain filled with blood drawn from Emmanuel's veins. And sinners, plunged beneath that flood, lose all their guilty stains." A more contemporary hymn and songwriter, Andrae Crouch, says it this way: "The blood that Jesus shed for me, 'way down at Calvary, the blood that gives me strength from day to day, will never lose its power. It reaches to the highest mountain, and flows to the lowest valley. The blood that gives me strength from day to day will never lose its power." The blood of Christ is something to sing about, not to hide.

REDEMPTION

What did Jesus mean when he said, "And you shall know the truth, and the truth shall make you free. . . . If therefore the Son shall make you free, you shall be free indeed" (John 8:32, 36)?

Imagine yourself as a slave standing at the auction block. You have no rights and no recourse for any ill treatment you've received from the hands of your master. Half naked and bound by shackles, you stand under the scrutiny of potential buyers. Lust bids first, hoping to get you at a bargain price. Covetousness is willing to bid a higher price for your soul. Unfaithfulness, jealousy, and anger all put in their bid. And then from the back of the crowd a voice cries out, "I'll give my life for this slave." A hush falls on the crowd. The bidders turn around, disbelief etched on their faces. Each one wonders, "Who would be foolish enough to lay down his life for such an unworthy slave?" But the man steps forward with tear-stained eyes and says, "I repeat, I'll buy that slave and in return I'll give you my life." How true—"If the Son shall make you free, you shall be free indeed." The blood of Jesus Christ not only paid the price of redemption, but it also set man free from his bondage.

Under New Management

One further implication of redemption is that *the redeemed are now under new ownership and new management*. At one time you were under the jurisdiction of the devil. But now you are brought under the jurisdiction of Jesus Christ. Formerly you were living in the sphere of death and darkness. But now you live in the atmosphere of light and life. This means that both the ownership and management of your life have changed.

Today you see many signs in front of restaurants and small businesses, "Under new management." Normally when the new manager comes on the scene, he removes old policies and adopts new ones. He may remove the old decor and completely redesign the interior. He may get rid of old personnel and bring in his own team to manage the business effectively.

When Jesus Christ paid the price to set you free from

the bondage of sin, he brought you under new management. He removed the old policies and established new ones, found in the Word of God. He removed the old decor which included immorality, impurity, passion, evil desire, greed, anger, wrath, malice, slander, and abusive speech (Colossians 3:5, 8). He replaced those things with a new decor, such as "a heart of compassion, kindness, humility, gentleness and patience; bearing with one another, and forgiving each other . . ." (Colossians 3:12-13).

Furthermore, the Lord removed the old personnel who were once in control of your life, such as "the rulers, the powers, the world forces of this darkness, the spiritual forces of wickedness in the heavenly places" and replaced them with the Spirit of God (Ephesians 6:12; Romans 8:9).

This is a complete housecleaning. Paul described it when he wrote, "Therefore if any man is in Christ, he is a new creature; the old things passed away; behold, new things have come" (2 Corinthians 5:17).

Redemption therefore begins with the thought that man is enslaved to Satan and sin, and is so overwhelmingly indebted to God that he cannot pay it. But Jesus paid the price of redemption so that men could be set free from their bondage of sin. Once they have been set free from sin's bondage, the redeemed are under new ownership and new management.

The Debt Is Canceled

But what happens to that great debt which man owes God? Even though Jesus paid the debt with his blood, what happens to the debt? This brings us to the sixth application of redemption. *The debt of sin is canceled.* Suppose you suddenly lose your job and cannot make your mortgage payments. After a few months, the bank is ready to repossess your house. But on the day of repossession the bank calls you and says, "Mr. Jones, we were ready to repossess your house by noon. But a gentleman walked in here at 11:55 A.M. and paid off your entire mortgage. The house now belongs to you—paid in full."

This is what happened at Calvary. When Jesus cried out

on the cross, "It is finished," that is exactly what He meant. The debt of sin was canceled because the price had been paid. Paul framed this truth in the following words: "And when you were dead in your transgressions and the uncircumcision of your flesh, He made you alive together with Him, having forgiven us all our transgressions, having canceled out the certificate of debt consisting of decrees against us and which was hostile to us; and He has taken it out of the way, having nailed it to the cross" (Colossians 2:13-14). How can we be sure that God has the power to forgive us? Because only the one offended has the authority to forgive the offender. And since we have sinned against God, he alone has the authority to forgive us.

Recall the story which Jesus told his disciples when speaking about forgiveness. He said, "For this reason the kingdom of heaven may be compared to a certain king who wished to settle accounts with his slaves. And when he had begun to settle them, there was brought to him one who owed him ten thousand talents (about $10 million). But since he did not have the means to repay, his lord commanded him to be sold, along with his wife and children and all that he had, and repayment to be made. The slave therefore falling down, prostrated himself before him, saying, 'Have patience with me, and I will repay you everything.' And the lord of that slave felt compassion and released him and forgave him the debt" (Matthew 18:23-27). Because that slave owed this debt to a king, only the king could release him from that debt.

Though you and I could never pay the price for our release, because the debt was too great, Jesus paid it for us. He was both able and willing to give his life for us. That's why God can be both holy and just to release us from that debt.

Now having looked at the subject of redemption, let's focus on several lessons which will be helpful as we consider day-to-day living.

What Lessons Can We Learn from Redemption?

You No Longer Have to Obey Your Old Masters

The first lesson is that *you no longer have to obey sin or Satan*. Since you have been released from the former managers of your life, and have been placed under new management, you do not have to give the old managers the time of day.

The man who joins the military is taught to salute an officer whenever one approaches. He also has to dress properly every day, keep his room neat, snap to attention when ordered to do so, say "Yes, sir" and "No, sir," go to bed at a specified time, and get up at a ridiculous time. He is constantly under the orders of his officer.

The day comes, however, when the enlisted man is discharged from military service. The next time he sees an officer coming toward him, he is under no obligation to salute that officer. If he chooses to look foolish and salute an officer while in civilian dress, that's up to him. But he is under no obligation to salute. He doesn't have to say "Yes, sir" or "No, sir." The officer could demand that the discharged soldier snap to attention, but that former soldier can stand slump-shouldered if he wants. The officer could demand that the discharged soldier wear a military outfit, but he could tell the officer to get lost. He has no responsibility whatever to obey.

Likewise, though you have established many habit patterns from the old life, you no longer have to yield to those sinful patterns. You can now look at a beautiful girl without lusting after her. You have the right to speak your mind without swearing. You have the right to turn down the next cocktail, and you can praise God instead of cursing him.

The apostle Paul said it well when he wrote, "For sin shall not be master over you, for you are not under law, but under grace... But thanks be to God that though you were slaves of sin, you became obedient from the heart to that form of teaching to which you were committed, and having been freed from sin, you became slaves of righteousness" (Romans 6:14, 17-18).

REDEMPTION

Some of your former friends may think you're a little weird for making such a sudden change in your life. But that's their problem. If your former friends have a difficult time knowing how to treat you, recognize that this problem has existed for many years. Peter himself wrote, "For the time already past is sufficient for you to have carried out the desire of the Gentiles, having pursued a course of sensuality, lusts, drunkenness, carousals, drinking parties and abominable idolatries. And in all this, they are surprised that you do not run with them into the same excess of dissipation, and they malign you; but they shall give account to Him who is ready to judge the living and the dead" (1 Peter 4:3-5).

Your Life Is Not Your Own

Second, *your life no longer belongs to you.* You have no right to do with it as you please. Your body is not to be used as a target for drugs, illicit sex, obesity, workaholism, or any other sinful lifestyle. The Scriptures make it clear that you belong to God first by creation. This is why the Psalmist wrote, "Come, let us worship and bow down; let us kneel before the LORD our maker" (Psalm 95:6). Our proper attitude toward God should be one of unconditional abandonment—"Lord, I am your creation. Do with me as you see fit."

We not only belong to God by creation; we also belong to him by redemption. Jesus paid the great price for our redemption, and we have no right to abuse our bodies. Paul states, "Or do you not know that your body is a temple of the Holy Spirit who is in you, whom you have from God, and that you are not your own? For you have been bought with a price: therefore glorify God in your body" (1 Corinthians 6:19-20). Our bodies have become a sanctuary for the Holy Spirit. When we abuse our bodies and indulge in the lusts of the flesh, we are degrading both the tremendous sacrifice which Christ was willing to make on our behalf and that Holy One who has taken up residence in our bodies.

Abusing our bodies is not only immoral, it is illogical.

Suppose you were to buy a house. A few weeks later, after the close of escrow, the previous owner decides to move back into the house and take over management. You would be appalled at the owner's foolish move. But is that not what we do when we decide to take over control of our lives after the Lord has come to live within us? Redemption means that we no longer belong to ourselves.

How Should We Respond to Redemption?

What is the best response to redemption? It is to *use your freedom wisely*. Paul says, "For you were called to freedom, brethren; only do not turn your freedom into an opportunity for the flesh, but through love serve one another" (Galatians 5:13). One of society's great problems is the repeat offender. Many prisoners return to prison because they don't know how to use their freedom properly. No sooner are they out of prison than they adopt their old lifestyle and get themselves into trouble again. This is exactly what the apostle Paul warns the believer to avoid.

Redemption—a word emphasizing a purchase, a price, a deliverance from bondage and indebtedness, and a change of ownership. The song writer captured the concept well when he wrote, "Redeemed! how I love to proclaim it. Redeemed by the blood of the Lamb. Redeemed by His infinite mercy. His child and forever I am."

Now that you have been set free from the enslavement of sin you have the ability not only to experience God's forgiveness, but to forgive yourself and others. As you read on you'll learn how to wipe the slate clean.

CHAPTER
9

WIPING THE SLATE CLEAN
FORGIVENESS

Throughout my years of formal education, I was tormented by a loathesome habit that plagued many of my teachers. The habit annoyed me so much that I often found myself ready to attack the chalkboard. What habit am I referring to? Scratching the chalkboard with a squeaky piece of chalk? No. Though that would send chills up my spine, it happened too infrequently to bother me. What really irritated me were those times the teacher, writing on the board as he was explaining his subject, would run out of chalkboard space. Whenever it happened he would lightly erase a part of the board, leaving indistinguishable letters seeping through a white blotch. Then he would write over the white chalk smear. The result was an unintelligible mess resembling early cuneiform. This would so unnerve me that I would have loved to grab the eraser from the teacher, clean off the board completely, and then say, "Okay, *now* you can go on with the lesson."

Our spiritual lives are something like that chalkboard. They are covered with so many blotches of sin that it's not only difficult for others to see a clear spiritual distinctive, but we can't even understand or read ourselves accurately. We send out mixed signals, resulting in a garbled, unintelligible life message. What we need is for someone to wipe the slate clean and help us begin anew.

The Bible tells us that such a person has already arrived on the scene, making it possible for us to have our slate wiped clean. His name is Jesus Christ. And the process of cleaning the slate and starting over is called forgiveness. This chapter will deal with forgiveness by answering some pertinent questions about God's great act of mercy. Let's begin by investigating the need for forgiveness.

Why Does Man Need to Be Forgiven by God?

Man Has Offended God's Character

One of the main reasons man needs to be forgiven by God is that *he has offended God's holy character*. Like the person who writes graffiti on the sides of a building, man often offends God's character intentionally. He gets a thrill from ruining anything that is pure or upright. Consider, for instance, what Hollywood has done with the sanctity of marriage. The Scriptures say, "Let marriage be held in honor among all, and let the marriage bed be undefiled; for fornicators and adulterers God will judge" (Hebrews 13:4). Hollywood has taken that beautiful relationship which God has designed for a man and woman and rejected it as old-fashioned, replacing it with sex outside of marriage or extramarital affairs as the natural way of life. What was once evil and unnatural is being considered good and natural.

Paul commented on this attitude when he wrote: "For the wrath of God is revealed from heaven against all ungodliness and unrighteousness of men, who suppress the truth in unrighteousness.... For even though they knew God, they did not honor Him as God, or give thanks; but they became futile in their speculations, and their foolish heart was darkened.... and exchanged the glory of the incorruptible God for an image in the form of corruptible man and of birds and four-footed animals and crawling creatures.... For they exchanged the truth of God for a lie, and worshiped and served the creature rather than the

Creator, who is blessed forever. Amen. For this reason God gave them over to degrading passions; for their women exchanged the natural function for that which is unnatural, and in the same way also the men abandoned the natural function of the woman and burned in their desire toward one another, men with men committing indecent acts and receiving in their own persons the due penalty of their error. And just as they did not see fit to acknowledge God any longer, God gave them over to a depraved mind, to do those things which are not proper ..." (Romans 1:18, 21, 23, 25-28). Much of man's offense toward God is intentional.

But man also offends God's holy character unintentionally. There are times he is not aware of breaking or violating the laws of God. You may have sometime been traveling at one rate of speed, then entered a zone where the speed is lowered, but were unaware of it either because you did not pay attention to the signs or because the signs were blocked by a tree or some other obstruction. You stand guilty of violating the speed limit even though you didn't know you were doing it. This is the reason God gave us his law—so we would know when we violate his holy character. Paul testifies, "What shall we say then? Is the Law sin? May it never be! On the contrary, I would not have come to know sin except through the Law; for I would not have known about coveting if the Law had not said, 'You shall not covet' " (Romans 7:7).

A few months ago our family was eating at a local spaghetti house. I happened to be wearing white slacks, which I knew was a dangerous thing to do while eating spaghetti. I was very careful, though, and made certain that my napkin covered my slacks. After dinner, we went shopping. It was while we were shopping that my son looked at me and began to laugh. "You should see the back of your trousers," he giggled. "They're covered with spaghetti." I turned around and looked, and he was right. Whoever had sat in the seat before me had spilled spaghetti and it was never cleaned up. What was once a pair of clean trousers was now splotched by red spaghetti stains. It was unintentional, but the trousers were still stained.

Whether we intentionally or unintentionally sin against God, our sin violates God's law and offends his holy and righteous character.

God Must Punish Sin

There is another reason man needs to be forgiven by God. Man needs forgiveness not only because he has offended God's holy character, but because God must punish sin. Paul specifies the penalty of sin: "For the wages of sin is death ..." (Romans 6:23). Without forgiveness, man must pay the penalty. Justice demands that sin be punished. Without forgiveness man will be separated from God throughout eternity, for that is the meaning of spiritual death. This brings us to the next important question.

What Does God Do When He Forgives?

The Scriptures use a number of analogies to describe God's act of forgiveness. For instance, *he releases us from paying sin's penalty.* The writers of the New Testament use many words which are translated "forgive." For instance, the word *aphiēmi* means "to release," "to remit," or "to cancel." This word is used in the Lord's prayer where it says, "and forgive us our debts, as we also have forgiven our debtors" (Matthew 6:12). When we pray after this manner we are asking God to cancel the debts which we owe him.

Another word used for forgiveness is the term *karizomai*, which means "to show favor" or "to give freely." Paul chose this word when he wrote, "and when you were dead in your trangressions and the uncircumcision of your flesh, He made you alive together with Him, having forgiven us all our transgressions" (Colossians 2:13). When we were spiritually apart from God and living in sin, God showed us special favor by forgiving us our transgressions and making us alive together with him.

A third word is the term *apoluo*, translated "to set free," "to release," or "to pardon." Jesus Christ used this along with the first word, *aphiēmi*, in his parable of the king and his servant that we quoted in the previous chapter. Remember the story: the servant owed his master a fabulously large debt which he could never hope to repay. But when he begged his master to forgive the debt, it was canceled. Here's how Matthew put it: " 'Have patience with me, and I will repay you everything.' And the lord of that slave felt compassion and released (*apoluo*) him and forgave (*aphiēmi*) him the debt" (Matthew 18:23-27).

This servant's debt was canceled and he was released from paying the penalty of owing the king such a large debt. This is what is meant by forgiveness. God releases us from paying sin's penalty and cancels the debt.

God also *casts our sins into the depths of the sea*. The prophet Micah wrote, "He will again have compassion on us; He will tread our iniquities underfoot. Yes, Thou wilt cast all their sins into the depths of the sea" (Micah 7:19). The sea is so deep that its depths have yet to be discovered. Every day ships leave New York harbor loaded with garbage which is taken out to sea and dumped into its depths. This is exactly what God does with our spiritual garbage: He takes it out to sea and dumps it into the depths.

The Lord also *casts our sins behind his back*. Hezekiah, king of Judah, had become mortally ill. But when he prayed to God for restoration of health, God added fifteen years to his life. After his illness and recovery, the king wrote the following words: "I said, 'In the middle of my life I am to enter the gates of Sheol; I am to be deprived of the rest of my years.' I said, 'I shall not see the LORD, the LORD in the land of the living; I shall look on man no more among the inhabitants of the world. . . . O Lord, by these things men live; and in all these is the life of my spirit; O restore me to health, and let me live! Lo, for my own welfare I had great bitterness; it is Thou who hast kept my soul from the pit of nothingness, for Thou hast cast all my sins behind Thy back' " (Isaiah 38:10, 11, 16, 17). This means that God no longer focuses upon our sins. He does not concern himself with them, for they are behind his back.

One further description of forgiveness is that God *no longer remembers our sins*. Through Isaiah the prophet, God declared, "I, even I, am the one who wipes out your trans-gressions for My own sake; and I will not remember your sins" (Isaiah 43:25). God not only forgives, he forgets. How can God forget? Isn't he omniscient? Yes, he knows every-thing. When the Bible says he forgets our sins, it means he does not remember them against us. They are no longer counted against us. Therefore we also have the ability to forget (by not counting their sin against them) when people offend us or sin against us.

What Did It Cost God to Forgive?

God's forgiveness is not a cheap act of leniency, nor does he waive the penalty for sin. God demands that sin be punished and places the most severe punishment—death—on the offender.

But God, who is rich in mercy, took his own innocent and righteous son, placed our sin upon him, and then punished him as though he were the worst transgressor who ever lived.

Suppose your child were innocently riding his bicycle down the sidewalk. Suddenly three young bullies pop out from behind a hedge and begin to push him around. They call him names, make fun of him, push him off his bicycle, and break his bike. You see what's taking place, but by the time you arrive on the scene, the bullies are gone. You be-come angry for what they did to your child, but instead of punishing the three older children, you take your child home and punish him. That wouldn't make any sense, would it? And yet, that's what God did to his own son. When he sent Jesus into the world, the world scorned him, rejected him, and attempted to push him around. God was angry with man for abusing his son, and he took his son to the cross and punished him in place of the men who re-jected him. Understandably, we would never love those three bullies enough to punish our child and then offer them forgiveness. But God loved us enough to punish his son for our sins and to offer us forgiveness.

Is forgiveness costly? It is when you consider that it

cost God to give up what he loved the most—his only son. So when you think of forgiveness, remember its price.

What Is the Extent of God's Forgiveness?

If forgiveness hadn't cost God so much, we might be concerned how much sin God would forgive or how often he would forgive. But because God willingly punished his innocent son for our guilt, we can be assured that *all* of our sin, without exception, has been cancelled. God offers many examples which show us the extent of his forgiveness. He forgave Moses of murder, David of adultery, Peter of denying the Lord Jesus Christ, Paul of persecuting the Church. He forgave the disciples for running away from his son. So whatever sin you feel you may have committed, God is in the business of forgiving it all.

The Unpardonable Sin

But you may be wondering whether forgiveness *extends to the unpardonable sin*. It was Jesus who said, "Therefore I say to you, any sin and blasphemy shall be forgiven men, but blasphemy against the Spirit shall not be forgiven. And whoever shall speak a word against the Son of Man, it shall be forgiven him; but whoever shall speak against the Holy Spirit, it shall not be forgiven him, either in this age, or in the age to come'" (Matthew 12:31, 32). Many people think they have committed the unpardonable sin. We know the unpardonable sin could not be murder, for Moses was forgiven that. The unpardonable sin could not be adultery or immorality, for David (as well as the woman caught in adultery) was forgiven. What, then, is the unpardonable sin?

According to Matthew's gospel, the unpardonable sin is the act of attributing to Satan the power of the Holy Spirit which was working through Christ. Jesus cast out demons by the power of the Holy Spirit, but the eyewitnesses said he was casting out demons by the power of Satan. They were attributing the Spirit's power to Satan. And as long as they persisted in attributing Jesus' work to Satanic power, there was no forgiveness.

Since the Lord Jesus Christ is not walking this earth

and performing great works by the power of the Holy Spirit, men are not attributing his works to the power of Satan. Therefore I do not believe that the unpardonable sin can be committed today. So whether it be adultery, homosexuality, lying, murder, child abuse, having a child out of wedlock, or other such acts of rebellion, they are forgivable.

The Sin unto Death

Some people are troubled by the biblical passage that speaks of *the sin unto death*. There are those who fear for their life because they believe they have committed the sin which will result in physical death. The apostle John refers to the sin unto death when he writes, "If anyone sees his brother committing a sin not leading to death, he shall ask and God will for him give life to those who commit sin not leading to death. There is a sin leading to death; I do not say that he should make request for this. All unrighteousness is sin, and there is a sin not leading to death" (1 John 5:16, 17).

It's important to note that John is not saying that a specific sin leads to death. A more accurate translation would read "sin unto death" rather than "*a* sin" or "*the* sin unto death." Various passages throughout Scripture give evidence that God sometimes disciplines a believer by removing him from earth. He disciplined Ananias and Sapphira for lying to the Holy Spirit when they testified that they sold a piece of property for a certain amount of money and gave all the proceeds to the church, when in reality, they kept back some of the price for themselves. Peter responded by saying, "'Ananias, why has Satan filled your heart to lie to the Holy Spirit, and to keep back some of the price of the land? While it remained unsold, did it not remain your own? And after it was sold, was it not under your control? Why is it that you have conceived this deed in your heart? You have not lied to men, but to God.' And as he heard these words, Ananias fell down and breathed his last; and great fear came upon all who heard of it" (Acts 5:3-5).

Furthermore, God disciplined certain Corinthian believers for abusing the Lord's table. When Paul spoke about partaking of the elements, he warned his readers, "Therefore whoever eats the bread or drinks the cup of the Lord in an unworthy manner, shall be guilty of the body and the blood of the Lord. But let a man examine himself, and so let him eat of the bread and drink of the cup. For he who eats and drinks, eats and drinks judgment to himself, if he does not judge the body rightly. For this reason many among you are weak and sick, and a number sleep" (1 Corinthians 11:27-30).

On another occasion, one of the believers in Corinth was living immorally with his father's wife (probably his step-mother). Because the church did not discipline the man for his immoral lifestyle, the apostle Paul announced that he was going to deliver the man over to Satan so that Satan would take his life. Paul wrote, "I have decided to deliver such a one to Satan for the destruction of his flesh, that his spirit may be saved in the day of the Lord Jesus" (1 Corinthians 5:5).

We know that God does not use this kind of discipline on everyone who lies or who is immoral or who abuses the Lord's table. At times he does, but remember this is discipline and not condemnation. According to the Scriptures, "There is therefore now no condemnation for those who are in Christ Jesus" (Romans 8:1). The fact that God disciplines us guarantees that we will not be condemned. Paul writes, "But when we are judged, we are disciplined by the Lord in order that we may not be condemned along with the world" (1 Corinthians 11:32). Because God takes someone home earlier than might have been does not mean that the sin has not been forgiven. That sin is covered by the blood of Christ as well as other sins. But perhaps because the believer refuses to deal with the sin through confession, or possibly because God wants to set an example for others, he removes that person from the earth.

Sins of the Future

Another concern that people have when they think of the extent of forgiveness is whether it *extends to the sins of the*

167

present and future. According to the Scriptures, God's forgiveness extends to the past, present, and future. When Christ died on the cross, all of our sins were future, since we were not yet born. When God wipes the slate clean, it is thoroughly clean.

How Should We Respond to God's Forgiveness?

Some people use God's forgiveness as a blank check to sin as much as they please, and then claim that everything is covered by the blood. But Paul spoke to this very issue when he wrote, "What shall we say then? Are we to continue in sin that grace might increase? May it never be! How shall we who died to sin still live in it?" (Romans 6:1, 2). As Christ identified with us on the cross when he died for sin, we too identify with him be dying to sin. Our response to God's forgiveness should be twofold: We should keep ourselves clean by walking in the light and we should forgive others as God has forgiven us. Let's focus on that first response.

Walk in the Light

It is imperative to keep ourselves clean by walking in the light. The apostle John writes, "But if we walk in the light as He Himself is in the light, we have fellowship with one another, and the blood of Jesus His Son cleanses us from all sin. If we say that we have no sin, we are deceiving ourselves, and the truth is not in us. If we confess our sins, He is faithful and righteous to forgive us our sins and to cleanse us from all unrighteousness. If we say that we have not sinned, we make Him a liar, and His word is not in us" (1 John 1:7-10).

What does it mean to walk in the light? Walking in the light means continuous exposure to truth. The person who wants to sin doesn't want a lot of exposure. This is why most sin happens in the darkness. Jesus addressed the issue when he said, "And this is the judgment, that the light is come into the world, and men loved the darkness rather than the light; for their deeds were evil. For everyone who does evil hates the light, and does not come to the light, lest his deeds should be exposed. But he who practices the truth comes to the light, that his deeds may be manifested as having been wrought in God" (John 3:19-21). Those who want to sin do not feel comfortable around God or God's people. They are not going to spend much time reading the Scriptures. They don't welcome listening to a sermon. They would rather not be reminded of sin. They feel more comfortable with a crowd which practices sin and enjoys the security of darkness.

As we are constantly exposed to the truth, though, the Holy Spirit is able to show us where we are falling short of God's standard. This should encourage us to confess our sin and experience a cleansing by God and intimate fellowship with him again.

Do you recall the account when Jesus was washing the disciples' feet? When Christ came to Peter, the disciple responded, "'Never shall You wash my feet!' Jesus answered him, 'If I do not wash you, you have no part with me.' Simon Peter said to Him, 'Lord, not my feet only, but also my hands and my head.' Jesus said to him, 'He who has bathed needs only to wash his feet, but is completely clean; and you are clean, but not all of you.' For He knew the one who was betraying Him; for this reason He said, 'Not all of you are clean'" (John 13:8-11). Jesus knew that all but one of the disciples were spiritually clean. Therefore, he who is clean needs only to be washed periodically through confession of sin.

If a person takes a shower and then walks outside and gets his feet dirty, he doesn't have to go back into the house to take another shower. He needs only to wash his feet. Likewise, when we trust in Christ, we are thoroughly cleansed and forgiven of our sin. Just because we periodically do sin against the Lord, we don't need to be thoroughly cleansed again. But we do need to deal with those sins and receive cleansing for fellowship. While the major cleansing removes the penalty of sin, the periodic cleansing restores fellowship with God.

Walking in the light not only means continuous exposure to truth, but also means immediate confession of known sins. What is confession? Is it merely a verbalizing of guilt? No. The biblical concept includes three essentials. The first is that you agree with God that you have sinned against him. The word translated "confess" comes from a Greek word which means "to say the same as." When you confess your sin, you and God agree that what you did was wrong. You don't look for an excuse or attempt to blame someone else. You agree that your act has violated God's holiness and you acknowledge that you are the one to blame.

Confession is also remorse for the sin which you have committed. There are those who are guilty of "easy confessionism" where they merely mouth certain words and feel that their oral rehearsal will take care of their guilt. The very opposite of that opinion is the example of David after he committed adultery with Bathsheba. He was filled with remorse. With a tear-stained face, David cried, "How blessed is he whose transgression is forgiven, whose sin is covered! How blessed is the man to whom the LORD does not impute iniquity, and in whose spirit there is no deceit! When I kept silent about my sin, my body wasted away through my groaning all day long. For day and night Thy hand was heavy upon me; my vitality was drained away as with the fever-heat of summer. I acknowledged my sin to Thee, and my iniquity I did not hide; I said, 'I will confess my transgressions to the LORD;' and Thou didst forgive the guilt of my sin" (Psalm 32:1-5).

David realized that he had made a fool of himself. He knew that he had brought disdain to the name of God. He realized that he had given occasion to the enemies of the Lord to blaspheme the name of God (2 Samuel 12:14). So when David confessed his sin, he confessed in great sorrow.

Confession is also an expression of not wanting to sin again. Those who believe in an "easy confessionism" already make plans for the next sin as they verbalize their confession to God. But not so with true confession. In another Psalm, David pours out his heart before God concerning the same sin of adultery by writing, "Purify me with hyssop, and I shall be clean; wash me, and I shall be whiter than snow.... Create in me a clean heart, O God, and renew a steadfast spirit within me.... Restore to me the joy of Thy salvation, and sustain me with a willing spirit. Then I will teach transgressors Thy ways, and sinners will be converted to Thee" (Psalm 51:7, 10, 12, 13). David had no plans to sin against God again. He wanted a clean heart and a joyful spirit. He wanted to teach others the ways of the Lord. He wanted to be useful to the Lord again.

Suppose I were to jog ten miles and then when I arrive home, I hop in the shower, put on clean clothes, and go out and mow the grass. Ridiculous? You'd better believe it. It's foolish for anyone to work up a good sweat, take a shower, put on clean clothes, and go out again to work up another sweat. Once you shower you don't make plans to get sweaty again. Likewise, when we confess our sin to God, seeking his cleansing, there should be no thought in our minds of going out and sinning again.

Forgive Others

We should forgive others as God has forgiven us. You read earlier about a slave who was released from paying the penalty of his debt to the king. How did he respond to the king's great compassion and forgiveness? Jesus continued the parable, "But that slave went out and found one of his fellow-slaves who owed him a hundred denarii; and he seized him and began to choke him, saying, 'Pay back what you owe.' So his fellow-slave fell down and began to entreat him, saying, 'Have patience with me and I will repay you.' He was unwilling however, but went and threw him in prison until he should pay back what was owed. So when his fellow-slaves saw what had happened, they were deeply grieved and came and reported to their lord all that had happened. Then summoning him, his lord said to him, 'You wicked slave, I forgave you all that debt because you entreated me. Should you not also have had mercy on your fellow-slave, even as I had mercy on you?' And his lord, moved with anger, handed him over to the torturers until he should repay all that was owed him. So shall My

171

heavenly Father also do to you, if each of you does not forgive his brother from your heart" (Matthew 18:28-35).

Here was a slave who owed his master over ten million dollars, while someone else owed him only about eighteen dollars. And yet, though the slave's master released him of the ten million dollar debt, the slave was not willing to forgive his debtor eighteen dollars. We are like this unmerciful slave when we refuse to forgive those who ask us. No matter how much we have been offended, it is not as much as we have offended God. That's why the apostle Paul wrote, "And be kind to one another, tender-hearted, forgiving each other, just as God in Christ also has forgiven you" (Ephesians 4:32). That's the standard—"just as God in Christ also has forgiven you."

But how has God forgiven us? What characteristics do we discover in God's forgiveness?

God forgives us when we ask him for forgiveness. He does not give a carte blanche forgiveness to all men. We must ask for it. And when we do, he gives it. In the same way, we must be willing and available to offer forgiveness to those who want it. But what if that individual rejects my offer? If that is the case, we are free from pursuing the matter. All we can do is to pray for the offender.

Second, God forgives whatever needs to be forgiven. There is no sin which is too great or too small for God. If we distinguish between what sins we will forgive and what sins we will not forgive, then we are not following God's pattern for forgiveness. He does not make such distinctions.

Third, the Lord forgives as often as we sincerely ask. The emphasis here is on the word *sincerely*. The apostle Peter was very generous when he offered to forgive someone seven times, because the rabbinical law said that one needed only to offer forgiveness three times. But God's forgiveness is always available as often as we need it. He does not count the number of times we ask him and then offer us just one more chance. His forgiveness is available as often as we need it and as long as we are sincere in asking for it.

FORGIVENESS

If a person is sincere in asking, and yet seems to have a recurring problem, then he or she should be willing to seek counsel or help for that problem. If a husband asks his wife's forgiveness for his infidelity but then tells her, "I may be unfaithful again, but if I am, I'll expect you to forgive me," he is not sincere about his request for forgiveness. The individual who is being controlled by a debilitating habit such as alcohol abuse should not flippantly ask for forgiveness, but should seek help in dealing with the main problem. But where there is sincerity, forgiveness should be offered as often as it is needed.

When God forgives, he also removes any thoughts of taking vengeance. To say, "I'll forgive you" while at the same time you tell yourself, "Boy, am I going to get even with him" is not to forgive as God forgives. When the Lord cancels the debt, there is no thought of vengeance or getting even. Seeking vengeance is putting ourselves on the same level as the servant in the parable who refused to forgive an eighteen dollar debt when he owed his master over five hundred thousand times that amount.

One other quality of God's forgiveness is that God treats a forgiven offender as pardoned. Remember the Corinthian believer who was living immorally with his father's wife? The apostle Paul expected to turn that man over to Satan for the destruction of the flesh, so that the man's soul would be spared. But this man repented of his sin and sought the forgiveness of the church. Many in the church were not willing to forgive him. So the apostle had to write a second letter to Corinth and tell them, "Sufficient for such a one is this punishment which was inflicted by the majority, so that on the contrary you should rather forgive and comfort him, lest somehow such a one be overwhelmed by excessive sorrow. Wherefore I urge you to reaffirm your love for him" (2 Corinthians 2:6-8).

Because this man was not being forgiven, he was becoming overwhelmed with sorrow and isolation. Paul encouraged the church to affirm their love for him once again.

God does not keep score of our offenses against him. When Paul writes about love, he says that love, "does not

173

act unbecomingly; it does not seek its own, is not provoked, does not take into account a wrong suffered" (1 Corinthians 13:5). The wife who says she forgives her husband but anxiously waits for him to slip again so that she can rehearse all of his past mistakes has not truly forgiven him. The husband who tells his wife, "I'll forgive you, but things will never be the same again" is not offering true forgiveness. God doesn't keep score of wrongs suffered. Neither should we.

Furthermore, God treats the offender as pardoned by focusing on the offender's needs. God realizes that we need his fellowship, a clear conscience, and his total acceptance. Think for a moment of someone who has offended you in the past. What does he or she need from you? Certainly not a guilt trip. If that individual is truly sorry for what he has done and has asked for your forgiveness, he needs your affirmation of love. He needs to be treated as pardoned.

Ask Forgiveness of Others

A third response to God's generous and sacrificial act of forgiveness is that *we should ask forgiveness from those we have offended*. Whether we offend others intentionally or unintentionally, we need to ask their forgiveness. Jesus said, "If therefore you are presenting your offering at the altar, and there remember that your brother has something against you, leave your offering there before the altar, and go your way; first be reconciled to your brother, and then come and present your offering" (Matthew 5:23-24). What does this mean?

First, you are aware that you have offended someone. He knows and you know that you've annoyed him. You may have misjudged him and said something unkind. You may have slandered his character. Perhaps you cheated him in some way, or unintentionally slighted him. Whatever the offense, he has been hurt by your actions and has made it known to you directly or indirectly. A word of caution at this point.

If you have had feelings of jealousy, anger, or bitterness toward another, but he is unaware of it, you would be unwise to contact him and say, "By the way, you may not know it but I've been bitter toward you for years, so forgive me." That is not what this passage demands. If you take that approach, you may receive his forgiveness, but you'll also receive his suspicion from then on. Why? Because he never knew that there was a problem between the two of you. But now he begins to wonder what else is going through your mind about him. In this passage, the offense of which Jesus speaks is already known to both parties.

You, the offender, must take the initiative to wipe the slate clean and restore fellowship. Before you worship God, whom you cannot see, straighten out the strained relationship between you and the other person, whom you can see. First be reconciled to your brother, and then present your offering at the altar.

Think of a brother and sister fighting one another. They refuse to talk to each other. Later the boy comes to his dad and expresses how much he appreciates him. Dad says, "Johnny, I'm glad you love me. But show how much you love me by apologizing to your sister. It hurts me to see you two not getting along with each other. Prove your love for me by asking your sister to forgive you." This is precisely what God is saying. "Before you come to me and offer thanks and praise, make up with your brothers and sisters. People will know that you are my children when you both offer and ask for forgiveness."

Another aspect of asking forgiveness from one you've offended is making restitution. Remember Zaccheus? Luke records the event. "And when Jesus came to the place, He looked up and said to him, 'Zaccheus, hurry and come down, for today I must stay at your house.' And he hurried and came down, and received Him gladly. And when they saw it, they all began to grumble, saying, 'He has gone to be the guest of a man who is a sinner.' And Zaccheus stopped and said to the Lord, 'Behold, Lord, half of my possessions I will give to the poor, and if I have defrauded anyone of anything, I will give back four times as much.' And Jesus said to him, 'Today salvation has come to this house, because he, too, is a son of Abraham'" (Luke 19:5-9).

If your offense included cheating someone out of money, consider repaying the amount. If you borrowed something and then returned it broken or in poor condition, why not replace it, or offer to have it repaired? If you cheated someone out of time and got paid for work you didn't do, you may want to repay the person by giving him the work that should have been done.

Medical science tells us that, if not checked, cholesterol building up in the arteries can be harmful or even lethal. When we allow misunderstandings, hurt feelings, anger, jealousy, slander, and other offenses to collect in our relationships with others, this too can be harmful and even lethal. Those offenses must be removed so that communication and love can flow freely between you and others.

But what if the offended person will not forgive you? I believe that God holds you accountable to ask. But he holds the offended one accountable to grant forgiveness. If the person refuses, you have still fulfilled your obligation. Just keep close to the Lord so that you don't harbor feelings of resentment. Keep your conscience clear before God and allow God to work in the other person's life.

Do you know of someone you've offended? Then respond to God's magnanimous act of forgiving you by asking that person for his forgiveness.

Wipe the slate clean. That's what God does for you when you confess your sins to him. He is then ready to write a new chapter in your life. Since God has been so merciful to you, why not respond by walking in the light, forgiving others as he has forgiven you, and asking forgiveness of those you've offended?

As God has announced new life to you, so should you be willing to announce new life to others. That's the next subject—justification.

10

ANNOUNCING THE NEW LIFE
JUSTIFICATION

The judges of our land have been given authority to send a man to prison or to set him free. The underlying principle is that the innocent go free while the guilty are sent to prison. But it doesn't always work out that way. Sometimes the guilty are released and the innocent are imprisoned.

But in God's court of heaven, there are no innocent. So how can a man be set free if he is guilty? That's where justification enters.

What Is Justification?

If you were to eavesdrop on a typical Sunday School class, you'd probably hear a statement like, "Today we're going to study a very important truth. However, this truth is shrouded in a word which sounds very complicated. I'm referring to *justification*. But an easy way to remember the meaning of *justified* is to break it into the phrase 'just-as-if-I'd-never-sinned.'"

Such an approach to justification may prove to be a useful teaching tool; unfortunately, this approach waters down the truth. Like an L. A. smog, it both clouds and distorts reality.

Justification is neither a declaration of one's innocence nor the mere forgiveness of sins. Let's look at that teaching tool once more—"just-as-if-I'd-never-sinned." God never looks at man as though he had never sinned. God never pronounces a man innocent of his sins. Man stands guilty before God, because he has defamed God's holy character and has violated his righteous laws. In many courts today it is not unusual for judges to declare the innocent guilty and the guilty innocent. But God keeps good records. When he makes a judgment, it is accurate. ". . . the judgments of the LORD are true; they are righteous altogether" (Psalm 19:9). When a driver pushes his car over the speed limit and passes a police officer, that officer may either estimate the driver's speed and pursue him, hoping to get a conviction, or he may use radar which takes the guesswork out of the estimation. In God's court, there is no guesswork. God's radar locks onto our sin and knows the precise degree of our guilt. Though he justifies the one who comes to him, he does not pronounce that man innocent.

Some people equate justification with forgiveness. But forgiveness is negative (the putting away of sins). Justification is positive (the counting of righteousness). In his *Systematic Theology*, Dr. Lewis Sperry Chafer says, "To forgive means subtraction while justify means addition." A judge can pardon a man but can't make him righteous; God can do both. If justification, then, is not a declaration of one's innocence or the act of forgiveness, what is it?

Justification is God's gift of pronouncing man righteous in spite of his guilt. Let's look at this definition in three phases. consider first the gift aspect.

A Gift

Justification is a gift from God, according to the apostle Paul, who writes, "Being justified as a gift by His grace through the redemption which is in Christ Jesus" (Romans 3:24). What are the characteristics of a gift? A gift, obviously, is not earned. We give gifts to our children at Christmas time because we love them. But suppose a parent refused to give a gift unless his child worked hard for it. An unreasonable decision? Definitely, because it would then no longer be a gift, but a wage. The same analogy holds for justification. It is not earned. It can only be received as a gift. "Now to the one who works, his wage is not reckoned as a favor, but as what is due. But to the one who does not work, but believes in Him who justifies the ungodly, his faith is reckoned as righteousness" (Romans 4:4-5).

Gifts are also expressions of love, respect, or honor. You give gifts to your children and close friends out of love. You may give other gifts to an acquaintance out of respect or honor. God's love gift to the world was his son: "For God so loved the world, that He gave His only begotten Son, that whoever believes in Him should not perish, but have eternal life" (John 3:16).

Recognition of Man's Guilt

A second phase of justification is its recognition of man's guilt before God. I said earlier that justification is not a declaration of man's innocence. Why? Man is guilty. "For all have sinned and fall short of the glory of God" (Romans 3:23). The word translated "have sinned" means to "miss the mark." The very first sin you ever committed caused you to miss the mark. Man doesn't have to commit some gross sin to be declared a sinner. Just as a person who kills another is declared a murderer, and the man who steals only once is a thief, so the very first sin that a man commits qualifies him as a sinner. James puts it in these words: "For whoever keeps the whole law and yet stumbles in one point, he has become guilty of all" (James 2:10).

Because man is a sinner by nature and practice, he is continually falling short of God's glory. The meaning of falling short is "to be behind" or "to be deficient." No matter how hard man tries to keep up with God's expectations, he continually falls behind.

A year after I graduated from seminary, I had the opportunity to go on a trip into the wilderness of northern Minnesota. The crew included two Dallas Theological Seminary professors (Dr. Howard Hendricks and Dr. Bruce Waltke), five Dallas students, and two of us who had been out of school for a year. Of the nine-man crew only one had any experience in the wilderness. We spent three days in the virgin boundary waters above Eli, Minnesota. It was quite an experience to be able to drink the crystal clear water in the lake without fear of becoming ill. To sit around the crackling fire at night listening to the cry of the loons was an experience of great serenity. But there was another side of our wilderness journey. That three-day excursion included a grueling task called "portaging." We had to travel over several miles of rugged terrain from one lake to the next, loaded to the hilt with backpacks and a canoe on our shoulders. I don't recall how much those canoes weighed, but I do remember that after three days in the wilderness, I never wanted to portage again in my life. Though we took turns carrying those canoes single-handedly, when it was your turn, you prayed for a sprained ankle. The weight of the canoe pressed mercilessly into your shoulders. No matter how you positioned the canoe, you hurt. And even after three days of carrying that weight, I never got used to it. Nor did I want to.

What does this have to do with man's sin and that he is continually falling behind God's glory or standard? Suppose you were assigned to run a marathon against one of the world's greatest marathon runners, Frank Shorter. You are told that you must run in hiking boots, carrying a seventy-five-pound backpack and a three-man canoe, while Shorter is permitted to run in his lightweight racing shorts, shirt, and shoes. "You've got to be kidding," you'd probably say. "First of all, I can't run a marathon. Second, there's no way I could ever run against Frank Shorter and hope to win. And to be loaded down with a seventy-five-pound backpack and a three-man canoe could only guarantee losing the race."

You've got it. Whenever man tries to match God's standard while carrying his weight of sin with him, he can only lose. He is always deficient when he stands before God. And God recognizes man's deficiency. He knows man stands guilty before him and always falls short of his standard. But in spite of man's guilt, God justifies the one who is willing to trust in him. This brings us to the third phase of justification.

JUSTIFICATION

A Pronouncement of Righteouness

Justification is a legal pronouncement of righteousness. Notice the role that justification played in the court system of the Old Testament. "If there is a dispute between men and they go to court, and the judges decide their case, and they justify the righteous and condemn the wicked, then it shall be if the wicked man deserves to be beaten, the judge shall then make him lie down and be beaten in his presence with the number of stripes according to his guilt" (Deuteronomy 25:1-2). Under Mosaic law, the wicked were to be condemned and the righteous were to be justified. But in God's court of law, the wicked who repent of their sin and turn to God are declared righteous. How is that possible? Let's observe the role that each person of the Godhead plays in man's justification.

Jesus Christ made it possible for God the Father to declare the sinner righteous. And how was that accomplished? Jesus allowed his Father to transfer man's sins to himself, and then to transfer his righteousness to sinful man. A concise statement concerning this transaction is recorded in 2 Corinthians: "He made Him who knew no sin to be sin on our behalf, that we might become the righteousness of God in Him" (2 Corinthians 5:21). When Jesus was willing to receive our sins and pay the death penalty for them, he made it possible for the Father to justify the sinner.

And what was the Father's role in justification? God the Father declared the sinner righteous and removed the sentence of judgment against him by transferring his sins to Christ and Christ's righteousness to sinful man.

What then is the Holy Spirit's relationship to justification? The Holy Spirit develops the potential righteousness that we have in Christ into actual righteousness. Just as a child has the potential to walk, but will never do so unless he is encouraged by his parents, so the believer has the potential of living a righteous life because he was given Christ's righteousness. It is the responsibility of the Holy Spirit to encourage, to motivate, and to empower the believer to actually walk in righteousness.

We can say that justification is neither a declaration of one's innocence nor the mere forgiveness of sins, but it is God's gift of pronouncing man righteous in spite of his guilt. Let's investigate further.

How Can a Man Be Justified?

Not by Self-Effort

Most of the religions of the world, and even some branches of Christianity, teach that man can be justified by his own self-effort. The Reformation was born out of Martin Luther's struggle with this very question. Luther wanted to be right in the eyes of God. He prayed, helped people, and did penance with the hope that God would declare him righteous. Still he knew that his efforts were in vain. And then one day, a passage of Scripture penetrated his confusion with brilliant clarity: "The righteous man shall live by faith" (Galatians 3:11). He immediately realized that *man is not justified by his personal merits.*

Man has a two-fold problem when it comes to personal merits. First, he usually compares himself with the wrong standard, which in this case is other men. It's not difficult to find someone who is worse off than ourselves. We can always find someone who will swear more, eat more, drink more, steal more, and be more sensual than ourselves. The problem with this approach is that God doesn't use sinful man as the standard for comparison. Instead, he compares man with his Son.

Remember the parable of the tax collector and the Pharisee? It is Jesus' account of how a man is justified—"And He also told this parable to certain ones who trusted in themselves that they were righteous, and viewed others with contempt: 'Two men went up into the temple to pray, one a Pharisee, and the other a tax-gatherer. The Pharisee stood and was praying thus to himself, "God, I thank Thee that I am not like other people: swindlers, unjust, adulterers, or even like this tax-gatherer. I fast twice a week; I pay tithes of all that I get.' But the tax-gatherer, standing some distance away, was even unwilling to lift up his eyes to heaven, but was beating his breast, saying, "God, be merciful to me, the sinner!" I tell you, this man went down to his house justified rather than the other; for everyone who exalts himself shall be humbled, but he who humbles himself shall be exalted'" (Luke 18:9-14).

The Pharisee in this parable was a self-righteous man. He based his righteousness both on good works (such as fasting and paying tithes), and on not doing what other people do (such as swindling or committing adultery). Because he was righteous in his own eyes, he thought he was righteous in God's eyes. But he used the wrong standard for comparison.

Another problem which man has is that he always sees greater merit in his achievements than God sees. God is not impressed with what we do, because our good works do not deal with sin. It has been said that "beauty is in the eyes of the beholder." An artist may invest many months in what he considers to be a masterpiece. But when he attempts to sell it, potential buyers may not think the work of art is worth the canvas on which it's painted. Likewise, "righteousness is in the eyes of the beholder." What you and I consider righteous in our eyes is not what God considers as righteousness in his eyes.

Self-effort is not limited to one's personal merits. It may also include a free conscience. There are those who believe they are right in the eyes of God because their conscience is clear. But a clear conscience does not necessarily mean that a man has been declared righteous by God. Even the apostle Paul did not rely on his own self-evaluation. Paul testified, "I am conscious of nothing against myself, yet I am not by this acquitted; but the one who examines me is the Lord" (1 Corinthians 4:4). The conscience can be seared to the point where that which was once considered evil is now considered good. Man cannot trust his own heart. The prophet Jeremiah warns, "The heart is more deceitful than all else and is desperately sick; who can understand it?" (Jeremiah 17:9).

Justification Is by Faith

If man is not justified by self-effort, how then is he justified? *Man is justified by faith on the merit of Jesus' death.* Faith has always been the means of man's justification. Look at the testimony of Scripture: "For we maintain that a man is justified by faith apart from works of the Law. Or is God the God of Jews only? Is He not the God of Gentiles also? Yes, of Gentiles also, since indeed God who will justify the circumcised by faith and the uncircumcised through faith is one" (Romans 3:28-30). Paul also writes to the Galatians, "Nevertheless knowing that a man is not justified by the works of the Law but through faith in Christ Jesus, even we have believed in Christ Jesus, that we may be justified by faith in Christ, and not by the works of the Law; since by the works of the Law shall no flesh be justified" (Galatians 2:16). Paul adds further, "Now that no one is justified by the Law before God is evident; for, 'the righteous man shall live by faith.' ... Therefore the Law has become our tutor to lead us to Christ, that we may be justified by faith" (Galatians 3:11, 24).

The Law of Moses saved no one. It did, however, accomplish a very important task. It showed man that he could not live up to God's standard. The Pharisees thought they did live up to God's standard by keeping the Law. But they merely kept the external requirements of the Law. Jesus taught that the Law went beyond the physical act of sin. He showed how the Law also made requirements on a man's emotions and attitude. The Lord preached, "You have heard that the ancients were told, 'You shall not commit murder' and 'Whoever commits murder shall be liable to the court.' But I say to you that everyone who is angry with his brother shall be guilty before the court; and whoever shall say to his brother, 'Raca,' shall be guilty before the supreme court; and whoever shall say, 'You fool,' shall be guilty enough to go into the fiery hell" (Matthew 5:21-22). He further said, "You have heard that it was said, 'You shall not commit adultery'; but I say to you, that everyone who looks on a woman to lust for her has committed adultery with her already in his heart" (Matthew 5:27-28). The

JUSTIFICATION

Law could justify no one. It could only condemn the sinner by showing him that he has fallen short of God's standard.

Man can be justified by faith alone. But what is faith? The word is derived from the Greek *pisteūo*, meaning "to place confidence in," "to be pursued of," or "to trust." Sinful man is justified when he believes that Jesus' death was sufficient to settle the sin problem. He is persuaded that God actually credited our sin to Christ's account and Jesus' righteousness to our account. He is persuaded further that his own righteousness will not merit heaven.

I love music. I enjoy singing, playing my guitar, and listening to a variety of music. Suppose I got the brilliant idea to leave the pastorate and attempt to earn a living by singing. You'd be well within reason to do everything in your power to dissuade me. But to carry the episode further, let's say that one of the top Christian singers calls me and says, "Rick, though you've never met me personally, I want to make you an offer. I'll sing around the country and send all of my earnings to you. You'll receive a check in the mail every month. If you'll just trust me to sing instead of singing yourself, you'll be rewarded."

This is where faith enters. My first option is to believe that this top professional singer is a man of his word and will earn a living for me by singing so that I don't have to sing. My second option is to disregard his offer and insist on trying it my way by leaving the pastorate for a music career—which would guarantee certain failure.

Man is no more qualified to be accepted by God on his own merit than I would be accepted by music lovers on my personal merit. Man must place confidence in Jesus' death as the sufficient solution to the sin problem.

Paul wrote, "Much more then, having now been justified by His blood, we shall be saved from the wrath of God through Him" (Romans 5:9). Christ's death was the result of God's placing man's sin upon Jesus and then passing the death sentence upon him. Then when his righteousness was transferred to man, God could declare man to be righteous. Justification is not the result of self-effort, but rather of faith based on the merit of Jesus' death.

What Are the Benefits of Justification?

As I have studied the Scriptures, I've observed six major benefits for the person who is declared righteous by God.

Peace with God

As a starter, *the believer experiences peace with God*: "Therefore having been justified by faith, we have peace with God through our Lord Jesus Christ" (Romans 5:1). Peace with God is not like a peace treaty made between men. God's peace is permanent. When nations ratify a peace treaty with one another, it usually lasts until one of the parties breaks the agreement. But God does not break his agreement. When he justifies a man, he brings him into a permanent peace relationship with himself. God no longer considers man an enemy.

God's peace is not only permanent, it is also complete. By this I mean that God's peace not only guarantees that he withholds his judgment from us, but it goes a step further by making God available to help us put our life together.

Through the centuries, when one nation would conquer another, the victor often ravaged and killed the people of the land. If they thought it was to their advantage, they would enslave the people whom they conquered and rule them with a rod of iron. Russia is a cruel example of a nation who conquers and then removes the freedoms and rights of the people it overruns. In contrast, after World War II, when the U.S. defeated Germany and Japan, Congress enacted the Marshall Plan. This gave aid to these and other countries, to rebuild and eventually to govern themselves once again. Today both West Germany and Japan are living examples of a peace between countries which not only guaranteed no further judgment, but also guaranteed the resources to help them become strong nations once again.

Escape from Wrath

Justification also *spares the believer God's wrath*. Paul writes, "For the wrath of God is revealed from heaven against all ungodliness and unrighteousness of men, who suppress the truth in unrighteousness" (Romans 1:18). According to the words of the Lord Jesus, the unbeliever already has God's wrath upon him: "He who believes in the Son has eternal life; but he who does not obey the Son shall not see life, but the wrath of God abides on him" (John 3:36). Once a man believes in the Lord Jesus Christ, however, he is declared righteous and the sentence of death is removed. He no longer has to worry about God's judgment falling upon him when he dies, as Paul assures his readers when he writes, "Much more then, having now been justified by His blood, we shall be saved from the wrath of God through Him" (Romans 5:9). The justified believer is like the man sitting on death row who receives a pardon. The wrath of the Law no longer abides upon him.

Honor from God

A third benefit is that *the believer will be honored by God.* Paul informs the Roman believers, "For whom He foreknew, He also predestined to become conformed to the image of His Son, that He might be the first-born among many brethren; and whom He predestined, these He also called; and whom He called, these He also justified; and whom He justified, these He also glorified" (Romans 8:29-30). What does it mean to be glorified? The word *glorify* means "to honor." The Greek word *doxazo* means "to honor," and is used by the Lord when he refers to the ambitions of the Pharisees: When therefore you give alms, do not sound a trumpet before you, as the hypocrites do in the synagogues and in the streets, that they may be honored by men. Truly I say to you, they have their reward in full" (Matthew 6:2). Remember how the prodigal son was honored by his father? He was first honored with his father's warm embrace and acceptance. Then he was honored with a robe, ring, and sandals. Later he was honored as the guest of honor at a great banquet to which family and friends were invited.

In the same way, when we turn to God and are justified by him, he honors us with a warm embrace and an unconditional acceptance. He gives a robe of righteousness, and the Holy Spirit, symbolized by a ring. He gives us shoes which are the preparation of the gospel of peace, and then invites us to a great feast which we will enjoy with the Lord after the marriage of the Lamb. And the benefits continue.

Free from Condemnation

Another benefit of justification is that *the believer is free from condemnation.* Paul queries, "Who will bring a charge against God's elect? God is the one who justifies; who is the one who condemns? Christ Jesus is He who died, yes, rather who was raised, who is at the right hand of God, who also intercedes for us" (Romans 8:33-34).

Our court systems have a law called "the law of double jeopardy." This means that a person cannot be subjected to a second trial and penalty for the same offense. God's court of law is like that. Once man is declared righteous, he cannot be tried for sin anymore. He is free not only from God's condemnation, but also from man's condemnation.

This means that he should also be free from self-condemnation. Too often we walk around condemning ourselves when God doesn't condemn us. You may be wondering, "If God isn't accusing me, then who does accuse me when I feel so unworthy?" Condemnation usually comes from two sources: oneself and the devil. The Bible tells us that the devil is the accuser of the brethren (Revelation 12:10). He would love to keep you in despair by constantly reminding you of how bad you have been in the past, and how many times you fail in the present. But remember, it is not God who accuses you, for there is "no condemnation for those who are in Christ Jesus" (Romans 8:1).

Righteous from All Sin

A fifth benefit of justification is that *the believer is declared righteous from all sin.* Many people believe that God forgives some of their sins, but not all of them. Or else they think that he forgives their past sins, but doesn't forgive the present or future sins. The Bible teaches otherwise. When God declares a man righteous, he sees no sin in him.

JUSTIFICATION

If you want to see a good picture of some terrible sinners, look at the group that made up the church at Corinth. "Or do you not know that the unrighteous shall not inherit the kingdom of God? Do not be deceived; neither fornicators, nor idolators, nor adulterers, nor effeminate, nor homosexuals, nor thieves, nor the covetous, nor drunkards, nor revilers, nor swindlers, shall inherit the kingdom of God. And such were some of you; but you were washed, but you were sanctified, but you were justified in the name of the Lord Jesus Christ, and in the Spirit of our God" (1 Corinthians 6:9-11). When Paul preached his sermon in Antioch on his first missionary journey, he told the people how far justification reaches. He said, "Therefore let it be known to you, brethren, that through Him forgiveness of sins is proclaimed to you, and through Him everyone who believes is freed from all things, from which you could not be freed through the Law of Moses" (Acts 13:38-39). You are freed or justified from all things, including past, present, and future sins.

Suppose a man buys a second-hand business. When he pays the price for that business, he has paid for the company's debts of the past, present, and future. He is liable for all debts. When Jesus Christ died on the cross, he paid for your sins of the past, present, and future, being liable for all debts which you owed God.

Heirs of God

One other benefit of justification is that *the believer is made an heir of God*. Paul writes to Titus, "He saved us, not on the basis of deeds which we have done in righteousness, but according to His mercy, by the washing of regeneration and renewing by the Holy Spirit, whom He poured out upon us richly through Jesus Christ our Savior, that being justified by His grace we might be made heirs according to the hope of eternal life" (Titus 3:5-7).

I recently read in the *Wall Street Journal* that upon the death of Carl Rosen, president of Puritan Fashions Corporation (exclusive marketer of Calvin Klein jeans), his estate was divided like this: He wrote a will that left $50,000 to his main physician, established a $4 million trust for his children, and divided up his $20 million estate. Besides all the inheritance gained by his family and friends, his one son was made president of the company. But even though that inheritance was substantial, it could be lost through bad investments or it could cause jealousy and fighting within the family. Furthermore, that inheritance is only good as long as the heirs are alive. They won't be able to take any of it with them when they die.

God's inheritance isn't like that. God's is eternal. Furthermore, God's inheritance cannot be lost. The apostle Peter tells us how secure this inheritance is when he writes, "Blessed be the God and Father of our Lord Jesus Christ, who according to His great mercy has caused us to be born again to a living hope through the resurrection of Jesus Christ from the dead, to obtain an inheritance which is imperishable and undefiled and will not fade away, reserved in heaven for you, who are protected by the power of God through faith for a salvation ready to be revealed in the last time" (1 Peter 1:3-5).

Though the inheritance is not spelled out, we know that the Holy Spirit is a down payment: "In Him, you also, after listening to the message of truth, the gospel of your salvation—having also believed, you were sealed in Him with the Holy Spirit of promise, who is given as a pledge of our inheritance, with a view to the redemption of God's own possession, to the praise of His glory" (Ephesians 1:13-14). Part of that inheritance includes a place which Christ has prepared for every believer (John 14:2-3). It is also described in terms such as *crowns* and *rewards*. Whatever the specifics of the inheritance, we can be certain that it will far surpass anything we could have on earth.

We've learned a lot about all the great benefits God gives to those who have been justified by him. But are there not responsibilities which go along with justification? There certainly are.

What Are the Responsibilities of Those Who Have Been Justified?

The apostle James is very firm that though a man is justified by faith, his faith should be evident by his works. What are the responsibilities of those who have been justified?

Helping Others

James begins with *an interest in the needs of others.* "What use is it, my brethren, if a man says he has faith, but he has no works? Can that faith save him? If a brother or sister is without clothing and in need of daily food, and one of you says to them, 'Go in peace, be warmed and be filled,' and yet you do not give them what is necessary for their body, what use is that? Even so faith, if it has no works, is dead, being by itself" (James 2:14-17).

Man by nature is self-centered. He looks out for Number One. It is only through the miracle of the new birth that man changes his attitude. Too often in our modern society, people have been beaten and robbed, women have been raped, and others have been murdered as onlookers have stood and watched the crime, but have refused to come to the aid of the victim. When asked later why they didn't help, the usual response has been, "I just didn't want to get involved." The person who has been justified should be willing to get involved in the lives of others in order to meet their needs.

Obedience

A second responsibility of the justified believer is *a life of unconditional obedience to God.* James uses Abraham as an illustration of one whose faith could be seen through an unconditional obedience to God. James writes, "Was not Abraham our father justified by works, when he offered up Isaac his son on the altar? You see that faith was working with his works, and as a result of the works, faith was perfected; and the Scripture was fulfilled which says, 'And Abraham believed God, and it was reckoned to him as righteousness,' and he was called the friend of God. You see that a man is justified by works, and not by faith alone" (James 2:21-24).

Is James contradicting the apostle Paul? Absolutely not. He is complementing Paul's statement. True justification, though the result of faith, is demonstrated in works.

One way of telling whether a tree is alive is to look for its fruit. And yet the tree was alive before its leaves appeared and its fruit matured. Likewise, before God, justification is the result of faith. But before the eyes of men, justification is demonstrated by works. One such work is the act of reconciling yourself to someone who has offended you. We'll discuss that challenge in the next chapter.

11

GETTING
TOGETHER
RECONCILIATION

Many years ago I saw on television one of the most heart-rending films I'd ever seen. It was entitled *An Occasion at Owl Creek Bridge*. A prisoner was going to be hanged through a trap door in a bridge. The guards led the prisoner, with his hands bound, up to the gallows. They put a rope around his neck and placed a hood over his head. When the guards stepped back from the trap door, the executioner pulled the lever. With the sound of the trap door opening, you watched the prisoner drop through empty space. But his fall didn't stop at the end of the rope. The weight of the prisoner's body snapped the rope, plunging him into the cold, swirling torrents of the river. As the current carried him downstream, he struggled underwater to free himself. As I watched him struggle, my heart began to pound and I tried to breathe for him. At last he freed his hands, removed the hood, and with powerful strokes swam underwater, dodging the rain of bullets penetrating the water. Soon he was out of their range. As he came up gasping for air, I gasped with him.

After a brief rest he started to swim downstream. In the background I could hear dogs barking as they followed his scent. The prisoner continued to evade the guards throughout the film from one situation to another. I cheered when he succeeded in eluding his captors.

Finally, he came to a sandbar and dragged himself out of the water. When he collapsed on the bank of the river, he cried out with exhaustion and delight, "I'm a free man!" I was as excited as he that he was free at last.

After climbing up the riverbank, he saw a wooded area which would provide him with the cover he needed. Staggering from one tree to another, he frantically tried to reach the safety and security of his home. Soon the trees gave way to an open field, where the prisoner saw his house at a distance. As he shouted for joy, the door of his house swung open and his wife emerged. Their eyes met and they began to run toward each other.

The action is captured in slow motion as they run through gently waving flowers with romantic music in the background. Soon the couple is about to embrace. The atmosphere is alive with excitement. You know that within seconds the reconciliation will be complete. But just as they fly into each other's arms, the screen suddenly goes black. You're convinced that you've lost your picture. Nothing's happening. But in a moment you hear a horrible thud, and then a jerking and gurgling sound. And when the picture comes on again, you see a man dangling at the end of a rope. And you struggle with the realization that the reconciliation you thought you saw was but the microsecond of a hope that passed before the prisoner's eyes before he met his death. What seemed at first to be a reality was merely a dream.

Like the experience of this prisoner, reconciliation is often a mere dream for many people—whether it be reconciliation between man and God, or between man and man.

What Is the Meaning of Reconciliation?

What comes to your mind when you think of the word *reconciliation*? Perhaps you envision a husband and wife who were on the verge of divorce, but reconciled their differences and developed a lasting relationship. Or maybe your mind reflects on two friends who terminated their friendship because of a sharp disagreement. Then as time passed, one friend went to the other and sought to restore the relationship.

The biblical term *reconciliation* does imply an estranged relationship which is transformed into an intimate one. The focus of attention, however, is on the total change which occurs. The word *reconciliation* is derived from the Greek word *katalasso*, which means "to change completely." In its earlier stages, this word was used to refer to the exchanging of coins. Whenever a U.S. citizen makes a trip to a foreign country, he must exchange American dollars for that country's currency. And when he returns to the States, he reverses that exchange. Likewise, before an estranged relationship can experience healing, a complete change in one or both parties must occur.

When the Bible refers to reconciliation between God and man, it highlights two aspects. One focus is on *potential reconciliation*. When Jesus Christ sacrificed his life for the benefit of man, he made it possible for all mankind to have an intimate relationship with God. The apostle Paul refers to this potential reconciliation when he writes, "Namely, that God was in Christ reconciling the world to Himself, not counting their trespasses against them, and He has committed to us the word of reconciliation" (2 Corinthians 5:19).

Most people traveling to California have seen pictures of the Golden Gate Bridge. They're aware that it is probably the most familiar landmark of San Francisco. Until they visit California, they have no use for the Golden Gate Bridge. But once they journey to San Francisco, one of the first things they want to do is cross over the famous bridge. What was at one time merely a potential opportunity became an actual experience. That is the second aspect of reconciliation.

Reconciliation is an actual experience. Paul writes, "Now all these things are from God, who reconciled us to Himself through Christ, and gave us the ministry of reconciliation" (2 Corinthians 5:18). Though God made it possible for the entire world to be reconciled to himself, only those who are willing to cross the bridge will experience actual reconciliation and a total change. Is a complete change really necessary? Definitely!

Why Does Man Need to Be Reconciled to God?

Spiritual Helplessness

The New Testament indicates a number of reasons man has to be changed completely in order to come to an intimate relationship with God. One concerns his lack of spiritual strength. *Man is in a condition of spiritual helplessness.* Paul writes, "For while we were still helpless, at the right time Christ died for the ungodly" (Romans 5:6). Have you ever experienced physical helplessness?

A number of years ago, when our family was in Carmel for a few days, we went out to a seafood restaurant in Monterey. When our orders came, I sensed that something was wrong with my swordfish. But since the restaurant seemed to have a good reputation, I thought perhaps it was the sauce with which they basted it that caused the pungent odor. After eating about half my dinner, I joked with my wife, "If anything happens to me tonight, tell the paramedics it was the swordfish."

I felt fine as we turned in for the evening. I sat up and read until 11:30 P.M. and then fell asleep. About 2:00 A.M. I felt lightheaded and nauseated. Crawling out of bed, I made my way toward the bathroom. I no sooner walked through the door than I could feel myself beginning to fade. I called to my wife and told her she better call for help. The next thing I knew, I was looking up at several paramedics who had put monitors on my chest and prepared me for the trip to the hospital. I remember telling them, "It's not my heart, it's the swordfish." Paying no attention to what I way saying, they carried me into the ambulance and took me to the Monterey Hospital. Throughout the episode, I was too helpless to sit up or hold an intelligent conversation. About all I could get out was, "It's the swordfish." That's a helpless feeling.

The person who lives estranged from God is in a similar state of helplessness. Only his condition carries far greater consequences than the physically weak. Paul writes, "But a natural man does not accept the things of the Spirit of God; for they are foolishness to him, and he cannot understand them, because they are spiritually appraised" (1 Corinthians 2:14). This individual who is estranged from God does not have the ability or the strength to tune in to God. Like the paraplegic or quadraplegic who has no ability to move some of his muscles, the natural man is helpless to make himself right with God.

Man Is a Sinner

A second reason man needs to be reconciled to God is that *he is a sinner, a breaker of God's laws*. The apostle continues to describe man's spiritual condition by saying, "But God demonstrates His own love toward us, in that while we were yet sinners, Christ died for us" (Romans 5:8). The original language says that Christ died for man while he was being a sinner, emphasizing a present state of living. Man is a sinner by nature and by practice. And until his nature is changed by the supernatural work of the Holy Spirit, he will remain apart from God. To unite God with a sinner, without changing the sinner's nature, is like trying to mix oil and water. By its very makeup, oil separates from water. They are different in nature and do not mix. So God, who is holy and pure, cannot mix with man, who is unholy and impure. One of the two natures must change. And since God is unchangeable, it is man who needs to be reconciled to God.

Man Is an Enemy of God

Another reason man needs reconciliation is that *he is an enemy of God*. God did not wait until man decided to become his friend before he sent Jesus to this earth. The apostle informs his readers, "For if while we were enemies, we were reconciled to God through the death of His Son, much more, having been reconciled, we shall be saved by His life" (Romans 5:10). Jesus did not die for his friends, he died for his enemies.

By nature, man is the enemy of God. He is hostile in his attitude toward God and in his relationship with God. He considers that God is his enemy rather than his friend. Furthermore, man does not want to subject himself to the laws of God, for they interfere with his lifestyle. Paul stated it well when he wrote, "For the mind set on the flesh is death, but the mind set on the Spirit is life and peace, because the mind set on the flesh is hostile toward God; for it does not subject itself to the law of God, for it is not even able to do so; and those who are in the flesh cannot please God" (Romans 8:6-8). Mankind is alienated and hostile toward God, and continues to engage himself in evil deeds (Colossians 1:21).

There are certain groups throughout the world who have maintained hostility toward one another for centuries. The hostility between Arabs and Jews is not unique to this century. It existed in biblical days. And no matter what man attempts to do, the Middle East crisis continues. Any peace settlements that are made are merely temporary. In fact, there will be no true peace in the Middle East until the Prince of Peace returns to this earth. Likewise, until man comes to the Prince of Peace, enmity will continue between God and man.

Separation from Christ

Another condition which necessitates man's reconciliation to God is that *he lives apart from Christ*: "Remember that you were at that time separate from Christ . . ." (Ephesians 2:12). The fact that man is separate from Christ means that his day-to-day living continues as though Christ doesn't exist.

The spiritual world is as foreign to him as is the civilized to someone brought up in a jungle. Years ago, five young missionary men were martyred by the Auca Indians living in the jungles of Ecuador. One of the martyrs was Nate Saint, whose sister Rachel later spent some time living among the Aucas. A young Auca mother named Dayuma ran away from the tribe. Rachel Saint made contact with her and took her in. Rachel decided to bring Dayuma and her young son to the United States. And what an experience it was for them! Imagine this young Indian woman who had never been out of the jungle. Her entire life had been confined within a very small geographical area. But suddenly she was removed from the jungle and brought to this country in a "big bird," where nothing compared with anything with which she was familiar. The new country had tall grass huts. Huge animals seemed to zoom by her on big black jungle paths which had no trees. The animals made a lot of noise and didn't sound like anything she'd ever heard in a jungle. Most of the people she met had a strange color of skin. Their language sounded like a bunch of grunts to her. I imagine that her experience with the United States could be likened to one any of us might have if a spaceship descended into our backyard and took us to another planet.

The natural man who lives apart from Christ is unaware of the spiritual dimension which surrounds him, so he continues life apart from Christ.

Excluded from Heavenly Citizenship

Another reason man needs to be reconciled to God is that *he is excluded from a heavenly citizenship*. When the apostle Paul speaks of this, he refers to it as the commonwealth of Israel. He writes, "remember that you were at that time separate from Christ, excluded from the commonwealth of Israel . . ." (Ephesians 2:12). The person who is not reconciled to God is a citizen of the world. He has a one-dimensional citizenship. But when he is reconciled to God, man experiences a dual citizenship, expressed in these words: "For our citizenship is in heaven, from which also we eagerly wait for a Savior, the Lord Jesus Christ" (Philippians 3:20).

In spite of all of its problems, America is still seen by many people around the world as "the land of the free and the home of the brave." Is it any wonder America is a haven for the underprivileged of the world? People come to the United States because they want to experience the rights, privileges, and freedoms that we have and too often take for granted.

Those who are citizens of heaven have been given

many privileges which are not available to those who are citizens of the earth alone. The citizen of heaven has experienced the forgiveness of sins, eternal life, peace with God, power for living, and understanding of man's future, a day-to-day walk with God, and other blessings.

A Stranger to God's Promises

Consider another reason for man's need to be reconciled to God. *He is a stranger to God's promises.* "Remember that you were at that time separate from Christ, excluded from the commonwealth of Israel, and strangers to the covenants of promise . . ." (Ephesians 2:12). The word for covenant is the Greek *diathēkē* meaning "a testament, a will, a covenant or promise." God established many covenants with Israel. His covenant (agreement) with Moses promised blessing if the people obeyed God and curses if the people rebelled (Deuteronomy 28-29).

Remember when Howard Hughes died? Everybody wanted to get a piece of his estate. Different individuals came up with hand-written wills, supposedly written by Howard Hughes. All the wills were proved to be hoaxes, so those people received nothing from the estate.

God has made many promises with those who have been reconciled to him. They alone are heirs of God's blessings: "The Spirit Himself bears witness with our spirit that we are children of God, and if children, heirs also, heirs of God and fellow-heirs with Christ . . ." (Romans 8:16-17). Only the reconciled qualify to be heirs of God to receive his promises, while the unreconciled receive nothing but judgment.

Hopelessness

Paul continues to press his reasons for man's need to be reconciled to God by writing, "remember that you were at one time separate from Christ, excluded from the commonwealth of Israel, and strangers to the covenants of promise, having no hope . . ." (Ephesians 2:12). I can think of no worse condition than that of *hopelessness.* You may stand beside the bed of a loved one who is dying. As long as he continues to breathe, you have hope. But then the doctor comes in and informs you, "I'm sorry. It's just a matter of time." That's when you experience that hopeless feeling.

What is hope? When the Bible speaks about hope, it conveys the idea of assurance. The person who is not reconciled to God has no assurance of the future. He doesn't know what's going to happen to him when he dies. Even as he faces life's difficulties, he has no assurance that God will hear or answer his prayers. He has no assurance that God will help him through life's problems, or that all the events taking place in his life are working within a divine plan and toward a purpose for good. He is without hope.

A Practicing Atheist

Consider one more reason man needs to be reconciled to God. *Man is a practicing atheist*. Paul concludes his description of the man outside of Christ by saying, "remember that you were at that time separate from Christ, excluded from the commonwealth of Israel, and strangers to the covenants of promise, having no hope and without God in the world" (Ephesians 2:12). Paul uses an interesting word in this phrase which is translated "without God." It is the Greek word *atheos*, from which we derive our term "atheist." The man who is without God is living as though God does not exist. He is like a sick man who has all the proper medicine to help him, but refuses to take it. Therefore, from a practical standpoint he lives without medicine. So the man who lives without God is a practicing atheist.

Now if man needs to be reconciled to God, and yet cannot accomplish this task by himself, how can reconciliation take place?

Who Has the Ability to Bring Reconciliation between Man and God?

The Scriptures are quite clear that the candidates for this great task are limited. In fact, there is only one individual who ever lived on this planet who has the ability to reconcile man and God. Paul wrote to Timothy describing that person. He says, "For there is one God, and one mediator also between God and men, the man Christ Jesus, who gave Himself as a ransom for all, the testimony borne at the proper time" (1 Timothy 2:5-6). The only person who could qualify to mediate between God and man must understand man perfectly and identify with him completely. Likewise, he needs to understand God perfectly and identify with him completely. *Jesus understands man perfectly and can identify with him completely.*

The apostle John wrote, "But Jesus, on His part, was not entrusting Himself to them, for He knew all men, and because He did not need anyone to bear witness concerning man for He Himself knew what was in man" (John 2:24-25). The Lord always understood the motives and the reasoning of those who loved him and those who rejected him. He knew what was in the heart of man.

But he also completely identified with man. The writer to the Hebrews explains, "Since then the children share in flesh and blood, He Himself likewise also partook of the same, that through death He might render powerless him who had the power of death, that is, the devil; and might deliver those who through fear of death were subject to slavery all their lives. . . . Therefore, He had to be made like His brethren in all things, that He might become a merciful and faithful high priest in things pertaining to God, to make propitiation for the sins of the people" (Hebrews 2:14-15, 17). Jesus was both 100% God and 100% man. He knew man perfectly and identified with him.

Jesus also understood God perfectly and identified with him completely. Luke describes the account of the seventy disciples returning to the Lord and telling him what they had experienced in their ministry. Luke states, "At that very time He rejoiced greatly in the Holy Spirit, and said, 'I praise Thee, O Father, Lord of heaven and earth, that Thou didst hide these things from the wise and intelligent and didst reveal them to babes. Yes, Father, for thus it was well-pleasing in Thy sight. All things have been handed over to Me by My Father, and no one knows who the Son is except the Father, and who the Father is except the Son, and anyone to whom the Son wills to reveal Him" (Luke 10:21-22). The reason the Lord understood God is because he identified with God completely. The apostle John writes, "For this cause therefore the Jews were seeking all the more to kill Him, because He not only was breaking the Sabbath, but also was calling God His own Father, making Himself equal with God" (John 5:18). Jesus testified of himself, "I and the Father are one" (John 10:30). The Lord also told Philip, "He who has seen Me has seen the Father . . ." (John 14:9).

Have you ever wondered why God chose Moses to go down to Egypt to deliver Israel from the clutches of Pharaoh? The Bible does not attempt to answer that question. But one possible reason is that Moses was both Hebrew and Egyptian. He was Hebrew by birth and Egyptian by culture, having been raised in Pharaoh's court. So Moses could identify with both the Hebrews and the Egyptians.

In a similar way, Jesus Christ was both God and man, descending from heaven but reared on earth. He knew God and he knew man, because he was God in the flesh.

How Did God Accomplish Reconciliation between Himself and Man?

What process did God go through so that man could come into a personal relationship with himself? I see a four-fold process.

Hopelessly Alienated

God recognized that man was hopelessly alienated from him. He knew that if it were up to man, there would be no reconciliation. Paul refers to this problem when he writes, "As it is written, 'There is none righteous, not even one; there is none who understands, there is none who seeks for God; all have turned aside, together they have become useless; there is none who does good, there is not even one'" (Romans 3:10-12). Even though man is unaware of his alienation, he knows something is wrong. He just doesn't know what it is.

When I was a child, my grandfather bought himself a Great Dane. It was so huge that the first time I met him, he wagged his tail and hit me across the face. One day the Great Dane got loose and ran down to a neighbor's farm. The neighbor called my grandfather, who hopped into his car and went after the dog. When he found him, the dog was rolling around in a manure pile. My grandfather grabbed a blanket, put it around the dog, and dragged him into the car. When they arrived home, they no sooner got out of the car than Baron jumped up on my grandfather, wanting to play. He couldn't understand why my grandfather didn't want to be near him. When he raced over to my grandmother, she also turned away from him. That poor dog was hopelessly alienated from the family. It wasn't until Baron was thoroughly washed that he was welcomed into the family once again.

The average man does not recognize how nauseating and smelly his sins are before a righteous and holy God. God wants him to be reconciled, but first he needs to be cleansed by the blood of Christ. Or as Paul put it when he wrote to Titus, "He saved us, not on the basis of deeds which we have done in righteousness, but according to His mercy, by the washing of regeneration and renewing by the Holy Spirit, whom He poured out upon us richly through Jesus Christ our Savior" (Titus 3:5-6).

Reconciliation

What's the second step in the process of God's reconciling man to himself? Having seen man's hopeless alienation, *God wanted man to be reconciled to himself.* God does not delight in bringing judgment upon man. Rather, God's desire is that all come to repentance and enjoy a personal relationship with him: "The Lord is not slow about His promise, as some count slowness, but is patient toward you, not wishing for any to perish but for all to come to repentance" (2 Peter 3:9). Remember the story of the prodigal son? The father wanted the son to be reconciled to him, but the son wanted freedom to do as he pleased. Many a parent has shed tears over a son or daughter who wants to do his own thing. The parent takes no pleasure in disciplining the child. The parent does not delight in the estranged relationship. Instead, the parent painfully awaits for the child to return home.

God Takes the First Step

God did not stop at merely recognizing man's alienation and wanting man to return to him. *God took the initiative for man to be reconciled to him.* Man would never take the first step; therefore, God had to approach man. Man was "helpless"... "sinning against God"... and the "enemy of God." Man wanted nothing to do with God, and yet the Lord took the first step for reconciliation. "For God so loved the world, that He gave His only begotton Son, that whoever believes in Him should not perish, but have eternal life" (John 3:16).

Why is it that people remain alienated from one another? Most often it's because neither party wants to take the first step toward reconciliation. God could have played man's game by saying, "I won't move toward you until you first come and apologize to Me." But that is not the way God operates. He took the initiative to move toward man. And now the ball is in man's court.

Forgiveness

What happens when man accepts that reconciliation? *God forgives man when he accepts the terms of reconciliation.* The Gospels describe it so beautifully when talking about the prodigal who hit bottom. Luke writes, "But when he came to his senses, he said, 'How many of my father's hired men have more than enough bread, but I am dying here with hunger! I will get up and go to my father, and will say to him, "Father, I have sinned against heaven, and in your sight; I am no longer worthy to be called your son; make me as one of your hired men."' And he got up and came to his father. But while he was still a long way off, his father saw him, and felt compassion for him, and ran and embraced him, and kissed him. And the son said to him, 'Father, I have sinned against heaven and in your sight; I am no longer worthy to be called your son.' But the father said to his slaves, 'Quickly bring out the best robe and put it on him, and put a ring on his hand and sandals on his feet; and bring the fattened calf, kill it, and let us eat and be merry; for this son of mine was dead, and has come to life again; he was lost, and has been found.' And they began to be merry" (Luke 15:17-24).

This is the same reaction God has to anyone who is willing to admit that he has sinned against God. When he comes to his senses and turns to God, the Lord opens his arms and welcomes him with a warm embrace.

What Are the Results of Reconciliation?

If you were to turn to God and experience reconciliation, what would happen? Though we could list many outstanding results, consider the following four.

God's Friend

Man ceases to be God's enemy and becomes his friend. James makes it clear that the friend of the world is an enemy with God (James 4:4). But Jesus informed his disciples, "Greater love has no one than this, that one lay down his life for his friends. You are my friends, if you do what I command you" (John 15:13-14). First, Jesus brought man near to God: "But now in Christ Jesus you who formerly were far off have been brought near by the blood of Christ" (Ephesians 2:13). The man who is not reconciled to God is like the swimmer who is caught in an undertow and is being pulled out to sea. At first he doesn't recognize his plight. Then as he looks toward the shore, he notices that he is drifting rapidly away from the coastline. So he begins to swim back toward the shore, but his efforts are in vain. The harder he swims, the more he seems to drift out to sea. When he cries for help, the lifeguard hears him and runs to a boat, rows out to the man, and saves him.

Likewise, it's not until man is able to recognize how far he has drifted from God, and is willing to cry out for help, that Jesus Christ will come to his rescue and deliver him from being pulled out into a sea of despair by the undertow of sin. Once man is delivered and brought near to God, he no longer sees God as an enemy, but considers him a friend.

RECONCILIATION

Furthermore, Jesus not only changed man from being God's enemy to being his friend, he also changed that enmity by making peace between man and God. Paul writes, "For He Himself is our peace, who made both groups into one, and broke down the barrier of the dividing wall" (Ephesians 2:14). The peace treaty between God and man was signed by God centuries ago. But only when man is willing to sign on the dotted line will peace go into effect. When you sign the treaty by confessing Jesus Christ as your Savior and Lord, you can cry out, "It is finished. The battle is over. It is finished. There will be no war. It is finished. The battle has ended. It is finished. And Jesus is Lord."

A Complete Salvation

Another beautiful result of reconciliation is that *man experiences a complete salvation*. The writer to the Hebrews testifies, "Hence, also, he is able to save forever those who draw near to God through Him, since He always lives to make intercession for them" (Hebrews 7:25). Jesus has delivered man from sin's penalty (Romans 6:23). The reconciled man will not be condemned, because he has received Christ's righteousness. Furthermore, he is delivered from sin's power: "For sin shall not be master over you, for you are not under law, but under grace" (Romans 6:14). The apostle also writes, "But I say, walk by the Spirit, and you will not carry out the desire of the flesh" (Galatians 5:16).

But man is delivered from something else. He will eventually be delivered from sin's presence. Speaking of the New Jerusalem, the apostle John writes, "And nothing unclean and no one who practices abomination and lying, shall ever come into it, but only those whose names are written in the Lamb's book of life" (Revelation 21:27). Temptation will be past. Man's salvation will be complete.

Boasting of God

Another interesting result when a man is reconciled to God is that *man boasts about God*. What does man usually boast about? He brags about his accomplishments. He displays his trophies, ribbons, newsclippings, and so forth. Or he may boast about his ability in athletics, music, communication, or creativity. He may boast about his position in life and enjoy all of the titles which he has acquired over the years. Many boast about their bank accounts and glory in their houses, cars, and other possessions. Others glory in their authority and love to rule over others. This is what makes the reconciled person unique. While the average person demonstrates his pride in things, the one who is reconciled to God should be proud of God and display him to others.

Ambassador for God

What else happens when a man is reconciled to God? *Man becomes God's ambassador to the world.* The average person lives for himself. His decisions and motivations are usually self-oriented. But the one who has been reconciled to God has a new orientation. Paul puts it this way: "Therefore, we are ambassadors for Christ, as though God were entreating through us; we beg you on behalf of Christ, be reconciled to God" (2 Corinthians 5:20). A country sends its ambassadors to a foreign country. Often there are dangers and perhaps hostility within that country against the ambassador. But in spite of the problems, the ambassador represents his country in that foreign land. He is expected to live as one who represents his country and leader.

As citizens of heaven we have been placed here on earth to serve as God's representatives to the world. We should not be afraid to tell the world of our heavenly citizenship. And we certainly should not be reluctant to talk about the One who reconciled us, for it is he whom we represent. Furthermore, we should clearly explain to others how they too can become ambassadors of the King of kings and the Lord of lords.

What Are the Requirements for Man to Become Reconciled to God?

If man is going to be reconciled to God, *he must first change his attitude toward God.* Realize that God is not your enemy, but your friend. He wants you to come to him so that he can give you life in abundance. He wants to make you a citizen of heaven, cleanse you from sin, and give you the assurance of eternal life. So recognize that he is your friend.

Second, *believe that what God says is true.* People often remain alienated from one another because they refuse to believe each other. When the United States speaks out, Russia doesn't believe a word we say. When Russia speaks out, the U.S. is convinced that it is lying. The person who wants to be reconciled must believe that when God reveals himself to be holy and declares that man is sinful, he needs to accept God's value judgment of his life. When we are willing to believe what God says about himself and about us, then we are prepared for the final step.

Accept God's terms for reconciliation. And what are his terms? They are simply put by the apostle John: "But as many as received Him, to them He gave the right to become children of God, even to those who believe in His name, who were born not of blood, nor of the will of the flesh, nor of the will of man, but of God" (John 1:12-13).

What Are the Responsibilities of Reconciliation?

Does reconciliation carry any responsibility? Yes! I've observed three major responsibilities for the person who has been reconciled to God. First, *he is responsible to proclaim the word of reconciliation to man:* "Namely, that God was in Christ reconciling the world to Himself, not counting their trespasses against them, and He has committed to us the word of reconciliation" (2 Corinthians 5:19). We are responsible to tell others that reconciliation is possible for everyone. If a man invented a cure for cancer, it would be his moral responsibility to inform the world that a cure is available. And though he cannot force people to take the cure, he is responsible to make them aware of it.

Second, the believer should inform people that they must be reconciled to God by personal choice. This is why Paul says, "Therefore, we are ambassadors for Christ, as though God were entreating through us; we beg you on behalf of Christ, be reconciled to God" (2 Corinthians 5:20).

It's like the doctor who tells his patient, "You've had the medicine for a long time now. Why don't you help yourself by taking it?"

But along with proclaiming the word of reconciliation to others, *the believer should also help others to reconcile with one another.* Jesus said, "Blessed are the peacemakers, for they shall be called sons of God" (Matthew 5:9). As God has made peace with us by bringing us to himself, so we should encourage others to be at peace with one another. Rather than encouraging husbands and wives to divorce, we should encourage them to deal with their differences, make peace with one another, and reunite if possible.

There is one other responsibility we need to fulfill: *to practice reconciliation on a personal level.* It is far easier to tell others to bury their differences and reunite as friends than to carry out that responsibility ourselves. But when we fail to practice reconciliation in our own personal lives, we are like the obese person who sells diet plans to other obese people. Jesus' haunting words break through the hypocrisy: "Physician, heal thyself."

Are you estranged from someone? Have you done everything in your power to make reconciliation possible? Are you willing to take the first step to bring about peace in that relationship? Your willingness and your strong desire to be reconciled does not guarantee that it will happen. But God expects you to take the initiative and to do whatever you can to restore healing and reconciliation. That response is evidence that you have already committed yourself to a higher purpose, which the Bible calls sanctification. Read about it next.

12

COMMITTING TO A HIGHER PURPOSE
SANCTIFICATION

The concert pianist, astronaut, entrepreneur, professional athlete, and medical doctor have several characteristics in common. Each one has committed himself to strive for excellence. Each one has set a high goal for himself and has passed many others who, for one reason or another, have dropped behind in the race to the top or have dropped out of the race altogether.

The Christian also runs in a race—the race of life. In this pursuit he has the choice to strive for self-serving goals or to commit himself to a higher purpose. The former choice will lead him to mediocrity in his Christian life; the latter will lead him to progressive sanctification.

Let's investigate the meaning and practical application of sanctification.

What Is Sanctification?

The Westminster Catechism defines sanctification as "the work of God's free grace, whereby we are renewed in the whole man after the image of God, and are enabled more and more to die unto sin and live unto righteousness." Dr. Abraham Kuyper, late Professor of Systematic Theology at the University of Amsterdam, in his book *The Work of the Holy Spirit*, defines sanctification like this:

"Sanctification is God's work in us, whereby He imparts to our members a holy disposition, inwardly filling us with delight in His law and with repugnance to sin." How do these rather formal definitions translate into everyday language?

Both convey several key ideas about sanctification. It is a work of God in us, an inward change in our nature or disposition, and a commitment to a higher purpose, "dying to sin and living to righteousness," or "delighting in His law and treating sin with repugnance." To better understand, let's consider first some misconceptions about sanctification. Then we will look at the degrees of sanctification, and the uses of the word.

Misconceptions of Sanctification

There are two major *misconceptions about sanctification.* Some equate sanctification with sinless perfection. They are convinced that the sanctified person no longer sins. Several verses in John's first epistle prompt their belief: "No one who abides in Him sins; no one who sins has seen Him or knows Him. . . . No one who is born of God practices sin, because His seed abides in him; and he cannot sin, because he is born of God. . . . We know that no one who is born of God sins; but He who was born of God keeps him and the evil one does not touch him" (1 John 3:6, 9; 5:18). A number of people have told me that they are totally sanctified and therefore no longer sin. Whenever a man informs me that he is an example of sinless perfection, I'm tempted to talk with his wife—and if it's a woman who feels she's achieved sinless perfection, I'd like to talk with her husband.

Do these verses teach that man can reach sinless perfection in this life? Not likely. The emphasis of each verse is on the practice of sin. The present tense is used in each of these verses, conveying a continuous action. So John is saying that the one who is born of God does not keep on sinning or make it a habit. John was well aware that the old nature has not been eradicated. That's why he wrote in 1 John 1:8, "If we say that we have no sin (meaning no sin nature), we are deceiving ourselves, and the truth is not in us."

The believers of Corinth were sanctified, according to the apostle Paul. "And such were some of you; but you were washed, but you were sanctified, but you were justified in the name of the Lord Jesus Christ, and in the Spirit of our God" (1 Corinthians 6:11). The Greek word translated *sanctified* is in the aorist tense, which indicates a past action. Therefore, the Corinthians *were* sanctified. However, even though they had been sanctified, many of them were arguing with one another, walking in pride and arrogance, misjudging each other; some were immoral, and some were even doubting the resurrection. They certainly were not sinlessly perfect.

Another misconception is that sanctification is the same as a second blessing. The theory goes something like this. A person is justified (declared righteous) at conversion, but is not sanctified until later in life.

We've already discovered, however, that the Corinthians were washed, justified, and sanctified simultaneously. Sanctification is not some experience which one must wait for after conversion. It occurs at conversion. On the other hand, sanctification is also progressive. And the believer will become progressively more sanctified in his Christian life as he continues to yield to the authority of God's Holy Spirit. Does this imply that there are various degrees of sanctification? Very definitely.

Degrees of Sanctification

There are three degrees of sanctification: positional, progressive, and ultimate. Let's consider the first.

When I use the word "positional," I am referring to the believer's standing before God. Positional sanctification is made possible by the Lord Jesus Christ. It is described in the book of Hebrews: "By this will we have been sanctified through the offering of the body of Jesus Christ *once for all.* . . . For by one offering He has perfected *for all time* those who are sanctified" (Hebrews 10:10, 14). We stand before God as those who have been sanctified once for all.

Because we possess the righteousness of Christ, God sees us as completely sanctified.

Suppose a soldier's wife is expecting her first child when her husband is called to active duty. When his little boy is born, the soldier is separated from his wife and child by thousands of miles. Though the separation is painful, the soldier is thrilled with the news of being a father. They decide to name the child after his father, because whenever the mother looks at her son, she sees a definite resemblance of her husband in her child's face. The child is the soldier's son, but a year passes before the soldier gets the opportunity to return home and see his son. During that long interim the child is no less his father's son. The boy positionally belongs to that soldier, even though the child has not yet experienced the relationship.

In a similar manner, every believer stands sanctified before God, but his experience may not always reveal that relationship. This is why progressive sanctification is essential in the believer's life.

Progressive sanctification refers to the ministry of the Holy Spirit in the believer's life, turning him away from old habits, attitudes, and goals, and turning toward a higher purpose in life. The apostle writes, "For this is the will of God, your sanctification; that is, that you abstain from sexual immorality; that each of you know how to possess his own vessel in sanctification and honor, not in lustful passion, like the Gentiles who do not know God; and that no man transgress and defraud his brother in the matter because the Lord is the avenger in all these things, just as we also told you before and solemnly warned you. For God has not called us for the purpose of impurity, but in sanctification. Consequently, he who rejects this is not rejecting man but the God who gives His Holy Spirit to you" (1 Thessalonians 4:3-8). Progressive sanctification is another name for growth in the believer's life, where his desire for sin lessens and his desire for righteousness greatly increases. We'll concentrate on this aspect of sanctification later in this chapter.

The third degree of sanctification is called ultimate

sanctification and is accomplished by God the Father. Paul refers to this when he writes, "Now may the God of peace Himself sanctify you entirely; and may your spirit and soul and body be preserved complete, without blame at the coming of our Lord Jesus Christ" (1 Thessalonians 5:23). Eventually every believer will see his experience and his position coincide perfectly. This is the time when the church will stand before Jesus Christ as an unblemished bride. Jude comments: "Now to Him who is able to keep you from stumbling, and to make you stand in the presence of His glory blameless with great joy, to the only God our Savior, through Jesus Christ our Lord, be glory, majesty, dominion and authority, before all time and now and forever. Amen" (Jude 24-25). One day every Christian will experience a sin-free, stain-free life.

Sanctification in Scripture

Now, having considered some of the misconceptions about sanctification and the three degrees of sanctification, notice *how the word is used in Scripture.* The Hebrew word for sanctification is *kadash,* which means "to be hallowed," "to consecrate," or "to dedicate." The Greek word is *hagiazo,* meaning "to consecrate," or "to sanctify." Three other words which come from the same root are "saint," "holy," and "sanctuary." The sanctuary is a "consecrated place." Though there are many uses for this word, let's focus on the five most common.

Inanimate objects. Inanimate objects can be sanctified. God told Moses to sanctify Mount Sinai. "And you shall set bounds for the people all around, saying, 'Beware that you do not go up on the mountain or touch the border of it; whoever touches the mountain shall surely be put to death.' ... And Moses said to the LORD, 'The people cannot come up to Mount Sinai, for Thou didst warn us, saying, "Set bounds about the mountain and consecrate it"'" (Exodus 19:12, 23). When the people consecrated Mount Sinai, they sanctified it.

It is not uncommon today for people to sanctify inanimate objects. Whenever our family has moved into a new house, we've sanctified it or dedicated it to the Lord. Whenever our church has built a new building, we've dedicated that building to the Lord. When our family sanctifies a home, we are committing that house to a higher purpose than merely to live in it. And when we sanctify our church buildings, we are committing them to a higher purpose than merely using them as a gathering place.

Oneself. Another way the word is used is when people sanctify themselves. God told Moses, "'Go to the people and consecrate them today and tomorrow, and let them wash their garments; and let them be ready for the third day, for on the third day the LORD will come down on Mount Sinai in the sight of all the people.' . . . 'And also let the priests who come near to the LORD consecrate themselves, lest the LORD break out against them'" (Exodus 19:10-11, 22). When the people consecrated (sanctified) themselves and the priests sanctified themselves, they were committing themselves to God for a higher purpose. Again, this is a common practice today.

I came to know Jesus Christ as my personal Savior at the age of nine, but I can vividly recall the evening at church camp, when I was twelve years old, that I dedicated myself to the Lord for full-time service if he so chose. When missionaries leave for the foreign field, churches usually hold a commissioning service. In doing this they are sanctifying the couple to a high purpose. When a pastor first comes to a church, the church holds an installation service, setting that pastor aside for a special work. Furthermore, parents bring their children to the Lord and sanctify them in dedication services. People sanctify themselves when they commit themselves to God's purposes.

Jesus Christ. A third use of the term relates to the Lord himself. Jesus was sanctified by his Father according to the Lord's own testimony. When the Jews took up stones to stone him, Jesus responded by asking, "'Do you say of Him, whom the Father sanctified and sent into the world, "You are blaspheming," because I said, "I am the Son of God?"'" (John 10:36). When the Father sanctified Jesus, he did not make Jesus more holy, but set him apart for a higher purpose than remaining in heaven. That higher purpose was to come to the earth and die for the sins of men.

God. Believers are also exhorted to sanctify God. The apostle Peter writes, "And who is there to harm you if you prove zealous for what is good? But even if you should suffer for the sake of righteousness, you are blessed. And do not fear their intimidation, and do not be troubled, but sanctify Christ as Lord in your hearts, always being ready to make a defense to everyone who asks you to give an account for the hope that is in you, yet with gentleness and reverence; and keep a good conscience so that in the thing in which you are slandered, those who revile your good behavior in Christ may be put to shame" (1 Peter 3:13-16). The believer is exhorted to place Jesus Christ on the throne of his life, acknowledge him as the one in control, and submit to his authority. As long as our conscience is clean, we do not need to fear the intimidation of those who misjudge us. When we set Jesus Christ as the controlling one in our lives, we have nothing to fear and nothing of which to be ashamed.

Unbelievers. Yet another use for the word sanctification concerns those who do not profess Christ. Unbelievers may be sanctified by believers. When Paul gives instructions to those who find themselves in a mixed marriage, he says, "And a woman who has an unbelieving husband, and he consents to live with her, let her not send her husband away. For the unbelieving husband is sanctified through his wife, and the unbelieving wife is sanctified through her believing husband; for otherwise your children are unclean, but now they are holy. Yet if the unbelieving one leaves, let him leave; the brother or the sister is not under bondage in such cases, but God has called us to peace. For how do you know, O wife, whether you will save your husband? Or how do you know, O husband, whether you will save your wife?" (1 Corinthians 7:13-16).

In this passage *sanctification* certainly does not mean "holy" or "righteous." What then does it mean? In every marriage the two parties influence one another. If the unbeliever is willing to live with the believer, he will be exposed to God's ministering to him. As long as he remains married to the Christian woman, or the unbelieving woman remains married to the Christian man, the unbeliever can be influenced for good by the life of the Christian. Peter writes, "In the same way, you wives, be submissive to your own husbands so that even if any of them are disobedient to the word, they may be won without a word by the behavior of their wives, as they observe your chaste and respectful behavior. And let not your adornment be merely external— braiding the hair, and wearing gold jewelry, or putting on dresses; but let it be the hidden person of the heart, with the imperishable quality of a gentle and quiet spirit, which is precious in the sight of God" (1 Peter 3:1-4).

So the main idea of sanctification is that of "setting aside someone or something for a holy or godly purpose." With that statement in mind, let's summarize the uses of the word sanctification. It was used with the utensils for the tabernacle which were set aside for holy purposes. When a person sanctifies himself, he sets himself apart from the world system and commits himself to God and his purposes. Jesus was set aside by his Father for a high and holy purpose—to die for sinful man. Believers are exhorted to set aside Jesus Christ as Lord of their lives. And certain unbelievers are set aside by a believing spouse, so that God can work in their lives and eventually bring them to Christ.

Therefore, though sanctification suggests purity and holiness, the most consistent use of the word suggests a setting aside of a person or object from that which is common to a higher purpose.

How Can a Believer Experience Progressive Sanctification?

Since all of us are sanctified positionally by Jesus Christ and will eventually be sanctified ultimately by God the Father, how can the believer be daily sanctified by the Holy Spirit?

Earlier I said that progressive sanctification is a result

of the Holy Spirit's ministry in the life of the believer. But the Holy Spirit does not sanctify the Christian without his cooperation. The believer is responsible to cooperate with the Spirit. So let's investigate five responsibilities of the believer in cooperating with the Holy Spirit.

Personal Commitment

The beginning point is a personal commitment. *The believer should make an initial presentation of himself to God*: "I urge you therefore, brethren, by the mercies of God, to present your bodies a living and holy sacrifice, acceptable to God, which is your spiritual service of worship" (Romans 12:1). When one presents or dedicates himself to God, he turns from his sinful desires and commits himself to God's control of his life. Sometimes this is referred to as yielding to the Lordship of Christ, being filled with the Holy Spirit for the first time, receiving the baptism of the Spirit, and so forth. The act of presenting is an act of dedication. It is similar to sanctifying Christ in your heart.

Though the apostle used the term *body*, he refers to the total person. The Lord not only wants control of the body, but also of the mind, will, and emotions which affect the body. Think about a wild horse. As long as the horse runs wild, he is not good to anyone. But when that horse submits to his trainer and allows the trainer to ride him, the horse has been broken. And though the horse has the same physical strength and abilities, once he is broken by submitting to the will of the trainer, the horse becomes useful to man.

As long as we are in control of our own lives and doing the things we want to do, we are of little use to God. But when we willingly accept God's control and submit our bodies to him, he then is able to channel us toward useful purposes.

We often begin our Christian journey by wanting Christ's salvation but not necessarily his sanctification. We still have too many plans of our own and don't care for God to interfere with our future. But as the Lord allows us to go through some difficult circumstances, we begin to compromise with him and allow him some control over our life. But even that isn't enough. We need to come to that point of saying with John the Baptist, "He must increase, but I must decrease" (John 3:30).

We never receive more of the Holy Spirit than when we first receive him. But we do need to relinquish more of the control of our lives to him. This begins with an act of presentation, an act of dedication, an act of consecrating our lives to God. Once we make the initial decision to present ourselves to God, it is easier to deal with smaller issues such as, Who will be in charge of my financial life? or Whom should I consult as I develop plans for my future? Every Christian needs to make an initial presentation of himself to God. But he shouldn't stop there.

Setting Aside Sin

Every believer also needs to continually lay aside sinful habits, practices, and attitudes. Many believers could be referred to as "barnacled Christians," who are like ships at harbor. They are tied to the dock for long periods of time and do nothing but collect barnacles. A ship is built to sail on the ocean, and the Christian has been created to accomplish God's purpose in life (Ephesians 2:10). Barnacled Christians need to pull up anchor and begin moving out into life's seas, carrying a cargo full of holy habits, good works, and godly attitudes, free of the barnacles which hinder progress.

The writer to the Hebrews used another analogy, that of laying aside the old life. He wrote, "Therefore, since we have so great a cloud of witnesses surrounding us, let us also lay aside every encumbrance, and the sin which so easily entangles us, and let us run with endurance the race that is set before us, fixing our eyes on Jesus, the author and perfecter of faith, who for the joy set before Him endured the cross, despising the shame, and has sat down at the right hand of the throne of God. . . . Pursue peace with all men, and the sanctification without which no one will see the Lord. See to it that no one comes short of the grace of God; that no root of bitterness springing up causes trouble, and by it many be defiled; that there be no immoral or godless person like Esau, who sold his own birthright for a single meal. For you know that even afterwards, when he desired to inherit the blessing, he was rejected, for he found no place for repentance, though he sought for it with tears" (Hebrews 12:1-2, 14-17).

The writer highlights three essentials for winning a race. First, the runner must remove anything that would encumber his running. There's a great difference between jogging in a cotton or nylon outfit. There is also quite a difference in the weight of running shoes. Competitive runners wear the lightest clothing possible, unencumbered by extra weight. A Christian's spiritual encumbrances may include unhealthy habits, negative attitudes, old relationships, or even present relationships which keep him from becoming a winner for God.

Winners also run with endurance. They don't give up. They don't throw in the towel. Anyone who wants to be a marathon runner needs to put endurance, which is the result of conditioning, at the top of his priority list. Many runners lose races because they run out of energy before they reach the finish line.

Paul makes a similar point when he writes, "And let us not lose heart in doing good, for in due time we shall reap if we do not grow weary" (Galatians 6:9). Many of us could advance much further in our Christian lives if we wouldn't allow ourselves to get discouraged or burn out because we haven't learned to pace ourselves. Some Christians initially immerse themselves in church activities, but eventually burn out. A good runner learns how to pace himself so that he can finish the race with endurance.

The third characteristic of a winner is that he has a goal in mind and keeps his eyes on that goal. I can't think of anything that would be more discouraging than running a race without a finish line. You'd never know when you had gone far enough, or whether you were on target. The goal for the Christian is the example of the Lord Jesus Christ: "fixing our eyes on Jesus, the author and perfecter of faith, who for the joy set before Him endured the cross, despising the shame, and has sat down at the right hand of the throne of God" (Hebrews 12:2). Jesus ran the race, endured the pain, and completed his task. As the believer runs in the race of life, he must continually lay aside his sinful habits, practices, and attitudes, focus on Christ and run with endurance.

But how can the believer actually lay aside these things? The Scriptures provide two helpful principles: the principles of avoidance and flight.

The Holy Spirit can develop greater sanctification in your life if you are willing to avoid every form of evil. Paul writes, "For this is the will of God, your sanctification; that is, that you abstain from (avoid) sexual immorality." ... "abstain from every form of evil" (1 Thessalonians 4:3; 5:22). The apostle Peter wrote a complementary exhortation, saying, "Beloved, I urge you as aliens and strangers to abstain from (avoid) fleshly lusts, which wage war against the soul" (1 Peter 2:11). How can you carry out that principle? You can avoid attending places of questionable entertainment. You can avoid reading trashy books or pornographic magazines. You can avoid attending risqúe movies, or renting home video movies which display nudity or sexually suggestive material.

The second principle emphasizes fleeing from evil. Paul told Timothy, "Now flee from youthful lusts, and pursue righteousness, faith, love and peace, with those who call on the Lord from a pure heart" (2 Timothy 2:22). The writer of Proverbs talks about a young man who is confronted by a harlot. The harlot says to him, " 'Come, let us drink our fill of love until morning; let us delight ourselves with caresses.' ... With her many persuasions she entices him; with her flattering lips she seduces him. Suddenly he follows her, as an ox goes to the slaughter, or as one in fetters to the discipline of a fool, until an arrow pierces through his liver; as a bird hastens to the snare, so he does not know that it will cost him his life" (Proverbs 7:18, 21-23). This young man did not flee; he behaved like an ox going to the slaughter.

What a contrast between that young man and another

young man who had a similar opportunity. His name was Joseph. The Bible calls Joseph a handsome young man (Genesis 39:6). The book of Genesis records the event— "And it came about after these events that his master's wife looked with desire at Joseph, and she said, 'Lie with me.' But he refused and said to his master's wife, 'Behold, with me here, my master does not concern himself with anything in the house, and he has put all that he owns in my charge. There is no one greater in this house than I, and he has withheld nothing from me except you, because you are his wife. How then could I do this great evil, and sin against God?' And it came about as she spoke to Joseph day after day, that he did not listen to her to lie beside her, or be with her. Now it happened one day that he went into the house to do his work, and none of the men of the household was there inside. And she caught him by his garment, saying, 'Lie with me!' And he left his garment in her hand and fled, and went outside" (Genesis 39:7-12). Joseph first avoided the temptation as much as he could. But when he was being confronted continuously, he ran away.

Reading the Scriptures

Another responsibility the believer has in sanctification is that *he should read the Scriptures systematically.* What do I mean by "systematically?" I'm referring to a steady and consistent reading program. Most people work best under some kind of a system or regular procedure. If you don't have a system for reading the Scriptues, you will probably read them haphazardly.

Jesus prayed to his Father, "Sanctify them in the truth; Thy word is truth" (John 17:17). The Lord recognized the value of being exposed to the Scriptures because they help us to see the higher purpose which God has for us and they encourage us to make a commitment to that higher purpose.

The Psalmist wrote about the excellent value of the Scriptures. He looked to them for the endurance and strength which he needed as he ran the race of life. "My soul weeps because of grief; strengthen me according to

Thy word. . . . And I shall lift up my hands to Thy commandments, which I love; and I will meditate on Thy statutes. Remember the word to Thy servant, in which Thou hast made me hope. This is my comfort in my affliction, that Thy word has revived me. The arrogant utterly deride me, yet I do not turn aside from Thy law. I have remembered Thine ordinances from of old, O LORD, and comfort myself" (Psalm 119:28, 48-52).

The Psalmist also learned the restraining value of Scripture: "How can a young man keep his way pure? By keeping it according to Thy word. With all my heart I have sought Thee; do not let me wander from Thy commandments. Thy word I have treasured in my heart, that I may not sin against thee . . . I have restrained my feet from every evil way, that I may keep Thy word. I have not turned aside from Thine ordinances, for Thou Thyself hast taught me. How sweet are Thy words to my taste! Yes, sweeter than honey to my mouth! From Thy precepts I get understanding; therefore I hate every false way" (Psalm 119:9-11, 101-104).

The Scriptures further provide guidance for everyday living. "O how I love Thy law! It is my meditation all the day. Thy commandments make me wiser than my enemies, for they are ever mine. I have more insight than all my teachers, for Thy testimonies are my meditation. I understand more than the aged, because I have observed Thy precepts" (Psalm 119:97-100).

Your system may include reading the Bible every day for fifteen minutes, or reading a portion of both the Old and New Testaments. You may enjoy a systematic reading from Genesis through Revelation. Or perhaps you prefer reading a chapter each day. It is not so important what system you use as it is that you develop some kind of systematic reading of the Scriptures.

Association with Mature Christians

Another responsibility of the believer is *to associate himself with mature Christians.* Solomon wrote, "He who walks with wise men will be wise, but the companion of fools will suffer harm" (Proverbs 13:20). With similar counsel the writer to the Hebrews said, "Remember those who led you, who spoke the word of God to you; and considering the result of their conduct, imitate their faith" (Hebrews 13:7).

We tend to be conformists. Very few want to buck the current of public opinion. That's why Paul wrote, "And do not be conformed to this world, but be transformed by the renewing of your mind, that you may prove what the will of God is, that which is good and acceptable and perfect" (Romans 12:2). Many believers could be classified as "chameleon Christians" because they change their attitudes and behavior according to their surroundings. If they are with Christians, they look and act like Christians. But if they are with non-Christian friends, they take on those characteristics.

In my later teen years, I had the privilege of being supported by a number of mature Christian men. They spent time praying with me, counseling me, and encouraging me in my Christian walk. I developed a boldness for witnessing by following the example of one man. I established a consistent prayer life by following the example of another. I developed a deep desire for studying the Scriptures by following the example of a third. The more I associated myself with such men, the more I experienced a personal spiritual growth and the sanctifying work of God's Holy Spirit. Things I once enjoyed I willingly put aside as encumbrances to my spiritual growth. I adopted new habits and attitudes.

If all of your associates are either non-Christians or immature Christians, you will see little need for progressive sanctification because of the tendency to compare yourself with the wrong group. The Bible emphasizes looking at spiritually mature leaders and imitating their faith.

Self-discipline

One final responsibility for the believer is that *he should discipline himself to achieve that which is excellent.* Paul writes, "Do you not know that those who run in a race all run, but only one receives the prize? Run in such a way that you may win.

And everyone who competes in the games exercises self-control in all things. They then do it to receive a perishable wreath, but we an imperishable. Therefore I run in such a way, as not without aim; I box in such a way, as not beating the air; but I buffet my body and make it my slave, lest possibly, after I have preached to others, I myself should be disqualified" (1 Corinthians 9:24-27).

Self-control in all things. That's Paul's emphasis. And what is self-control or discipline? It is learning to say no to what may be good in itself, but not helpful, in order to achieve that which is excellent. The word literally means "to be inwardly strong."

The apostle mentions the need of discipline for two purposes: godly living in the present and spiritual reward in the future. The believer should discipline himself for godly living in the present, according to Paul's exhortation, "But have nothing to do with worldly fables fit only for old women. On the other hand, discipline yourself for the purpose of godliness; for bodily discipline is only of little profit, but godliness is profitable for all things, since it holds promise for the present life and also for the life to come" (1 Timothy 4:7-8).

What are the qualities of a disciplined physical exercise program? Consistency should be near the top of the list. The body builder who lifts weights once every other month will make little progress. Likewise, the individual who wants to lose weight, but exercises sporadically, will be fighting an uphill battle. There must be consistency.

Another quality is addition. The body builder adds more weight to his iron-pumping equipment, while the weight reducer may add more repetitions to his exercise program. It is estimated that a runner loses one hundred calories per mile. If you want to lose three hundred calories in a day, you'll have to run three miles. But if you want to run off more calories, you'll have to increase the number of miles, especially if you maintain the same calorie intake.

The third quality of discipline for the body is proper diet. You need to eat both the right kinds of food, as well as the right amounts of food. But how does all of this relate to

SANCTIFICATION

a spiritual exercise program?

When one disciplines himself for godliness (progressive sanctification), he needs to be consistent in that spiritual program. Second, he needs to add some special qualities to his life. Peter wrote about this process, saying, "For by these He has granted to us His precious and magnificent promises, in order that by them you might become partakers of the divine nature, having escaped the corruption that is in the world by lust. Now for this very reason also, applying all diligence, in your faith supply moral excellence, and in your moral excellence, knowledge; and in your knowledge, self-control, and in your self-control, perseverence, and in your perseverance, godliness; and in your godliness, brotherly kindness, and in your brotherly kindness, love. For if these qualities are yours and are increasing, they render you neither useless nor unfruitful in the true knowledge of our Lord Jesus Christ. For he who lacks these qualities is blind or short-sighted, having forgotten his purification from his former sins" (2 Peter 1:4-9).

Along with consistency and adding other Christian qualities to life, maintaining a proper spiritual diet is critical. That diet would include prayer, Bible reading and study, using spiritual gifts in serving, and other balanced practices. When one disciplines himself for godly living in the present, he will also be disciplining himself for spiritual reward in the future.

Paul writes, "For momentary, light affliction is producing for us an eternal weight of glory far beyond all comparison, while we look not at the things which are seen, but at the things which are not seen; for the things which are seen are temporal, but the things which are not seen are eternal" (2 Corinthians 4:17-18). The Lord also says, "Do not lay up for yourselves treasures upon earth, where moth and rust destroy, and where thieves break in and steal. But lay up for yourselves treasures in heaven, where neither moth nor rust destroys, and where thieves do not break in or steal; for where your treasure is, there will your heart be also" (Matthew 6:19-21).

We are often called the "now generation." We want

everything immediately, if not sooner. But the Bible has an eternal focus and a temporal focus. As we discipline ourselves for the present, we will be rewarded in the future.

What is your purpose in life? For what are you living? Someone has written, "The good is the enemy of the best." That is true especially in the Christian life. If a believer becomes a nominal Christian, he has sacrificed the best at the altar of the good or the mediocre.

God wants us to commit ourselves to higher purposes. That process is known as sanctification. You have been sanctified by the Lord Jesus Christ, and you will be sanctified ultimately by God the Father. But right now, the Holy Spirit needs your cooperation for you to daily experience progressive sanctification. And as you allow God's Spirit to sanctify you each day, you will begin to enjoy your unearned status as a greatly appreciated member of God's family, which he has given you by adoption.

13

GAINING STATUS IN THE FAMILY
ADOPTION

The wedding of the century was celebrated July 29, 1981. A shy, nineteen-year-old girl, a kindergarten teacher in London, agreed to become the bride of Prince Charles, heir apparent to the English throne. Within minutes, Diana Spencer was elevated to the status of Princess Diana.

In a similar way, everyone who establishes a personal relationship with Jesus Christ receives both membership into the royal family of God and status as an adopted son.

Let's take a closer look at this process of joining God's family and gaining status in it by learning how to enter this royal family.

How Does a Person Join God's Family?

Joining the family of God is much like becoming a member of any family—one must be born into it. How is one born into the family of God? You'd be right to say that a person is born into God's family by believing in Jesus Christ or by receiving Christ as his personal Savior. But the apostle John emphasizes three aspects of being born into God's family. Observe John's words: "But as many as received Him, to them He gave the right to become children of God, even to those who believe in His name, who were born not of blood, nor of the will of the flesh, nor the will of man, but of God" (John 1:12-13).

Receive Christ

The first aspect of being born into God's family is *to receive Jesus Christ*. Before John wrote about receiving Christ, he said, "He came to His own, and those who were His own did not receive Him" (John 1:11). Who were Jesus' own? John was referring, of course, to the Jewish people. Jesus Christ was a Jew, born in Bethlehem and reared in Nazareth. His own people referred to him as "the carpenter's son," in spite of the miracles he performed, the claims which he made about himself, and his impeccable character. The Jewish nation rejected Jesus as anything other than a man.

Many of the Jewish people accepted him as a prophet, according to Matthew's testimony. "And when He had entered Jerusalem, all the city was stirred, saying, 'Who is this?' And the multitudes were saying, 'This is the prophet Jesus, from Nazareth in Galilee'" (Matthew 21:10-11).

Other Jews accepted Jesus as a political revolutionary. Still others followed him because he was able to provide for their physical needs, giving them food and healing. Jesus himself spoke of a kingdom which he was about to establish, so many of the Jews anticipated his delivering them from the yoke of the Roman government. And that is as far as the Jews were willing to go with this Nazarene.

In what ways did they not receive him? For one thing, the Jews did not receive Jesus' claim to be equal with God. Consider the time when Jesus spoke of his sheep: "'My sheep hear My voice, and I know them, and they follow Me; and I give eternal life to them, and they shall never perish; and no one shall snatch them out of My hand. My Father, who has given them to Me, is greater than all; and no one is able to snatch them out of the Father's hand. I and the Father are One.' The Jews took up stones again to stone Him. Jesus answered them, 'I showed you many good works from the Father; for which of them are you stoning Me?' The Jews answered Him, 'For a good work we do not stone

You, but for blasphemy; and because You, being a man, make Yourself out to be God'" (John 10:27-33). The Jews rejected Jesus Christ on the basis of his claim to deity.

When one receives Jesus, he must receive him as God. One must thoroughly believe that, "In the beginning was the Word, and the Word was with God, and the Word was God. . . . And the Word became flesh, and dwelt among us, and we beheld His glory, glory as of the only begotten from the Father, full of grace and truth" (John 1:1, 14).

Believe in His Name

One is not only brought into God's family by receiving Jesus. John adds, "even to those who believe in His name" (John 1:12). One must also *believe in his name*. And what name would that be? The name Jesus, meaning "Savior." But one must not merely believe that Jesus is the world's Savior.

A bachelor may be eligible for all the women in the world, but he is meaningful only to the one whom he selects to be his wife, and who receives him as her husband. Likewise, Jesus Christ is eligible to be the Savior of the world, but he is meaningful only to the one whom he selects to be his child, and to the one who receives Jesus as his Savior and Lord. This is what believing in his name means—making that Savior personal.

Born of God

The third aspect of coming into the family of God is *to be born of God*. John makes it clear that man is not brought into God's family through natural birth. Nor does he enter God's family by a mere act of his own will. He comes into God's family by being born "out of God" (*ek*—out, plus *theou*—God). Physical birth comes from both a man and a woman. But a person's spiritual birth comes from only one source—God.

In order to see the similarities between the natural and the spiritual birth, notice some of birth's essentials. First there is an act of love. For physical birth to occur, a husband and wife are brought into a sexual union, expressing love to one another. And though in spiritual birth the sexual union is missing, there is nevertheless an act of love:

"For God so loved the world, that He gave His only begotten Son, that whoever believes in Him should not perish, but have eternal life" (John 3:16).

Another essential is an implanted seed. Before physical birth can occur, the husband's seed is planted within his wife. Likewise, the Bible reveals that God's seed has been implanted in the believer. "Little children, let no one deceive you; the one who practices righteousness is righteous, just as He is righteous; the one who practices sin is of the devil; for the devil has sinned from the beginning. The Son of God appeared for this purpose, that He might destroy the works of the devil. No one who is born of God practices sin, because His seed abides in him; and he cannot sin, because he is born of God" (1 John 3:7-9). John refers here to the lifestyle of sin. Though the believer may sin at times, because he possesses God's seed, he will eventually take on characteristics of his Father.

My two sons bear a number of my characteristics. They possess some of my physical characteristics, mannerisms, and attitudes, some which they have inherited and others which they have unconsciously or consciously adopted for themselves. If for some reason they were to reject everything they had ever been taught, and consciously attempted to remove all mannerisms and attitudes which they picked up over the years, they would still bear my resemblance. In the same way, even though we do fail God, those who possess God's seed within them will demonstrate some of his mannerisms, attitudes, and character.

A third essential of birth is the gestation period. In the physical realm, that period is generally nine months. But in the spiritual realm, gestation could be quite extensive. Most Christians can look back over their lives before they trusted in Christ and remember different times when God seemed very real to them. Perhaps they were impressed with God when they were a small child. Or maybe during their teenage years, God somehow broke through to them. But their birth may not have taken place until later. For some individuals the gestation period could be a few months, while for others it could include many years of preparation by the Spirit of God.

I believe that many people are living in a gestation period and are ready for delivery, but there are too few obstetricians to make the delivery. That is what Paul was referring to when he wrote, "For 'Whoever will call upon the name of the Lord will be saved.' How then shall they call upon Him in whom they have not believed? And how shall they believe in Him whom they have not heard? And how shall they hear without a preacher? And how shall they preach unless they are sent?" (Romans 10:13-15).

Another essential is the moment of birth. Though the gestation period may be extended, and the process of delivery may take several hours, the actual birth occurs in a moment. I recall the night I had the opportunity of leading one of the members of our church to Christ. I don't know how many years he had been in gestation, but I do know that many of his friends had been praying over the years for him. His wife was a believer, and so he daily observed the seed of God manifesting itself through her life. One evening, after he and his wife had visited our church, I called on them at their home. As I became acquainted with the couple, I realized that though he had some religious background, he did not have a personal relationship with Christ. The delivery took several hours, during which I explained the claims of Christ and answered his questions. It was a painful delivery as I asked him, "Can you think of any reason why you should not receive Jesus Christ as your Savior right now?" He lowered his head, stared at the floor, and finally looked up at me and said, "No, I can't think of any reason why I shouldn't receive Christ right now." As he invited Christ into his life, the expression on his face gave glowing evidence that a babe in Christ had just been born. Though the gestation and delivery took time, the birth was instantaneous.

You may be in the gestation phase, the delivery phase, or have already experienced the new birth. If you've been born anew, you are part of God's family. And as a member of God's family, the Lord has given you a special status.

What Status Does One Receive in God's Family?

The status that every new believer receives in God's family is two-fold: he becomes a child of God by birth and he becomes a son of God by adoption. Consider first that *the believer becomes a child of God by birth*. What is the significance of being a child of God?

A Child of God by Birth

The fact that you've become a child of God means that you belong to the largest family on earth. Whether you travel to Moscow, Peking, Bogotá, Cuba, New York, or Los Angeles, you will find other family members. They may speak a different language and live a different culture, but you will know you are with other members of God's family.

A large family has its merits. My step-mother is one of thirteen children. All of the family members have both a physical and spiritual relationship, since each one has received Christ as personal Savior. Whenever they gather for a reunion, laughter and singing fill the atmosphere. They share both their joys and concerns. A sense of unity, security, and support envelops them. They give to one another rather than take. The sheer size of the family of God should likewise provide a sense of security, belonging, and support.

Becoming a child of God also means that you belong to the most prominent family on earth. The Christian who is status-conscious could go a long way in dropping names. His Father is not a president of a mere bank, large corporation, or the most powerful nation on earth. The believer's Father is the ruler over all things. He not only owns the cattle on a thousand hills, he also owns the thousand hills. He has the authority to elevate and put down kings.

I participated in my share of squabbles as a child over whose dad was the toughest or the most important. I can recall arguing with a friend, "My dad can beat up your dad anytime." When you're a child, your dad is omnipotent, omniscient, and seemingly omnipresent. But as you advance in years, you become aware of his clay feet. But the believer's Father is really omniscient, omnipotent, and

ADOPTION

omnipresent. He has no clay feet. The believer is a child of
the most prominent Being in existence.

Furthermore, your Brother is the Lord Jesus Christ (Hebrews 2:11). Remember when you were a child and got the
upper hand in a scuffle? You may have gotten into a fight
with a kid who had an older brother. What was his threat?
Right: "I'm going to get my older brother after you, and he'll
take care of you." I could never use that threat, because I
had no brothers at all. (But I did have an older sister who
bailed me out of some skirmishes.)

The Lord Jesus Christ, our older Brother, is protector,
encourager, and counselor. He is willing to fight our battles
for us—if we allow him. He is willing to encourage us when
we want to throw in the towel. He will counsel us if we will
listen. I couldn't think of a better family to belong to than
one where God is my Father and Jesus is my older Brother.

A Son of God by Adoption

I said earlier that the status of the believer is two-fold.
Not only does he become a child of God by birth, but *he
becomes a son of God by adoption.* And this is where I want to
focus the rest of the chapter. What is adoption? Let me
suggest a definition and elaborate on it. Adoption is "the
act of God, whereby children of God are given the status of
adult sons." Don't confuse it with human adoption.

Divine adoption is not identical to human adoption.
According to the customs of society, human adoption
takes an outsider and makes him a member of a family. It's
the legal way to create a father and son relationship. Divine
adoption differs in that one already is a child of God by
birth. Divine adoption does not make a person a member
of God's family; rather, it advances him to the position of
an adult son. This means that the believer receives all the
privileges, as well as the responsibilities, of the adult son.

What Are the Benefits of Being an Adopted Son?

Freedom from the Law

And what are the benefits and the responsibilities of
being an adopted son?

An adopted son is free from being treated like a little child. The apostle Paul writes, "Now I say, as long as the heir is a child, he does not differ at all from a slave although he is owner of everything, but he is under guardians and managers until the date set by the father. So also we, while we were children, were held in bondage under the elemental things of the world. But when the fulness of the time came, God sent forth His Son, born of a woman, born under the Law, in order that He might redeem those who were under the Law, that we might receive the adoption as sons" (Galatians 4:1-5).

God releases the believer from being under Law, which could not free men from sin. It only condemned man by showing him how far he had fallen short of God's standard. So Paul writes, "But before faith came, we were kept in custody under the law, being shut up to the faith which was later to be revealed. Therefore the Law has become our tutor to lead us to Christ, that we may be justified by faith. But now that faith has come, we are no longer under a tutor. For you are all sons of God through faith in Christ Jesus" (Galatians 3:23-26).

When my sons were still living at home, they were under my authority and my law. As small children they had very little freedom. They got up and went to bed when we told them to. They went outside to play and came back into the house when they were told. They did not always agree with the law that they were under, but they knew the penalty which followed any violation. As they grew into the teenage years, the laws became fewer and the freedoms greater. And now that they are grown sons, they are almost entirely out from under my law. Since both are away at school, they can stay out as late as they please. They may have to pay the penalty the next day when they attend an early morning class, but the decision when to get up and when to go to bed is theirs. The decision about how to invest their time is also theirs. No longer are they under my time restrictions. If either son mismanages his freedom and his grades take a nosedive, however, he may find himself back under law.

ADOPTION

But with God, we have been set free from law never again to be brought back under its authority. This does not mean that we have license to do whatever we please. God has established restrictions for our protection. But he wants us to use our freedom both for the benefit of others and for his own glory: "For you were called to freedom, brethren, only do not turn your freedom into an opportunity for the flesh, but through love serve one another" (Galatians 5:13).

God not only releases the believer from being under the Law, he also holds the new convert responsible to behave like an adult son. The Lord does not recognize a childhood stage of Christianity where one is permitted to misbehave and act childishly. In fact, when the Corinthians were acting as children, the apostle Paul rebuked them, warning, "And I, brethren, could not speak to you as to spiritual men, but as to men of flesh, as to babes in Christ. I gave you milk to drink, not solid food; for you were not yet able to receive it. Indeed, even now you are not yet able, for you are still fleshly. For since there is jealousy and strife among you, are you not fleshly, and are you not walking like mere men?" (1 Corinthians 3:1-3).

The writer to the Hebrews also rebuked his readers for behaving like children. He admonished them, saying, "Concerning Him we have much to say, and it is hard to explain, since you have become dull of hearing. For though by this time you ought to be teachers, you have need again for someone to teach you the elementary principles of the oracles of God, and you have come to need milk and not solid food. For everyone who partakes only of milk is not accustomed to the word of righteousness, for he is a babe. But solid food is for the mature, who because of practice have their senses trained to discern good and evil" (Hebrews 5:11-14).

God does not lower his standards for young Christians. No special Scripture has been written for the new believer in Christ. He is expected to maintain the same standard as the person who has been a Christian for many years. Qualifications for the elders of the church (1 Timothy 3:2-7) are not limited to church leaders. These same qualities should be characteristic of the individual who has been a Christian for a short while. Paul simply emphasized that before a person is given a position of leadership, these qualities should characterize his life.

The Holy Spirit

Another benefit of the adopted son is that *he has received the Holy Spirit*. Paul continues, "And because you are sons, God has sent forth the Spirit of His Son into our hearts . . ." (Galatians 4:6). The apostle told the Romans, "For you have not received a spirit of slavery leading to fear again, but you have received a spirit of adoption as sons . . ." (Romans 8:15). Every believer, no matter how long he has been a Christian, has been given an equal amount of spiritual resources. You will never receive more of the Holy Spirit than you have now, but he can receive more of you. It was Jesus who said, "For He gives the Spirit without measure" (John 3:34). The Holy Spirit does not come in parts and pieces. He is given as a whole.

I was driving in a six-cylinder car the other day, but one or two of the cylinders were not working properly. This decreased both the power of the car and the smoothness of its ride. A car can run well only when it is working on all cylinders. In the same way, though every believer has been given the Holy Spirit in full measure, he may experience a rough and powerless life because he has not plugged all the facets of his life into the Holy Spirit. When we disconnect ourselves from the Spirit in our financial lives, moral lives, family lives, social lives, or any other aspect of living, we will not measure up to our status as adopted sons. Nor will we experience the full life which God intends for us to enjoy.

A Relationship with the Father

A third benefit of being adopted is that *the believer can have an intimate relationship with his Father*. Paul writes, "And because you are sons, God has sent forth the Spirit of His Son into our hearts, crying, 'Abba! Father!'" (Galatians 4:6). Again Paul states, "For you have not received a spirit of slavery leading to fear again, but you have received a spirit of adoption as sons by which we cry out, 'Abba! Father!'" (Romans 8:15).

What is meant by the phrase "Abba! Father!"? It is the speech of a child to his father. It's a term of endearment and intimacy. It expresses both a relationship of delight and dependence.

I'm reminded of a wonderful experience I had when my boys were very young. My folks were visiting us when we lived in Winnipeg. I happened to be down in the basement working on a project when I heard laughter outside. Looking out the basement window, I saw my younger son playing in the sandbox while he was watching my older son and his grandfather kicking a ball back and forth. I quickly grabbed my 8mm camera and began shooting pictures through the window. As I was capturing these treasured moments on celluloid, I wanted to get a better picture of my younger son, so I tapped on the window. As he looked around and saw me in the window, his face broke into a delighted grin, and he cried out with delight, "Dada!" Though the movies are silent, it doesn't take an expert lip reader to interpret my son's words as he spoke those delightful and intimate words, "Dada!"

You've probably experienced similar situations where you were unaware of God's presence, being busy with your own life. But as God brought some unexpected blessing upon you, you responded with delight, "Oh, Father, thank you!" or "Abba! Father!"

This term not only expresses a delightful relationship, but also a dependent relationship. Jesus used the phrase as he poured out his soul to God in the garden. Mark's Gospel records, "And He was saying, 'Abba! Father! All things are possible for Thee; remove this cup from Me; yet not what I will, but what Thou wilt'" (Mark 14:36). Crises do come when you don't know where to turn. You wonder if God is aware of your deep hurt and unfulfilled need. You feel very much alone. As you look into the future, hope is diminished. You feel like King Jehoshaphat when he was surrounded by his enemies and cried to God, "O our God, wilt Thou not judge them? For we are powerless before this great multitude who are coming against us; nor do we know what to do, but our eyes are on Thee' " (2 Chronicles 20:12). And so you cry out, "O God, help me!" which being interpreted is "Abba! Father!" Because you are an adopted son, you can have an intimate relationship with your Father.

Led by the Spirit

A fourth benefit of being an adopted son is that *you are being led by the Holy Spirit.* Paul informed his readers at Rome, "For all who are being led by the Spirit of God, these are sons of God" (Romans 8:14). The word translated *led* means "to move," or "to be impelled by influencing the mind." Jesus Christ experienced this lifestyle according to Luke's Gospel. "And Jesus, full of the Holy Spirit, returned from the Jordan and was led about by the Spirit in the wilderness for forty days, being tempted by the devil" (Luke 4:1-2). It is the Holy Spirit who is willing to influence our minds as we allow him that opportunity.

Have you ever wondered why you want to do good? Why you want to please God? Why you want to help others? Paul answers that question in his epistle to the Philippians by writing, "For it is God who is at work in you, both to will and to work for His good pleasure" (Philippians 2:13). Even in the days of Moses, as the people worked on the tabernacle, it was the Spirit of God who gave them both the desire and the ability to accomplish his purpose. Notice how often the phrase "willing spirit" or the phrase "whose spirit moved him" is recorded in these two chapters of Exodus: "Take from among you a contribution to the LORD; *whoever is of a willing heart,* let him bring it as the LORD's contribution: gold, silver, and bronze" (Exodus 35:5). "And everyone *whose heart stirred him* and everyone *whose spirit moved him* came and brought the LORD's contribution for the work of the tent of meeting and for all its service and for the holy garments. Then *all whose hearts moved them,* both men and women, came and brought brooches and earrings and signet rings and bracelets, all articles of gold. . . . And all the women *whose*

heart stirred with a skill spun the goats' hair. . . . The Israelites, all the men and women, *whose heart moved them* to bring
material for all the work, which the LORD had commanded
through Moses to be done, brought a freewill offering to
the Lord. . . 'And He has *filled him with the Spirit of God,* in wisdom, in understanding and in knowledge and in all
craftsmanship; to make designs for working in gold and in
silver and in bronze, and in the cutting of stones for set-
tings, and in the carving of wood, so as to perform in every
inventive work. *He also has put in his heart to teach.* . . . *He has
filled them with skill* to perform every work of an engraver and
of a designer and of an embroiderer.' . . . Then Moses called
Bezalel and Oholiab and every skillful person *in whom the*
LORD *had put skill,* everyone whose heart stirred him, to
come to the work to perform it" (Exodus 35:21-22, 26, 29,
31-34, 35; 36:2).

Discipline

Let's consider one more benefit of being an adopted
son of God. *An adopted son is disciplined by his father.* Now, when
you first read that statement, you may question how discipline could qualify as a benefit. We tend to see discipline
negatively, as something that hurts. Often discipline is
considered the child of anger. But the Scriptures shed an
entirely different light on discipline, and show it as a benefit rather than a detriment.

In what way is it a benefit? Discipline is an evidence of
your father's love—"And you have forgotten the exhortation which is addressed to you as sons, 'My son, do not regard lightly the discipline of the Lord, nor faint when you
are reproved by Him; for those whom the Lord loves He
disciplines, and He scourges every son whom He receives"
(Hebrews 12:5-6). Have you ever wanted to spank someone
else's child? If you were to fulfill your urge, you probably
would not discipline so much as punish him. Your actions
most likely would not spring from love for the child, but
from desire for justice. But when you deal with your own
children, though you may feel anger, you deal with them
out of love. You want the best for them. You don't want

them growing up taking from others, or demanding their rights and making life miserable for everyone else. You want your children to grow into mature men and women. You want them to contribute to society. That's why your discipline is evidence of your love for them. The parent who refuses to discipline his children demonstrates his lack of concern for them.

Discipline is an evidence of your relationship with God. "It is for discipline that you endure; God deals with you as with sons; for what son is there whom his father does not discipline? But if you are without discipline, of which all have become partakers, then you are illegitimate children and not sons" (Hebrews 12:7-8). If you could get away with sin, then you could question whether you have a personal relationship with God. You know of young people who get away with lying, stealing, cheating. You may reprimand them, but since they are not your children, you don't discipline them. You probably would not allow your own children to get away with doing what is wrong. They may get away with actions of which you are unaware. But once you discover the problem, discipline follows.

The military has no authority to discipline those who are not in the armed services. A civilian cannot be court martialed. But the man or woman who is in the military had better comply with military standards. Discipline is evidence of relationship.

Another blessing of discipline is that it is an evidence that your father has your best interests at heart. "Furthermore, we had earthly fathers to discipline us, and we respected them; shall we not much rather be subject to the Father of spirits, and live? For they disciplined us for a short time as seemed best to them, but He disciplines us for our good, that we may share His holiness (Hebrews 12:9-10).

A child is not always aware of what is best for him. Children are often ignorant of the dangers in life. What may seem like a good thing to them may not be good at all. People can take advantage of children because they are naive.

Neither do we always know what is best for us. There are times that God withholds from us and we complain. At other times God takes us through troubled waters and we conclude that the experience could not possibly be good. But remember, God's purpose in life is not to make us comfortable, but to develop us into mature, adult sons.

Job enjoyed the good life. And then he lost everything, including his health, his family, and his wealth. But it was during that lonely time of despair, when God seemed to be so distant, that Job learned about himself and about the Lord. Eventually Job was able to come to the point where he could say, "I know that Thou canst do all things, and that no purpose of Thine can be thwarted. Who is this that hides counsel without knowledge? Therefore I have declared that which I did not understand, things too wonderful for me, which I did not know. Hear, now, and I will speak; I will ask Thee, and do Thou instruct me. I have heard of Thee by the hearing of the ear; but now my eye sees Thee; therefore I retract, and I repent in dust and ashes" (Job 42:1-6). Only after Job went through God's school of discipline was he able to come out as gold refined by fire. After the discipline came the blessing: "And the LORD restored the fortunes of Job when he prayed for his friends, and the LORD increased all that Job had twofold. . . . And the LORD blessed the latter days of Job more than his beginning. . . . And Job died, an old man and full of days" (Job 42:10, 12, 17).

One further blessing of discipline is that it is an evidence that your Father's purpose is to craft you into a mature believer. "All discipline for the moment seems not to be joyful, but sorrowful; yet to those who have been trained by it, afterwards it yields the peaceful fruit of righteousness" (Hebrews 12:11). When God disciplines you, he is crafting you into his own image, which includes a holy character and righteous behavior. Maturity means to become complete or whole. So many people are incomplete in character and behavior. They need to have the rough edges smoothed. They need to grow in knowledge and wisdom.

Moses was mature in age when he was herding sheep

on the back desert, but he was not mature in character. It wasn't until he spent forty years leading the people from Egypt and through the wilderness to the promised land that Moses became a mature man in character and behavior. Maturity is the result of God's loving discipline.

What Are the Responsibilities of An Adopted Son?

Now that we have seen the benefits of an adopted son, consider the responsibilities of sonship.

Like His Father

One obvious responsibility is that an adopted son *should be like his father.* The resemblance between a father and son includes both one's behavior and character. The adopted son of God should treat others as his Father treats him. Jesus taught, "You have heard that it was said, 'You shall love your neighbor, and hate your enemy.' But I say to you, love your enemies, and pray for those who persecute you in order that you may be sons of your Father who is in heaven; for He causes His sun to rise on the evil and the good, and sends rain on the righteous and the unrighteous. For if you love those who love you, what reward have you? Do not even the tax-gatherers do the same? And if you greet your brothers only, what do you do more than others? Do not even the Gentiles do the same?" (Matthew 5:43-47).

Too often we Christians have a "they and us" mentality; "they" being the unchurched and "us" the churched. We have a tendency to treat "them" with suspicion. A church can too easily become a closed corporation and never really penetrate the hurting world.

John Stott calls such believers "rabbit hole Christians." Applying this term to Christian college students, Stott writes, "You know—the kind who pops his head out of the hole, leaves his Christian roommate in the morning, and scurries to class, only to frantically search for a Christian to sit next to (an odd way to approach the mission field). Thus he proceeds from class to class. When dinner time comes, he sits with all the Christians in his dorm at one huge table and thinks, 'What a witness!' From there he goes to his all-

Christian Bible study, and he might even catch a prayer meeting where the Christians pray for the non-believers on his floor. (But what luck that he was able to live on the floor with seventeen Christians!) Then at night he scurries back to his Christian roommate. Safe! He made it through a day and his only contacts with the world were those mad, brave dashes to and from Christian activities." We should never treat the unchurched as persons to avoid, but rather as individuals to love. That's how our Father treats them.

As one's behavior should be like his Father's, so should his character. Jesus further says, "Therefore you are to be perfect, as your heavenly Father is perfect" (Matthew 5:48). The word translated *perfect* means "to be complete or whole." The apostle Paul wrote that his major objective was to perfect believers in the Lord. "And we proclaim Him, admonishing every man and teaching every man with all wisdom, that we may present every man complete in Christ" (Colossians 1:28). Just as you want wholeness for your children, so is this God's desire for you—to be like him.

A Peacemaker

Another responsibility of the adopted son is that *he should be a peacemaker.* "Blessed are the peacemakers, for they shall be called sons of God" (Matthew 5:9). Too often believers are troublemakers, walking around like infants in dirty diapers, making messes wherever they go. This is why Paul wrote that a church leader should not be pugnacious (1 Timothy 3:3). He is not to be a bully, demanding his rights and threatening those who don't give in to his whims. There can be no prima donnas in the church of Jesus Christ. This includes teachers, soloists, instrumentalists, church board members, and pastoral staff. "So then let us pursue the things which make for peace and the building up of one another" (Romans 14:19).

Discipline without Complaint

Another responsibility of an adopted son is that *he should receive his Father's discipline without complaint or discouragement.* The writer to the Hebrews concludes his remarks on discipline by saying, "Therefore, strengthen the hands that are weak and the knees that are feeble, and make straight paths for your feet, so that the limb which is lame may not be put out of joint, but rather be healed" (Hebrews 12:12-13).

Usually when we go through a period of discipline, we wonder whether God hears us or has interest in us any longer. God may bring you to the point where everything is beyond your control. The only choice before you is either to depend entirely upon him, or to nosedive into total despair. At such times, rather than asking God, "Why?" ask, "What can I learn from this experience?" God does not discipline us to discourage us or to hear us complain. He disciplines us for our good.

Walking in the Spirit

A final responsibility for the adopted son is that *he should walk in the Spirit.* "But I say, walk by the Spirit, and you will not carry out the desire of the flesh" (Galatians 5:16). This means that you and I are to walk in the sphere of the Spirit's influence.

A number of years ago, my younger son bought a hamster. Steven enjoyed taking the hamster out of his cage and playing with him on the floor. But there was a problem whenever our dog came into the house. One whiff of the hamster and the dog attacked. In order to allow the hamster freedom and still protect him from the dog, we bought a clear plastic ball with a lid. We'd unscrew the lid, put the hamster in the ball, screw the lid back on, and lay the ball on the floor. The hamster would stand up and run inside the ball, rolling it all over the floor. What about the dog? All he could do was run over and sniff the plastic ball. Once in a while he'd hit it with his nose, but there was no way he could get at the hamster. As long as the hamster was within the plastic sphere, he was both free and safe. But when he was out of his sphere, he was only free to get himself into trouble. He could be attacked by the dog or trampled by human feet.

ADOPTION

In the same way, the believer is to walk in the sphere of the Holy Spirit. As long as he is walking in the Spirit, he is protected from the onslaught of fleshly lusts. But if he refuses to walk in the Spirit, he is fair game to every conceivable temptation.

But what does it mean to walk in the Spirit? Just as that hamster was placed into the plastic ball and depended on the ball for his protection, so is the believer placed into Christ and surrounded by the Holy Spirit. As he consistently depends upon the Holy Spirit and submits to his authority, the believer will be Spirit-controlled and Spirit-led.

As an adopted son, you don't have to strive for status before God by competing with other believers. Others may be more gifted than you or more successful, but your status before God is not based on your achievements or how well you match up with other believers. Your status before God is determined only by what he has done for you. He has brought you into his family by a new birth, and has made you an adopted son. That position allows you to enjoy all of the benefits of sonship, yet requires that you accept all the responsibilities of a son.

Diana Spencer gained status in the royal family of England by saying, "I do," and by receiving Prince Charles as her husband. A person enters and gains status in the royal family of God in a similar way. He says, "I do," to Jesus and receives him as personal Savior. Then he begins to enjoy the benefits and to share the responsibilities of royalty.

EPILOGUE

Now that you have completed *Living Securely In An Unstable World*, it's possible you feel less secure than before you opened the book. Perhaps you've felt like a stranger reading about someone else's personal experience. You've been able to identify with very little of it.

It might be that though you've always been a religious person, you've neglected to make salvation personal. You've failed to admit your spiritual bankruptcy and invite Jesus Christ into your life, believing that he alone is your only way to heaven.

If this is true, recognize that you no longer have to be a stranger to God's family. He wants to be your Father. His Son longs to be your personal Savior. And his Holy Spirit craves to take control of your life and give you the ability to be what he designed you to become.

You can experience forgiveness of sins, life eternal and purpose in daily living if you will ask Jesus to take up residence in your life as a permanent guest.

He knocks at the door of your heart and asks to be invited into your life. Why not open the door and extend to him the invitation? You might want to pray something like this—

"Dear Jesus, thank you that before you even created the world, you planned for me to enjoy eternal fellowship: Thank you for choosing me. And thank you for taking my place on the cross. I know that I deserved that death because I am the one who has sinned.

"I invite you now to enter my life. I accept your forgiveness of my sins. And I ask you to make me what you want me to be.

"In Jesus' name I pray. Amen."

If you prayed this prayer and meant it, you have become a child of God. You can now experience all that he has for you. You now can live securely in a volatile world.

Why not tell a friend about your new discovery? And then take a moment to write to me and share your exciting news—Rick Yohn. 5300 France Avenue South, Minneapolis, Minnesota 55410.